TIME OF THE TOAD

Reflections on the Last Decade

JAMES COLEMAN

ISBN: 1450585280
ISBN-13: 9781450585286

TABLE OF CONTENTS

ACKNOWLEDGEMENTS

I thank my many daughters, especially Lisa Crawford, for the original suggestion of this book. And I owe more than they might imagine to all readers of *Nightingale at Large,* although they are responsible for none of the stumbles in my essays.

Special thanks are due my wife, Judith Dushku. She is always not only a serious reader of *Nightingale at Large* but my whole happiness in all respects. Additionally, I admire and am inspired by her work in these interesting times.

PREFACE

These brief essays are selected from my personal weblog *Nightingale At Large*. I want to return the weblog to its intended focus on Florence Nightingale and Social Medicine and this book will be the archive of the political observations and angry effusions I fell into writing during the George Bush presidency, a kind of "Journal of the Plague Decade" during which most of us were compelled to consume toad-meat.

The Bush presidency is a part of the Reagan Era (1976-to date) during which the forward motion of our society ceased, backlash prevailed, wars were continuous, and almost all benefits of the national economy were handed over to the very rich, an oligarchy that rules us now. One hundred and sixty years ago, Nightingale faced a similar deadly stagnation: Malthusian deceptions; a New Poor Law; entrenched orthodox medicine for-profit; a quagmire Crimean War; and a greedy, heedless gentry and its apologists. I want to return to writing about her experience of her plague years.

On March 20, 2004, in one of his more directly fascist speeches, George W. Bush announced that "The War on Terror" was "the inescapable calling of our generation." I do not believe we should take our callings from the likes of George W. Bush. Surely, the inescapable calling of our generation is public health, social medicine, epidemiology, and broad social reform. Our calling is to decisively move forward out of the Reagan Era. The Reagan Era has been a disaster for all but the very rich. The reactionary backlash that Ronald Reagan led—so contrary to the best in our history—must be reversed. Genuine reform must be our agenda. The reforms we are able to achieve will be the next small step toward the grand objective of socialism (which is to say, toward equality and democracy) and toward the personal ease and liveliness of mind we all desire.

We recognize that modern medicine, especially social medicine, can be a life saver; however, modern medicine did not come about through the self-interest of private medical practitioners or from the bottom line preoccupation of the pharmaceutical, chemical, instrument, and insurance industries. Modern medicine derives from hospitals (where funds and labs, statistics and staff expertise could be concentrated for the first time). And those hospitals derive from nurses who made the hospitals into clean, habitable, safe, and life-giving rather then life-taking places. This was Florence Nightingale's achievement in founding modern nursing. My family and friends, readers of *Nightingale at Large*, know that we need new Nightingales: reformers with status, learning, and commitment.

To anyone who might misunderstand my title, the following chapters focus on America's extreme inequality (the heart of the matter), the Bush presidency (our "Time of the Toad"), our media (ventriloquist dummies telling small tales), nonexistent Democratic Party opposition over the decade, and something about Barack Obama. My title is appropriated from Dalton Thrumbo's book of that title published in 1949. In it Thrumbo reflects on the inquisition by the House UnAmerican Activities Committee (flourished 1945-1960). That led to a period of intense anti-communist terror. Its effects are still with us. Thrumbo was one of more than 300 blacklisted Hollywood screenwriters and artists. He was imprisoned for Contempt of Congress after refusing to betray his friends and colleagues. This good man died in 1976. In the opening of his *The Time of the Toad* he wrote:

> All nations in the course of their histories have passed through periods which might be called the Time of the Toad: an epoch long or short as the temper of the people may permit, fatal or merely debilitating as the vitality of the peoople may determine, in which the nation turns upon itself in a kind of compulsive madeness to deny all in its tradition that is clean, to exalt all that is vile, and to destroy any heretical minority which asserts toad-meat not to be the delicacy which governmental edicts declares it.

INEQUALITY

Inequality Matters in Cincinnati
(Posted 05/14/2002)

How do you measure the degree of separation between those of us who lead contented lives in White, solidly middle income neighborhoods and the Black families in the background of the article by Mark Singer in the May 20, 2002 *New Yorker,* "A Year of Trouble," about the police shooting of an unarmed Black youth and the subsequent uprising in Cincinnati? Inequality matters, yet it is hard to get a handle on how much it matters. We—those reading *New Yorker* articles and those participating in the days of uprising, marching, and the boycotting in that racist city—are so far apart it is not easy to imagine how much inequality matters.

If the Black to White population ratio of cities in America were anything like those in South Africa (9 to 1) we would have a movement here similar to the movement in South Africa against Apartheid. Victory in that movement replaced a lot of formal and legal segregation—a good thing—but replaced it with absolute economic segregation. All that the ANC was able to do in South Africa, all that the international anti-Apartheid slogans ("Apartheid in South Africa, Burn it to the Ground!") did, was grand but limited. The more significant changes rested on promises, promises. Inequality was the victor. Inequality is what I saw in the townships of Johannesburg and what I felt from inside our gated, electrified, heavily policed, all-white guest house in Oranjezicht, Cape Town. Burning the formal trappings of Apartheid was as insufficient as the Cincinnati mayor's Commissions and Police Review Boards called up in response to the uprising there.

Looking back today from the perspective of Dakar, Senegal—where my wife and I are running an English language college—where Apartheid has never been reinforces the lesson. There are extremes of rich and poor in Dakar, yes, but inequality is ten times greater in South Africa. For you mathematicians, I am thinking the Gini coefficient and at least one order of magnitude. The obvious difference between Senegalese and Black South Africans in manner, culture, evidence of pride, real conversation across races, and freedom of movement floods over the liberal levies I have built against just such race-based observations.

The differences also describe something like the depth of humiliation portrayed in "Boesman & Leana," a film about South Africa I am now teaching. Its director and the American actors (Danny Glover and Angela Bassett) use the metaphor of madness to convey the depth of the humiliation. Humiliation and madness are husband and wife.

3

Here in the U.S. our very different population dynamics produce these small, periodic rebellions as in Los Angeles in 1992 and Cincinnati in 2001. Still, you have to ask about the humiliation (or madness) here, where there is only an economic segregation.

In the U.S., our City Councils, Mayors' Offices, police forces and fire departments, social service agencies, and other public officials commonly behave in racist ways, in ways so common that anyone has every right to call this a racist country. Given the extent of economic inequality, it would be amazing if they were not racist. Our systemic racism teaches officialdom to make an automatic conversion of structural economic disadvantage into human inferiority (and dangerousness or madness).

That conversion—poor equals inferior equals dangerous—is one of capitalist America's foundation lies. Unless the place holding official is a very thoughtful, courageous and independent-minded person, to hold a place is to be automatically racist. That is how much inequality matters. Ordinary functionaries exercise their racism constantly, justify it with old "true stories," and, at the same time, take it for granted. This racism is encouraged by the daily newspapers that also take race-based economic inequality for granted, furnish more "true stories," and always defend officialdom from top to bottom. Their denial must be brushed aside.

Although Blacks are only about 13% of our population, their contribution to our culture is enormously disproportionate. This has also been the case with Jews (about 4.5%) and it once was the case with the Irish. But the legacy of slavery and sharecropping and Jim Crow was not the legacy of the urban immigrant sweatshops, factory and construction labor, and upward mobility. The "whiteness" construct (color equals inferior) stuck with the Blacks while it was removed against the Irish only after public policy allowed them to became politically and economically significant in the cities.

We pigeonhole the Black contributions to culture (mainly as entertainment), as we did with Jews and the Irish until they succeed economically against the mean-spirited exclusion from equal education and fair enjoyment within the national economy. Money and narrow social cohesion matters far more than any position that Blacks may occupy in the arts, entertainment, athletics, the military, or in the law. Martin Luther King's loose assertion was that this was a Christian nation was mere convention. It is an unequal, mean-spirited, capitalist nation rooted in Christian hypocrisy. Too little is being done to change that.

Many things about Blacks come as a big surprise to most Americans. For instance, that there actually are only a few Black officials. I believe there are eight or nine African-American mayors of all cities over 40,000. The Association of Black Mayors reports that there are over 500 Black mayors in the U.S. and 9,000

Black elected officials in all cities of all sizes especially (hamlets to Atlantas). They are concentrated in southern cities and towns where nearly half of all African Americans live. However, there were only 1245 cities over 25,000 in 2000 and nearly 20,000 towns and cities in total. Thus, there are less that 3% with Black mayors. And forget about the U.S. Senate or state Governors where there are zero Blacks. The south is no longer rural; and, in any event, the issue is not Black mayors or officials in small southern towns.

There are 36 million African-Americans and over half (51.5% in 2002) live inside central cities. That is over twice the percentage of non-Hispanic whites living inside central cities. These deteriorating cities, like it or not, are segregated cities, unfairly taxed, and unfairly treated in federal policy and federal benefits.

Blacks are located inside central cities at twice the rate of Whites. They are unemployed or underemployed at twice the rate of Whites. They live at government-defined poverty level at twice the rate of Whites. Black median family income is also about half that of Whites, as is home ownership. Gross statistics, I know, but clear enough to stand against those who deny that Blacks, because they are Black, are systematically excluded from the benefits of the national economy.

Other figures are even more appalling. For instance, Blacks are 13 percent of our total population but nearly 50 percent of total prison population and that population stands at a world championship six million-plus. Then, also, the numbers for educational attainment and for infant mortality, birth weight, etc.

I believe the financial figures are the most telling. They are closer to the cause. In total net worth, Blacks, on average, stand at one sixth that of Whites. And if you eliminate home equity from the figure—and home equity is the main form of wealth for most ordinary people—net worth for Blacks vanishes to a rounded zero percentage. Income (the flow of dollars, usually wages and salary) is what most journalists focus on. But wealth or net worth becomes the more important figure once you are talking of the older population who are raising children. Net worth refers to an individual's or a family's total assets minus debts at a single point in time. Either way you look at it, with or without equity in homes, this is a fine measure of the enormous inequality that Black people, their children, and their heirs have visited upon them.

Many other countries and most "world aware" organizations would call such a racial disparity in net worth a human rights abuse. Nor is it inaccurate to call it a crime against humanity.

Demanding some minimal "reparations," based on the mountain of dollars of disparity in net worth is like begging for pennies. It is literally begging for pennies, independent of any judgment you make about that demand for "reparations" as a political tactic.

5

When talking about America—said to be virtuous and fair—we are obliged to make some of the obvious economic comparisons between Blacks and Whites. Then we are obliged to add comparative health statistics. Those are truly horrendous. Stories from Cincinnati or Los Angeles or Detroit or Boston are not enough.

No heart-warming stories about "progress" can stand against the reality of this peculiar "savage inequality" in America. When "Progress" stories are used to block talk of this horrific inequality—as is often the case—that talk is itself racist even when coming from some Black pastor or spokesperson.

History is involved here. First there was slavery and then Jim Crow, lynching and beatings, legal segregation, judicial and police-enforced unequal treatment, and finally, policy-created inequality. Inequality also must be measured in educational quality, segregated housing, epidemic health issues (including illegal drugs), and employment opportunity. All these measurements must be respected prior to anecdote, human interest story, analysis, or speculation. Measured again and again.

Then let those who are politely called "conservatives" juggle and minimize and deny as they do. They are playing White against Black. They are playing Rich against Poor, which is the functional meaning of "Conservative." However you slice it, inequality matters.

༄

The Filthy Rich on Nantucket
(Posted 06/07/2005)

The NY Times series "Class Matters" deserves more comment. The team of authors has finally ventured to touch the tiptop one tenth of one percent in American wealth, the filthy rich. Published last Sunday, this segment follows the culture-magazine, human-interest pattern established in the first eight: this tiny top group as they live (for a few weeks out of the year) on "the island of the really, really rich," Nantucket.

Nantucket is a 50 square mile island off Cape Cod. The first thing to know about Nantucket is that it is not Martha's Vineyard or Block Island. Those are closer islands beloved by day-trippers, anglers, sunbathers and casual sailors. Beloved by folks with kids, ordinary vacationers, gays, and even Black people living in or revisiting wonderful Oak Bluffs whose history dates back to freed slaves working the whalers and those who came to the Vineyard in the first half of the eighteenth century with their Protestant camp meetings. The camp meeting tents eventually became the tiny carpenter Gothic cottages that distinguish Oak Bluffs. No, Nantucket is further out, a more expensive ride, and has always been entirely dominated by the rich and those allowed to service them: Whaling magnates who build a town of Greek revival mansions when the island was the "whaling capital of the world," 1800-1840: then vacationing magnates of the Gilded Age, 1880-1929, whose largess scattered vacation mansions all around America (Vanderbilts, Melons, Duponts, like that); and now the engorged rich of the 1980-2000 boom times and the Bush bonanza who have now covered the island with their inevitably excessive private homes.

What kind of dollars are we looking at? Like 10,000 square foot vacation homes used only weeks in the year and providing alternative to their other vacation homes in Palm Beach, Aspen, the Hamptons, Sun Valley, wherever. We are talking 5-20 million dollar homes. We are talking one tenth of one percent at the top who own much of the country's wealth accumulation, that wealth at the expense of the bottom 90% of us. As I noted previously, the numbers are very crude because the government is discrete. It does not report detail at these elevated levels and probably no one knows how much income they do not pay any taxes on (conservative estimate is 30% unreported). "Household wealth"—the relevant measure—is generalized into the millions of families in the top 10% by government discretion.

The *Times*, using available public numbers and no analysis, gets no closer than 338,400 households each with an inflation adjusted net worth of over only God knows what. But, as I explained in the first post on this series, if you want to look at the super-rich, those who are the primary beneficiaries of the sharply growing income disparity (money from poor through the middle flowing to the very rich) in the United States, you must get to 12,000 or 15,000 households at the top of this pile of 338,400.

Still those 338,400 households is a useful number. Okay, an inflation-adjusted net worth well in excess of $10 million. These households will enjoy Bush's tax cuts over 15 years at an average yearly savings of about $200,000. At the pinnacle of the 338,400 there are about 12,000-15,000 obscenely rich households. They hold real power, the kind that buys politicians, buys whole accounting and law firms, buys and sells and moves corporations, drafts legislation and secures its passage, authorizes wars. They are filthy rich.

The way it works (politically and socially) is that the larger 338,400 households function, by and large, as the defenders and, in their way, minions and imitators of the very richest 12,000 to 15,000 households. The larger group takes its instruction in duties, politics, and culture from the very much richer and smaller group. The larger group is mobilized in defense of their "common" interests, including incidentals such as shifting the money necessary for a vacation home on Nantucket.

So, the *Times* tells a few stories of $10 to $60 million estates and the unpleasant people who inhabit them. I am not being merely snippety. I am honestly reflecting the inescapable content of the *Times* staff reporting. The article says these people "tend to be brash, confident, and unapologetic." The human-interest stories make it clear that what the *Times* means is "crude, nasty, and brutal in their dealings with others." In other words, the very rich of Nantucket (on those occasions when they choose to relax on that island) are unpleasant people who associate only with their unpleasant peers.

These people's multi-million dollar privacy has caused increasing closure of the island's traditional walkways and pathways to the sea. It has meant the buying up of adjacent houses to secure more "distance" from neighbors, securing beaches against public trespass, building 10,000 square feet homes featuring a half mile walk to the servant quarters. There are wine cellars for 2,000 bottles estimated at $300/bottle. It has come to mean $250,000 club memberships (mostly unused but "necessary, don't you know"). It means distress for the "old money" culture of the island (which is to say, offenses against "old" bad taste by new bad taste). It has meant endless litigation using big-name NYC or Boston lawyers to push the boundaries and traditional easements, as well as jokes between carpenters and plumbers and even florists about their new need for malpractice insurance. These service people naturally cannot afford to live on the island—nor can the school principal nor his teachers—and they fly in (about 400 each morning) for the day's work. It means endless waiter and boutique-keeper tales of the normally obnoxious behavior of the very rich.

Old Money goes "tut tut" and says, "shame has gone out the window," referring to a faux lighthouse built against code between the two wings of a new mansion. Old Money deplores the new super-sized yachts, hot second wives, and the staggered array of golf courses (one for themselves, another for new money, and another for new-new money where non-conforming golf balls and drivers are commonplace, I assume). "Shocking, really."

Nantucket forms the ideal gated community. It has the ocean for a mote. There are no franchise businesses (none, not just discretely hidden ones as on Hilton Head). There are no pleasant little outlying towns such as East and South Harbor on Arcadia Island off Maine where service people might live, or those on the Vineyard where artists live and day-trippers wander. And still—as always with the wealthy in and about all of these enclaves of theirs—many ordinary people come to gawk and dream and perhaps scheme to steal their way to their own little piece of the reflected glory of true wealth. Indeed, many people simply adore the rich. Perhaps there is a Latin name for this perversity. Unfortunately, they never meet any of the very rich and so the illusion of grace and generosity (from silly novels) is maintained. Because of wealth display, Nantucket continues to be visited by the *hoi polloi* as it has for generations. They leave made lesser. That is part of the point of conspicuous consumption.

Nantucket was once a beautiful island, but has become an odd one. Expect no parks or playgrounds. Do not bring the kids. You cannot see the forest for the things built of trees, those excessive homes. You have to take your pleasure looking at the inaccessible private property of others and admiring the work of their gardeners.

Today's paper ran seven "To the Editor" letters about this segment on Nantucket. Mostly it is nice people writing to defend the beauties and traditions of the island and worrying that if they say anything critical of the unpleasant rich they will be accused of "Envy," as one put it. They are embarrassed at the "palpable excitement" some feel when contemplating great wealth. Nice people, as I say, contemplating at a distance, I would hope.

One letter, however, is from a George Bush man—a Chairnan of Bush's Council of Economic Advisers, a Harvard economist. N. Gregory Mankiw. True to form, this letter is contentious, irrational, threatening, and very firm. A fine example of those qualities in 300 words or less. Bush people must take special instruction at the White House, Cheney wing. He argues that since the very rich experienced a decreasing share of the national wealth during the Great Depression, 1929-1934, and during the 1970's recession, therefore those who want to reduce income inequality [such as myself] must want to "put the economy through the wringer" as in 1929. I suspect all of us can think of other ways, ways that avoid the soup kitchens, the migrations of the jobless, the starvation and deaths the winter of 1929-30, but let that be. Mankiw says if we really want "economic prosperity for all" we must give up "the politics of envy." A nice circle of jabberwocky logic, and yet he manages to sound pompous rather than funny.

This is not really about some series run by the *New York Times*. Any paper or magazine could and many have run similar material. Such articles are valuable only in that they repeat the fact that the rich are getting richer and the rest of us are getting poorer at an accelerating rate, that "social mobility"—that dream of all immigrants—has become a lie, and that government policy facilitates this loss of fairness, opportunity, "social mobility," and a level playing field. What such articles never address is that such an extreme income inequality is literally destroying the lives of millions of good people. In order to flourish, it must continue destroying generation after generation.

John F. Kennedy's literalism was a false metaphor—"a rising tide lifts all boats"—not mere shallow optimism but rather a false analogy. Present today among us are the criminally rich, the filthy rich. Some of our boats sink lower, others tread water, a few enjoy backwater eddies for the illusion of success. And a very tiny number of boats rise up like ocean yachts atop the crest of a never-ending summer wave off Nantucket Island.

&

Our Broken Levee
(Posted 09/06/2005)

The levee protecting our pompous country from exposure to the elements has broken. We all saw who was left behind in New Orleans: the poor in their "squalid perches" (as the *Boston Globe* called them); the flocks and burdens of terrified children. We saw the black of the bodies floating there in the debris-filled water of the city. Even TV reporters, who normally do not take note of such facts, commented on the class and race of the survivors of Katrina.

A few survivors were appropriately angry: "This is a national disgrace"; "We need food and water and they sent us men with guns"; "They treated us like dogs!" There was some "looting" (better called "finding") and some lawlessness. That will be made into ballyhoo by the president who said the problem in New Orleans on the third day was "lack of security." But in spite of the scope of tragedy and the chaos created by long delayed and incompetent disaster response the great majority evacuated when told to do so. Those without cars or without money for emergencies ("I just live paycheck to paycheck") went to the shelters when, reluctantly, everyone abandoned their homes and neighborhoods.

A major urban center washed away along with many thousands of its disregarded citizens. There were children and the disabled everywhere, nursing home residents in their final isolation, desperate fathers and sons scavenging for survival. We all saw it. The facade of "greatness" exposed. We will now see if a massive government-funded recovery and rebuilding can accomplish what years of ignored studies and *New Orleans Times-Picayune* articles were urging, at far less cost. We will hope the survivors get some benefit from the social services that—now, at last, after the destruction of their city—fall their way.

President Bush and his colleague Gov. Haley Barbour of Mississippi—who is former chairman of the Republican Committee and a possible 2008 Republican nominee for the presidency—will do everything possible to patch up their reputation and put off criticism, as will the Democrats in Louisiana. Both of these rich Republicans (banking and oil for Bush and Griffith & Rogers—a top U.S. lobbying firm—for the governor) have been consistent advocates of cutting government social spending and turning that money over in the form of tax cuts that primarily benefit the very rich. As Bush has said "One of the last things that we need to do to this economy is fuel government."

They are now forced to briefly assume the white hats of the "nanny state" to which they have been so hostile. President Bush will attempt to shift most costs to the states and communities (as with education and health care); he will continue to gut the treasury with his illegal, deadly-in-every-way war in Iraq; he will continue the effort to hand Social Security savings to Wall Street and keep up his subsidy (exemption from fair taxation) on industrial fuel. But face-saving will require him to provide some federal assistance to New Orleans people and to those in other states who are supporting them. Face-saving will also mean backing off (for the time being) his latest gift to the superrich, eliminating the Estate Tax.

However he twists and turns, we pray that this last disaster can mark the effective end to his slash and burn anti-people presidency. This extremist, reactionary president has hidden long enough behind the facade of a Bible-belt "compassionate conservative."

Public school will not open in New Orleans this year. Although TV reporters will never comment, we can also use this opportunity to see those left behind by the American educational system. 92.7 percent of the public school students in Orleans parish, a consolidated school district, are Black, minority, and mainly poor. "White flight," motivated by deteriorating schools, low teacher qualifications and high teacher turnover, low salaries, inadequate textbooks and supplies, woeful housekeeping and maintenance services, and a general absence of parks, playgrounds, art and music and dance, sport facilities, theaters and auditoriums. These are the same children you just saw on television in New Orleans. The picture is duplicated in Chicago (87 percent people of color in the public school), Washington, D.C. (94 percent) and so on through St. Louis, Philadelphia, Cleveland, Detroit, Baltimore, New York City.

These children go to school in the deep isolation of their race and their poverty. The struggle for integration that took place after Brown v. Board of Education has been reversed. These inner-city schools are the result of conscious efforts to avoid integration. Jonathan Kozol's article in the September *Harper's* ("Still Separate, Still Unequal; America's educational apartheid") gives us some idea of the victim's reaction to their isolation and disregard, a polite and quiet anger in the manner of children:

> "It's more like being hidden." says a fifteen year old. Another adds "It's as if you have been put in a garage where, if they don't have room for something but aren't sure if they should throw it out, they put it there where they don't need to think of it again" And a sixteen year old said "Think of it this way. If people in New York woke up one day and learned that we were gone, that we had simply died or left for somewhere else, how would they feel?" "How do you think they'd feel?" Kozol asks her. "I think they'd be relieved."

In all our city centers education has returned to the 1896 lie of Plessey v. Ferguson ("separate but equal"). Any chronicle of these children would have the same powerful obviousness as the television newscasts from New Orleans.

> An eight year old observed, "We do not have the things you have, you have clean things. You have a clean bathroom. You have Parks and we do not have Parks."

Between 1967 and 2000 in New Orleans there was a 30 percent decline in white student enrollment followed by "a governmentally administered diminishment in value of the children of the poor" (Kozol). To all of these urban centers came cuts in salaries, cuts in maintenance, cuts in supplies. Along with this came more and more rigidly sequential styles of instruction, command and control emphasis, new schemes of reward and punishment, "standards" posted and constantly reiterated, drill, standardized exams.

Prepackaged commercial lessons taught by novice, inept, and underpaid teachers. It is this, along with nearly four years of drill-based literacy methods proliferating in our urban school that was codified in Bush's "No Child Left Behind" Law in 2002. That was a viciously racist law. There is no respectability in quibbling over details here.

As soon as the process of re-segregation began once more in New Orleans and the other cities in the early 1990's the achievement gap between black and white children began once more to widen. Yes, every particular up-tick is reported (4th grade reading in NYC, some math performance elsewhere); but the over-all decline continues while Bush—in that patented, infuriating way he uses to address every failed policy (Iraq, Health, New Orleans, Education)—keeps repeating "It's working." "It's making a difference." The statement is his deadly lie, enforced with sheer repetition, a lie accepted by large numbers of Americans. The truth, known to every poor child, is "We do not have the things you have."

And "Left Behind" is also the story of health in America. In 1970 New York City public schools had 400 doctors to address children's health needs. By 1993 the number was cut to 23, most of them part-time. The fact of racial demographics was the true cause. And it also happened in New Orleans. Last week, in New Orleans, the National Disaster Medical System—which promises 24/7 emergency medical response and delivery anywhere in the U.S. within 12 hours—did not arrive until three days after the expected, much foretold landing of Katrina.

We do not have "the greatest health care system in the world." It is only the most expensive. We rank dead last among the advanced nations. We have 279 physicians per 100,000 persons while Europe has 322. We are 26th from the top in infant mortality. Our life expectancy is lower that that of Europe. We pay for enormous corporate overhead, the "administrative costs" of identifying the unprofitable and denying them coverage, and CEO salaries. We pay for profit taking, for a criminal pharmaceutical industry (committing well beyond the crimes of big tobacco), and for selective, profit-driven HMO's. Health insurance, while costly enough to bankrupt some major corporations who provide it to their unionized workers, is beyond the reach of between 43 and 60 million Americans. Among the 50 most economically advanced nations, only the U.S. and South Africa do not provide government guaranteed health care to all citizens.

And yet something like 40-50 percent of Americans thinks we are a glorious nation. They must be thinking of landscape. The glory lie is the secret of Bush's appeal. Its believers are thinking like hillbillies who have a still in the back-and-beyond and "damn those federal revenuers!" They are thinking like thugs around a backyard barbeque in Hicksville saying "I've got mine; damn the government." Folks, we need a good government. Desperately. Our children's future depends on it.

We all saw the apartheid housing in New Orleans. Then we saw an apartheid rescue effort, now blamed on "bureaucracy" and "bungling" and about to be forgiven, as if no one was really responsible. And there is apartheid education. And apartheid health care.

You have to reach for words to describe the situation. "A failed state" one said; another said "a feral nation." One of our problems is that so many people really have a kind of faith that we are a great nation. Belief in the substance of things unseen. Or else they do really enjoy basking in the reflected narcissism and entitlement of the enormously wealthy, sucking on hollow celebrity as compensation for doing without the social services of an adequate nation. And all the while paying for someone else's excess.

Do people really know nothing of that aristocracy of wealth (only a few thousand families) who sit beside their social pool and swim in money, living far beyond the wildest dreams of any imaginary "rich uncle?" All the numbers are public. And the weakest must go to the wall to pay for that excess of the rich. That is not Christianity (a devalued commodity, more and more reduced to "pie in the sky by and by"), That is not even decent. And we saw it all on television.

Administration policy (also in full public view) facilitates the crime. This government functions as a funnel of money into the open mouths of the obscenely wealthy. This Administration's top priority (in spite of 9/11, in spite of the Iraq debacle, in spite of Katrina) has been to use the tax code to transfer wealth to the super rich. Soon the Senate will again scramble (for electoral pennies!) to permanently eliminate the estate tax (as the House has already voted). That will benefit the richest two percent of the population and shift $1.5 billion a week (about what the Iraq war is costing) from the public treasury to the private bank accounts of the heirs to the nation's twenty thousand richest families. They cannot wait; and they will not wait long. The Bush Administration is truly not a "tax and spend" government, it is an "oil and armaments" government, an everything-for-the-corporate-bottom-line government, and primarily an everything-for-the-rich government.

If we should want to change this we must force the government to serve a different "base," a different class. Some of this class was revealed to us by Katrina, others are anywhere you wish to look. It is a very different base and—if you have even a little bit of experience in the world—a better one. Who would claim that the existing government performs well in the international arena with its exclusive reliance on arms and its denigration of diplomacy, in managing a war in Iraq while ignoring and dictating to the very military who are trying to fight that loosing war, in disaster responses on the Gulf Coast, in response to our education crisis and to oil depletion and global warming? Yet it is exactly this clanking claim you hear everywhere. It is the song of the wealthy. Look into any detail of our present commonwealth (transportation budget amendments, federal contracts, regulatory exemptions, performance in crisis situations, service to the most needy). There is no "conspiracy." This is open policy. The music you hear is a parody of Whitman's American anthem "Song of Myself" sung by the 15,000 richest families, a song of harvesting the nation's wealth. The rest of us are left behind.

∽

Roaring Twenties, Roaring 2000s
(Posted 03/29/2007)

The *Times* today reported on income inequality in America based on the release of preliminary 2005 tax returns. Here are the key quotes:

- The new data shows that the top 300,000 Americans collectively enjoyed almost as much income as the bottom 150,000,000 Americans nearly doubling the gap from 1980.
- The top one percent received 21.8 percent of all reported income in 2005, up significantly from 19.8 percent the year before and more than double their share of income in 1980. The peak was in 1928, when the top 1 percent reported 23.9 percent of all income.
- The top tenth of one percent reported an average income of $5.6 million, up $908,000, while the top one-hundredth of a percent had an average income of $25.7 million, up nearly $4.4 million in one year.

A graphic supplemented the report from Piketty and Saez. You can easily find the excellent graphic not printed here; it dramatically shows the so-called "Great Compression" (which is to say, growing equality) from WWII to 1976 during which the share of the nation's income going to the top one percent declined while the share going to the bottom ninety percent increased. Take note, WWII to 1976! Since then inequality has increased.

The top one-hundredth of a percent (average income $25.7 million) of our vast 300 million people amounts to 300,000, and that chasm of separation between the rich and the rest of us is understated. The *Times* piece is based on preliminary tax return data and covers only those who have thus far filed (and the top income filings are often delayed), fails to cover about 30% of business and investment income to the top that the IRS say is normally "missed," ignores the cuts in government assisted health care, child care, and education (which are meaningless to the rich and crucial to the poor), and of course ignores unreported hidden income. In addition, the top has the advantage of every conceivable legal and accounting service helping them reduce their taxable income.

What these 300,000 share with us is the sunshine, air, and the condition of the downtown streets. That is about it.

Not only should Bush's tax cuts for the rich be eliminated (that is the easy one) but the tax rate on the rich should be increased while poor and middle class rates should be lowered. The newfound money could go to a national health care system, to eliminating poverty, and to reversing the trend toward bad education for the many. Nor is it too hard to show that these measures, even in the near term, would strengthen our economy, that is, strengthen all except the fortunes of the 300,000. However, this 300,000 rule. We do not. We may, if we like, sing "Democracy is coming to the U.S.A." but singing hope changes nothing.

Overthrowing the rule of the 300,000 will be no small matter. They will more than just kick and scream. They can be expected to do bloody murder. They control all that passes for political leadership in this country. That is where we differ from our Declaration of Independence founding fathers. They were willing to take on King George II. The functionaries in and around Washington D.C. today are in the pocket of the 300,000 and only willing to feel around in the pocket lint and between the couch cushions of the 300,000.

Part of the reason I feel today that such data is not only boring but also fundamentally depressing is because it shows that our problems are not at all mysterious ones. Most of the ugly things in our society flow from the inequality described in these numbers. The top 2% of Americans (to whom Bush provided his tax cuts) reported nearly half of all reported national income (48.5%). That reaches a peek touched in 1928. Following that 1928 peek of inequality, a combination of Great Depression, FDR, and WWII brought us the long period (1945-1975) during which government policy alleviated the poverty and our middle class came into being.

Surely, we have learned enough to do it again.

൭

Inequality Drives Abuse of Power
(Posted 04/02/2007)

Today in the NY *Times* Paul Krugman wrote, "I have a theory about the Bush administration abuses of power that are now, finally, coming to light. Ultimately, I believe, they were driven by rising income inequality."

Bravo! However, the *Times* editors smelled transgression in this Krugman's "Distract and Disenfranchise" column. They stuck in a phrase—"A unified theory of Bush scandals"—as it were a pullout quote (it was not) hoping to suggest that Krugman was over-reaching, speculating. The diminishment of the importance of Krugman echoes what these same editors always try to do to Albert Einstein (recently) or to any socialist, suggesting that he was an idealist vainly pursuing fantastic speculative conclusions. Thus, we heard of Einstein's "Quixotic pursuit" for a "unified theory," his "grand quest" for a "theory of everything."

Here is Krugman's argument: In 1980, when Ronald Reagan came to power, we were a middle-class nation and at least white voters could reasonably believe that vast injustices and inequalities were behind us and, therefore, we no longer needed Big Government to remedy inequity through taxes and social programs, as had been the case in FDR's time. And so they began to sell Republican politics-for-the-rich to the American people. Look what happened.

Since then—since about 1976—we have again become a deeply unequal society with an enormous and growing income gap between top and bottom, while the middle has been frozen in place for 30 years, an entire generation. American inequality is now at the level it was in the 1920s. The robber barons are back, thanks to 30 years of Reaganite Republicanism. Bush is only the 2000 through 2008 version.

Republicans (a party of tax cuts for the rich, privatization, and pro-corporate "supply side" economics) have had to rely or a narrowing set of tricks to win elections. They have relied on diversion: on 9/11; on "war on terror"; on a real war in Iraq [which, BTW, the rich are not paying for]; on security alarms and alerts; on appeals to a fundamentalist base the most outspoken of whom appear to worship the rich on bended knee. And they have relied on disenfranchising those sections of the population who overwhelmingly vote Democratic: the poorest, minorities, immigrants, and all who have been in the hands of the justice system.

Distract and also disenfranchise: their formula for winning. The most recent abuses to come to light are the Gonzales firings of federal attorneys who were investigating the disenfranchising of Black voters. They were investigating voter ID laws, racial redistricting, and the "felon purges" of voter rolls.

After making these excellent points, Krugman, as he often does, goes on to hope the Democratic Party can see the connections here and take advantage of them to win overwhelmingly in 2008. Krugman is a loyal Democrat. Win they may; but you have to ask, "Why should we care?"

The Democrats are only appearing to oppose the war while giving Bush an eighteen-month window to continue it and voting more than all the money he has asked. Restoring civil rights is on the Democrat's platform but not on their agenda. Nor are they fighting to make taxes more progressive (making the very rich pay a higher rate). And the Democrats showed little energy when they were deprived of the votes of the poor and minorities in the last two presidential elections. They lost through electoral crimes in Florida, Georgia, Texas, Ohio, etc. Ralph Nader was a minor factor. Now it appears that fighting disenfranchisement is "off the table" for Democrats. In fact, if Clinton-era patterns hold true we can expect the whole topic of inequality will be dropped by the liberal and "left" liberal voices of the Democratic Party as soon as one of their own (most likely Ms. Clinton) is elected to highest office.

There are excellent graphics at the *Too Much* site, including one that shows that the richest one percent of Americans is not paying their share of the Iraq war costs.

೦ೡ

Housing and Inequality
(Posted 07/15/2007)

Some say, "I don't care that others are making much more." Perhaps they are thinking of ball players or Bill Gates. I don't care either. I am thinking about the tiny class of the very rich, not a handful of sunshine celebrities. Perhaps the "I don't care" folks do stand a ghost of a chance for a better income. Nevertheless, national inequality is shaping their lives willy-nilly, more than they apparently know.

Today the *NY Times* reviews some wealth books and provides a poor article on philanthropy. You know the story: old Rockefeller papa used to thrown dimes from his carriage, his equivalent of loaves and fishes, and that built this great nation. The reviews, taken together with the article, promote the idea that there is nothing basically wrong with capitalism. It is only that capitalism has slid into a "winner take all" mode that should be restrained. You see, the *NY Times* is "liberal." For the rest we have anecdotes of generosity and social benefit, in fact crumbs from the table.

Some real history does emerge. John F. Kennedy did throw out aging socialist New Dealers and populated Camelot with anti-Robin Hood types who enacted tax-breaks for the rich, just to start the ball rolling. For a time, the wealthy had faced a 91% top tax rate on annual regular income over $400,000. This progressive taxation is what had held inequality in check, more or less, in the period from the thirties to the seventies,

The JFK Administration cut the rate to 70% on the strength of a false analogy ("a rising tide lifts all boats") and the ever-green false argument of "stimulus." The tax rate paid by the rich has been falling ever since. Dramatically. "Over the last quarter of the 20th century, America's richest 1 percent watched their incomes, after taxes and inflation, more than triple. In that same period, hourly worker wages actually shrank." [From Robert H. Frank's new book *Falling Behind.*]

Everyone's tax rate is now around 25%. That is not sharing the burden. That is not equity. While you are spending every dime and going into debt, the super-rich are harvesting the interest on their massive accumulation. While they are getting ever richer, and because they are, you are getting poorer. You will be giving over in taxes during your "mature years" about what your home is worth (and your home, in most cases, is your entire real wealth, your "estate"). The very rich will be giving over about the price of their second summer home or what they spent on their last boy's education. You are giving over something like the proportion of your annual income that you spend on all food and entertainment. They are giving over like the proportion they spend on booze or flights to the other coast.

In the sixties, the average home was about 1,000 sq. ft (3 bedrooms and 1 bath). In 1980 it was 1,600, then 2,100 in 2001 and 2,330 in 2005. Bigger is more expensive and—no surprise—the increase in home size tracks along with the rising inequality in the U.S. Mega-priced homes drive up the value of all homes in their area. Think of yourself as a middle class young couple with the beginnings of a family. The cost of relocating into a "nice" neighborhood rises after the first million dollar building or rebuilding takes place in a neighborhood with good schools. Rising housing costs hit you right in the urban and suburban areas where you wish to live.

Think of it in terms of schools. As you probably know, housing costs (and size) track right along with all measures of the quality of schools. Bigger equals better. This has to do with local tax rates, local school funding, and Department of Education criteria for federal dollars, as well as City Council and School Board decisions. If you want good schools for your kids you try to buy a bigger house in a "better" neighborhood and you take on more debt as well as working more hours. Also hours worked and debt accumulation track along with rising inequality.

You had best recognize that the rational life decisions made in behalf of your family have—under our current social condition of great and rising inequality—forced you into greater debt. That is also the case with your kids' higher education, if any. It is the same with your family's health. And this analysis does not even mention the impact of the enormous disposable income of the superrich on government policy (political contributions, influence, bribery, purchased propaganda and PR, "legal" exemption from regulation, and so forth).

Inequality hurts you. As Robert Frank puts it in *Falling Behind* (2007), the cost of achieving goals that most middle-class families regard as basic rises with the increased spending of the very wealthy in an unequal society. You may not care in the least about Bill Gates or rock stars; you may find the lifestyle of the rich and famous disgusting, or amusing, or whatever. Nevertheless, their excessive wealth is a major cause of all your nagging financial problems.

Note: A nice piece of social labor—beyond my abilities—would be to assemble wealth-tracking data into effective graphics: unequal wealth distribution, unequal income distribution, the historical pattern of tax breaks for the rich, actual philanthropic giving (which is insignificant and falling), various debt measures, housing costs and school quality by income group.

There was once an excellent blog, calpundit.com, done by Kevin Drum. For a long time I saved notes and graphics from his site. Drum now writes lighter stuff. One example from before: if the standard personal exemption (meaningful to us; meaningless to the rich) had kept up with inflation, it would be significantly greater (not $3,650 but $64,730 in 2009 dollars).

The change in emphasis in the federal tax code over the past 30 years has been truly stunning, and it does not get enough attention. For the middle class, the standard exemption has decreased significantly while payroll taxes have increased. For the rich, the top marginal tax rate has plummeted, the estate tax has been eliminated, and rates have been halved on capital gains (and soon on dividends if Bush has his way). The net result is that while an average family paid about 5% of its income in federal taxes in 1948 today they pay about 25%. During the same period, the effective tax rate on millionaires and multi-millionaires and billionaires declined from about 75% to 26%. Graphics best show that change over time.

Conservative economists continue to tell us that if we stay with their program a while longer things will turn around. They are lying through their teeth. Their standard fairy tale is that (a) millionaires are overtaxed and (b) this acts as a drag on growth. In fact, both are false. The rich are taxed quite lightly in the United States, and there is no evidence at all that higher rates on the rich would do anything except improve the national economy.

Economic growth is most robust when money is in the hands of people who spend it: the poor and the middle class. Thank you, Kevin Drum. Thank you, Robert H. Frank. And thanks to Thomas Piletty and Emanuel Saez for their inequality research.

∾

John Edwards on Inequality
(Posted 08/10/2007)

Presidential candidate John Edwards has often spoken of "Two Americas" and of America's "inequality." He is entirely alone in using this word. Perhaps he will use this theme to create a significant campaign for himself. Here is Edwards on "Two Americas" in his speech in Des Moines, Iowa during his previous run on Dec. 29, 2003:

> Today, under George W. Bush, there are two Americas, not one: One America that does the work, another America that reaps the reward. One America that pays the taxes, another America that gets the tax breaks. One America that will do anything to leave its children a better life, another America that never has to do a thing, because its children are already set for life. One America, middle-class America, whose needs Washington has long forgotten, another America — narrow-interest America — whose every wish is Washington's command. One America that is struggling to get by, another America that can buy anything it wants, even Congress and a president.

This theme has strength and great potential. Edwards said, "The time has come to stop promoting the wealth of the wealthy" and "A fundamental unfairness is at the heart of our economy and our society."

These are phrases worth having repeated as Edwards is doing. This is rhetoric but it is not mush; it is the opposite of hatefully untrue. Such rhetoric may turn the thoughts of its intended broad audience toward just how much damage has been done by all these years of a government that champions the interests of the very rich.

The "Two Americas" theme may enable Edward to approach the topic of a much-needed redistribution of America's one-sided wealth. The theme may enable him to give some substance to his call for strengthening working America, universal health care, and better education for our children. It may enable him to move his own and the other campaigns more toward expanding the social benefits of being a citizen of this country. No one is surprised that Edwards must avoid the label of "radical" (although that and all other nastiness will come). Edwards does not have the strength of commitment to carry that label into mainstream politics. The "Two Americans" theme may make dismissal impossible. He knows all this.

The propaganda-waxed ears of America cannot tolerate too much reality, but Edwards has a theme he can develop in spite of the wax. There really are two Americas: the parasitic few (very few) and the shamefully under benefited many, which includes the great part of the so-called middle class. For-profit health care is too expensive (and consequently almost non-existent for many). Too many are ground down by excessive hours of work in non-union, nickel & dime workplaces. Dishonest mortgages, credit card debt, and ceaseless job insecurity make life grim. Children's schools desperately need enhancement. Higher education should be free in a society that wants to advance, not something that depends exclusively on the level of parents income. Our infrastructure is decaying. People are forced into conformity and backwardness by the very punishment of it all. That may be the worst of it. They have no time beyond what it takes to absorb and repeat the simplest false mythology (our false exceptionalism, false superiority, fear of the foreign, build-in thoughtless "just do it" determination, all the average-joeisms).

Edward is a proven phrasemaker and campaigner. He denounces "the wild west of the credit industry," "abusive and predatory lenders robbing families blind," a system that rewards "wealth not work," "the special interests," etc.

At this early stage, he is sticking to mainstream solutions. These are not particularly interesting or important (matching funds for modest savings, raising the capital gains tax to 28%, expanded tax credits for childcare, expanded Earned Income Tax Credit, more rapidly increasing the Minimum Wage). What matters now is whether he develops his signature theme of "Two Americas." That theme itself is the ear-opener; that is what is drawing the ire of the hired sculptors of public opinion. It is populist. It is intended for Average Joe. Anything actually intended for the average Americans, designed only for them, angers the powers-that-be, the rich, the respectable, the well positioned.

I notice they are now getting angry with Edwards and promising that we will have heard the last of him inside a month or two. However much they bitch and moan and quibble about Hillary, she is not inspiring any anger from the powers-that-be. Most seem rather enthusiastic. We learned this week that substantial Republicans are contributing to her campaign, just in case the nation doesn't do "the right thing," elect a Bush surrogate and they will be required to help put Hillary in office for four years in perfect continuity with our eight years of George Bush, preceded—in yet more lock-step continuity—by eight years of Hillary's husband.

I wish John Edwards well. Just his repetition (Two Americas, the haves and the have-nots, the tax-favored and the tax punished, the rich and the poor) can have an effect, can introduce some reality, break some of the inertia, indifference, depression, and sloth, and thereby create a better condition for the struggle for socialism. Edwards will not lead that struggle, nor is it likely he will forestall it with a dramatic social democratic revival. However, his talk of these two Americas may bring the possibility closer.

Edwards begins another seven days through Iowa next Monday (Aug. 13) and the week will determine whether he continues his significant populist campaign. A quiet but distinct shift in his emphasis to a rhetoric about "One American" ("Together we can build One America and restore the American Dream") will indicate that Edwards has given up, capitulated, turned tail. I hope not

∽

Wall Street's Journal on Inequality
(Posted 10/13/2007)

Yesterday's *WSJ* piece "Inequality's Roots"—in addition to more numbers on the fact of growing American inequality—offers a bandwagon diversion. The *WSJ* tells us we should blame inequality on those big Wall Street salaries. This follows the outcry over defense contractor salaries and the alarm about manufacturing CEOs taking home too much money. When the *WSJ* is shocked at Wall Street salaries, how can it not be a diversion, a false flag? This is a secondary issue hiding the primary. The primary issue is the obscene accumulation of wealth by the ultra rich—all of them.

Yes, of course, these managers and CEOs are paid more than their social value. However, this revelation makes no more than popular, endlessly echoed diversionary journalism, journalism beside the point, journalism careful never to point a finger at the real wealth-hoarders. You might see my October 6, 2007 post on "The Executive Compensation Diversion." Here I will make the point without color charts or cartoons of bankers with bills stuffed into and falling from the pockets of their tent-sized pinstripe suits.

The base research (by the Steven N. Kaplan and Joshua Rauh of the University of Chicago) points out that non-financial CEOs only marginally increased their share of the top 0.01% (one percent) of earners between 1994 and 2005, a modest 5% increase. Given the hue and cry, you would think the CEOs and financial managers were stealing our money while the economy tanked but their research gives the lie to the alarm raised. It is a diversion for the masses performed by opportunist intellectuals who know better.

For the *Wall Street Journal* to blame inequality on big Wall Street salaries is a cynical joke. On the dock are managing directors with Adjusted Gross Incomes

(2004) above $500,000. This amounts to 6006 guys at Goldman Sachs, Bear Stearns, Lehman Brothers, Morgan Stanley, JP Morgan Chase, Credit Suisse First Boston, Deutsche Bank, USB, Merrill Lynch, and Citigroup. At the top, there were 1324 of the 6006 in the category above $31 million/year in Adjusted Gross Income (AGI).

The implicit "They are to blame" comes about by conjoining this information with a repetition of the big numbers about inequality in America. Many know that a growing share of the nation's wealth has accrued to a tiny slice of the country's wealthiest individuals. New data from the Internal Revenue Service shows that in 2005, the richest one percent of tax filers earned 21.2 percent of all income (including capital gains) and that exceeds the previous high set in 2000 at the peak of the stock market boom (and matching the high of 1929).

You cannot deny the inequality. You cannot deny exorbitant CEO and Wall Street salaries. Conjoin the two points with vague questions: "What's behind Wall Street's ascendancy?" etc. And if you might see through the journalistic trick, they remind you that they have thrown into their accusation top executives of financial companies, top employees of investment banks, hedge fund managers, venture capitalist and private equity managers. They also remind you that these guys charge large fees, the dogs!

Yes, this group has significantly increased its presence among the richest of the rich. Beyond that, they have increased their personal exposure to the public (their art collections, holidays, mixing with celebrities, etc.). Actually, it is more the fact that the magazines and newspapers have increased their personal exposure for them. The article neglects to emphasize that the group, taken overall, is not a very large presence among the richest of the rich. They are somewhere between three and five percent of the very rich.

All this salary and bonus exclamation points is over what amounts to three to five percent of the very rich. Folks, let it go. It does not really matter. You are being diverted!

In 2004, the 0.1% richest tax filers in the country represented 132,000 tax filers with incomes starting at $1.4 million. Of these they [Kaplan & Rauh] estimate, 5,000 were top executives at non-financial companies, 13,600 worked on Wall Street, 3,000 were partners at major law firms, and 1,000 were professional athletes plus a few other entertainers.

We should be most interested in the remaining 110,000 people in that group with incomes starting at $1.4 million. Major media journalism is not permitted to notice that much larger group. It is absolutely forbidden to attend to the top of the top, other than in the society, fashion, and "culture" stories (yachts, McMansions, charities, light personality sketches, financial coups, and bad shots).

Anyway, something like ninety five percents of the ultra rich are left out of the *Journal's* (and everybody's) court of outraged public opinion. "It is the executive salaries, stupid!" cries the *Wall Street Journal*.

Most of those blogging on this WSJ article went for the ploy, the diversion. Invited, they came to play the false, diversionary blame game. Some bloggers damn these takers of excessive salaries and bonuses. Others excuse them, saying "remember their long education and long hours" and mix up a thousand stories of self-interests with a few of stories of "creativity." Others sputter, "Stop calling us 'the rich,'" claiming we "Pay more taxes." "Quit vilifying the successful."

One blogger in the twenty-some gets it and points out that what these financial managers all have in common is the conversion of wealth into current income for those who are in a position to seek their expensive advice and recommendations. These are high net worth individuals able to employ the advisers to pension funds, banks, corporations, etc., on such arcane matters as hedge funds. This "Observer" is worried about the "world of low expectation and immediate gratification" out there and the operation of the "greater fool" economic model in finance. Good points.

I also recall a Bloomberg columnist had some good pieces on the exploitation of the "plebeian bottom" among money market pension fund holders.

Admittedly, it is difficult to establish a neat, cheap, journalism-level picture of growing wealth inequality. The variables are numerous: AGI vs. "wealth" vs. "return on investment" vs. taxes vs. tax evasion (on which the David Cay Johnston in *The Great Tax Shift* is the best I have seen) vs. corporate scams vs. government policy vs. corporate welfare, vs. the enormous money-based disparity in education, information, and services (such as lawyers and CPAs). You can search "Inequality" and spend hours.

To give credit due, Greg Ip of the *WSJ* l did have the good grace to conclude his article by observing that IRS data shows that median income American saw their AGI fall 2% between 2000 and 2005 when adjusted for inflation while the top earners grew theirs by 3%. However—discredit due—he also had to quote George Bush: "What needs to be done about the inequality of income is to make sure people have got good education, starting with young kids." Ip does not laugh at this from the Ignorance President nor take any exception, although he certainly knows that a correlation between education and financial success no longer exists in America.

And those young kids, I must ask, are they the ones with health insurance or the ones, as Bush said, "After all, [they can] just go to an emergency room"? Greg Ip's newspaper is not there to rake away the muck, nor will it allow serious fingers pointing toward that oligarchy of wealth that, in fact, does rule the country.

We are in for years of this muck on the subject of inequality in America. There will be more "Who is to blame for inequality?" articles that do not point a finger at any significant segment of the truly rich.

Some serious people will begin to worry about a broad, increasingly impoverished population of angry men. The angry may be men who cannot recognize the difference between a million and a billion. They may buy lottery tickets. They may not see why "equal" tax rates are inherently unfair. But they could suddenly cease sucking up to the rich and cry "Hang them!" And then serious people will worry that the wrong heads may fall, valuable, creative heads. And, indeed, some may. Serious people should have begun worrying earlier.

Who is to explain to the angry men that some people make salaries in hundred thousands, some in millions or even tens of millions, and yet they are not the problem? Their salaries—totaled—do not come close to identifying that oligarchy of wealth—the ten or fifteen thousand families, the top of the top one tenths of one percent in wealth holdings—who are truly influential and own our government, who are wedded to war and privatization, wedded to empire and hegemony, committed to wringing from the poor and middle class every last penny possible. There are others, functionaries (servants, actually) and only lightly rich, who may be guilty of social ignorance and of enabling the oligarchy, but they also may make some substantial and valuable contributions to our society. This group includes those who, if not "the salt of the earth," are at least worthwhile people and can be needed. A reasonable wealth incentive will remain as a social and economic driver for some time to come. This is especially so since many young people today cannot even imagine any major driver other than money.

However, try explaining any of this quickly to long damaged and truly angry men and women who will have American rough justice on their side.

∽

Truths about Taxes
(Posted 11/03/2007)

Let me see if I understand this. Republicans, who have consistently supported tax breaks primarily benefiting the rich using the evidence-challenged argument of "economic stimulus," want to continue their tradition by freezing the alternative minimum tax law while making permanent their other tax breaks for the top 2%. Okay, got it. Nevertheless, this week they say they will make up the tax revenue shortfall by "going after" hedge and private equity fund manager salaries.

As you might imagine they are not serious, and neither are the Democrats rushing to defend these well-rewarded managers and protect their juicy exemption from standard tax rates on their income. The Democrats are taking no definite position against the alternative minimum tax (which has not risen with inflation since it passed in 1969 and which has already punished 19 million middle class Americans through inflation and soon threatens another 35 million).

Now, can you tell me that the Democrats are courting doom or have they figured out that no one is paying any attention?

Both Parties, as a formal matter, are responding this week to the legally required obligation of Congress to pass law making up for a $50 billion shortfall in tax revenue (See Edmund L. Andrews, "In Handling Tax Breaks, Senators Face Touch Choices," *NYTimes* 11/3/07). Both parties, naturally, are propaganda-committed to "fiscal responsibility." The Republicans are taking good advantage of the extensive publicity—clearly designed to incite hostility and/or envy from ordinary middle-income people—against the hedge fund managers who have become multi million and billionaires by managing risky investments for the truly wealthy clients they serve (including packages of sub-prime housing loans) and, all the while, enjoying the lower capital gains rate of 15% on their income rather than paying the top ordinary income tax rate of 35%. There has been a lot of talk about this since the middle of the year. There have been endless articles on the exorbitant incomes of these hedge fund, private equity, and venture capital managers.

There is something fishy in this journalistic outrage in papers not known for their hostility to those blessed with luxury-class incomes. The point here is that today's Republican position allows some popular noise making by Republicans ("We are clamping down on that loophole," as the kids say, "Not!") and against Democrats who are defending the indefensible Princes of Wall Street.

The Democratic Party is putting its candidates in the position of defending, before the eyes of people, a coddling of the now unpopular little clique of specialized Wall Street managers. And, far worse, the party of labor and the little guy—who did not act against the alternative minimum tax law in 2006 (as many liberals including Paul Krugman thought would be automatic)—are not now speaking of fixing it.

The alternative minimum tax was originally passed to make up for the exemption from taxation that the rich enjoyed as a consequence of their ability to hire high-quality tax lawyers and accountants, develop "shelters," phantom "partnerships," have exotic trusts written for them, and make extensive use of depreciation, long-term capital gains, etc. The law provided an alternative higher tax schedule (28%). You will notice that this is nothing like an equitable or progressive tax but it

27

is at least some tax revenue. The alternative minimum tax, regardless of exemptions, must be paid on income over a certain level. That level was $50,000-75,000/year way back in 1969. You can see the details at Center on Budget and Policy Priorities.

The fault—"missed" by Washington D.C.'s tame economists—was that the law was not tied to inflation. As the alternative minimum tax kept reaching more and more people, it came to be called the "Stealth Tax" and in 2006 it struck 4 million middle class earners and 19 million this year. Without change it will hit 33 million by 2010. That is a lot of middle class people making $50,000/year to $100,000/year today who are in no way "rich."

Also—you can do the math—the law effectively protects the top incomes from paying their fair share and enshrines massive deficits as both a guarantee that they continue to be protected and a propaganda weapon against social welfare expenditure, which the rich somehow seem to regard as "their" money. None of this was the literal intent of the original law, poor as it was.

Pretty ugly situation actually; a way of legislating a "flat tax" by backdoor means and away from most eyes.

Why do the Democrats not oppose it? And why are they defending multi-millionaire hedge fund managers? That is because the Democrats have enjoyed substantial financial contribution from the hedge fund managers and now they are paying back their benefactors. *Moneyline*, the website, reports that 77% of hedge fund contributions went to the Democrats and those Democrats received more than half of the $6.3 million given by venture capital firms. Do they think Giuliani and his ilk are going to ignore using these facts? As with Giuliani's prostate cancer (that he claims would have killed him under "socialized medicine"), he will not only use but also inflate and mock the shame of Democrats.

In addition to selling out America's middle class tax payers for the sake of hedge fund managing patrons, the Democrats, in the face of Bush's enormous budget deficit and given Congress's legal obligation for find a "Pay as you go" solution, are again going to avoid fixing the alternative minimum tax. They will continue taking even more money from the middle class. So, where is the constituency they hope to attract in 2008?

I am not forgetting the values of the Democratic Party, labor, civil rights, blah-blah-blah. And Democrats can talk about keeping in place the popular child tax credits and the college tuition expense deduction, and some popular small business and R&D expense tax breaks. They can crow about and promise more of these (financially insignificant) measures. But watch them skirt the big reality. Today they are Clintonian Democrats. They are fiscal conservatives. They will pay down the deficit. The way they will do it is by raising tax revenue via the Alternative Minimum Tax on the middle class.

The trend line of tax sharing published in the *Times* in an article by David Leonhardt (October 31, 2007, "Plain Truth about Taxes and Cuts") is good. But look at this fact: the greatest acceleration of regressive taxation (portion of normal disposable family income paid in taxes) came after 1976 and continued well into the 1980s. The next greatest acceleration of regressive taxation came with Clinton-Bush and continues now, continues even though we now have reached and will soon surpass 1929 levels of inequality in America.

ञ

Going Nowhere
(Posted 11/24/2007)

Note that the flat-to-declining median annual personal income over all these Republican years: *Nixon (Republican) 1969-1974; Ford (Republican) 1974-1977; Carter (Democrat) 1977-1981; Reagan (Republican) 1981-1989; Bush, Sr. (Republican)1989-1993; Clinton (Democrat?) 1993-2001; Bush, Jr. (Republican) 2001-2008*

Excellent graphics appear from the Economic Mobility Project of what the *Economist* calls "the impeccably non-partisan" Pew Charitable Trusts. The Report's key sentence reads: "Between 1974 and 2004, white and black men in their thirties experienced a decline in income, with the largest decline among black men." And, by the way, the category of non-Hispanic White men and women amount to about 68% of the population while the category non-Hispanic Black men and women amount to about 13%.

There is just cause for anger here, long brewing. These men in their thirties are not called "the best and the brightest." As you probably know "the best and the brightest" do not do anger. They do apologetics and justifications for this clear injustice.

ञ

When the Cup Becomes Empty
(Posted 10/14/2008)

The cup metaphor (optimists see it as half full, pessimists as half empty) is a sort of reduction of everything to personal psychology. As with the spinning wheel ("What goes up must come down") and the swinging pendulum, the cup metaphor stands against facing the facts. They stand for giving up a necessary struggle for equity. Above all, these metaphors say, "Abandon principle as a guide to action."

When the President, the Congress, the Parties, and their candidates are not trusted, unions are diminished, social organizations have fallen to insignificance, and the churches are fragmented and given to shallow moralizing, these and other weak metaphor rule. They hide both cause and effect. In addition, the media and most politicians have made "Ideology" a dirty word, certainly "socialist," and even "liberal." These words at least reveal something of our understanding of cause and effect, our sense of where we stand. Thus, many appeals to equity, justice, fairness, and internationalism fall on deafened ears.

In another way to say almost the same thing—I do that a lot—we have the evidence of "What's the Matter with Kansas?" When George Packer, in the October 13 issues of the *New Yorker,* reported his interviews with voters in economically hard-pressed states, he found them repeating the dividing line hot button empty phrases from Bill O'Reilly, Lou Dobbs, and talk radio's minor personalities. All of these—I think it is fair to say—are racists and xenophobes.

SEIU people and college volunteers canvas for Obama in these depression states, careful not to wear Obama apparel as they approach doors and enter diners. Democrats add their talk about "the Bradley effect" and avoid denouncing overt racism while McCain/Palin pump out yet more of it (with White sport Hockey and White NASCAR meets as political venues this past weekend, There are "Town Hall" meetings at which the TV millions hear ordinary citizens call Obama "frightening," "an Arab" and "palling around with terrorists." All this gets an immediate media echo. I am told there were calls of "Kill him!" and that Utah schoolchildren on a school bus were chanting, "Obama is a Muslim." Background catcalls of "Traitor!" complete the picture.

People are still very nice to each other, by and large, but over the course of this looming Depression and during this growing fascism niceness may disappear. Attitudes will increasingly take on the tone of the media and politicking as they have already among many white males. Dominant rightist politics are now Reagan/Bush hateful, hypocritically Christian, and very reactionary. Democratic Party politics are weak and tentative; Obama still formulates carefully, moderately. The bit of strength shown by Edwards' was ignored or repudiated. Extreme inequality has settled in over these nearly fifty years while the always reactionary, self-defensive rich drive our society in the absence of any other leadership.

Trash metaphors, hot button phrases, and the surge in racist, xenophobic thinking are symptoms of our growing inequality.

∾

744,220 Low-Wage Workers in Los Angeles
(Posted 09/04/2009)

Several years ago, my good fortune was a brilliantly narrated personal report on a Mafia house party in Los Angeles. There were minor capos, charming and presentable thugs, lawyers, and family, all very intimate, chatting about crimes. For these people breaking the law is their life and limb and the key to their private well-being.

Compare that to my more recent misfortune at other much less "honest" Los Angeles house parties or dinner tables with the sort of people who declare, "You just can't get good help anymore," "My biggest problem is still my employees," and "Those people's salaries are outrageous."

Both are sets of people who, on the evidence of their party chatter, break the law routinely. The second, the more "respectable" set, break the law by not paying the required minimum wage for day-care, cleaning, house services, or gardening. As business owners, they refuse to pay time-and-a-half, enforce off-the-clock labor, illegally deny workers' compensation for injury, and threaten their employees when they complain or attempt to organize, which is also illegal. They talk about work classifications of their own private invention such as "contract labor" and "exempt industries." They sit around deploring the appearance of day laborers (43% of whom are in the west) yet they both employ and cheat them. "They're all illegals, you know."

These Los Angelenos attempt to excuse their illegal activity by making snide remarks and telling those prejudicial and one-sided stories that the richer often tell about the crimes of the poorer. Pretty nasty! In breaking wage and hour laws, which have been bedrock since the 1930s, they are stealing from their own employees. They are depriving their own extended communities (such as Los Angeles County) of purchasing power and needed tax revenue. And, since they live in communities where many others do obey these well-known wage and hour laws, they are being knowingly criminal. By routinely flouting laws, they inevitability spread their own disrespect for the law. This last is the hallmark of the professional criminal. It is a quality held in common with the folks at the above Mafia gathering whom, by and large, I prefer.

There have been many systematic studies of this criminal activity in the U.S. since Siobhàn McGrath in 2005 compiled her *A Survey of Literature Estimating the*

Prevalence of Employment and Labor Law Violations in the U.S. Today I came upon the first study that, to some extent, isolated California.

I do not intend to document every point I have made recently about California in *Nightingale At Large* ("The United States of California" "Dream of a Failed State" and "Health in California"). It is all too obvious. However, one of my points was challenged; so, here are some bullet points from a very recent piece of research. It is *Broken Laws, Unprotected Workers* and describes the experience in Los Angeles of its estimated 744,220 men and women in low wage employment. They lack voice or representation; they are fragmented by occupation, not unionized, and employers exploit most of them in some way at least once a week.

Why pick on California? Because it is the worst. Because it is the most dependent on this low wage population. Because of the evidence that California is attempting an economic recovery on the backs of this poorest group. Because California may become the frontline in turning back the "Reagan Revolution" that created all this shame. It is either that or provide a leading example of American economic catastrophe.

Here are bullet points:

- Only 8% of low-wage workers ever file for workers' compensation and that is mainly because of illegal obstruction
- NLRB law is commonly violated to obstruct of union organizing efforts
- Illegal retaliation is routine, even against the most modest complaints
- Workers are illegally denied access to workers' compensation.
- Illegal deductions are taken from pay, tips are stolen
- Workplace injuries result in illegal firing and denial of compensation
- Employers invent industry or occupational exemptions from the law and regular employees are illegally classed as "independent contractors."
- 89 percent of "in home" childcare workers are paid less than the legal minimum wage.

That these violations of the law are a deliberate decision of employers is proven in the fact that not all employers do violate. There are employers who offer health insurance, provide paid vacation and sick days, give raises, etc. Obviously, the decision whether or not to comply with the law is part of a broad business strategy characteristic of Ronald Reagan California.

Wage and hour laws became necessary because of routine capitalist theft of wages due. With the accumulation of injury people think more and more of socialism, a just and equitable society, one without such glaring economic inequality. Thus, these laws have been on the books and defended in the courts since the 1930s when American socialism was a real threat to the rich. And consequently many millions of dollars have been paid in compensation when groups of employees successfully brought rare lawsuits against employers.

The violations are not primarily in private household employment (only 13.7% in the above study) but also in restaurants & hotels (16.5%), apparel & textile manufacturing (12.55), retail & drug stores 10%), food & furniture manufacturing, transportation & warehousing, security, and residential construction.

As for a solution, we would not want government agencies enlarged to the point where they are able to monitor all low-wage employment for violations of the law. That would be like setting up a second society to monitor the first. But procedures and regulations can be modernized, whistle blower protections can be strengthened and non-governmental groups and agencies can be more effectively mobilized, supported, and respected as valuable watchdogs. People could be educated in the law.

Clearly, the most effective monitor is labor unions. That is proven. Where there is unionization there is compliance and, all too often, not otherwise. This makes the California union busting tradition and ethos a particular problem. An additional shame, some studies have show, is that children come out of California public school with no knowledge of our union traditions and their manifold benefits; in fact they often have learned all the clichés and lies of anti-unionism by the age of eighteen.

We might also look at mandatory reporting. I believe the considered view of some women's advocacy organizations is against mandatory reporting of abuses (because of retaliation, violation of autonomy, privacy, etc., and perhaps simply because such reporting subverts the growth of advocacy organizations). However, perhaps there is a role for those in confidential relationships with ordinary people (such as teachers, ministers, nurses, etc.) to responsibly report suspected workplace abuses. Perhaps someone has thought through this issue of mandatory reporting.

I do not want to enter La-La land here, but we also might consider renewing the respect for the law as part of a reinitiated "Civics" element in public school curricula. Civics has disappeared. Because the U.S. government has initiated so many violations of international law in the past 40 or 50 years, repudiated guidelines crafted by the United Nations, violated treaties, interfered in the internal affairs of other sovereign nations, authorized torture and invasions of privacy, etc. —has become, in short, a rogue nation—the traditional teaching of "Civics" was dropped from the public schools. "Cost-cutting"—already used to explain the lack of arts education, the inadequacy of science education, and the impoverishment of Special Education for children with disabilities—will also be used to explain the lack of Civics Education. No doubt.

In colleges, on the other hand, some teachers report that in order for the texts and materials they assign to have any creditability with students they must contain a strong element of criticism of U.S. foreign policy. Call it "The Jon Stewart factor." However, that is not Civics for ten-year-olds. The college generation, like their parents, may already be lost causes. The status of law may have to be reestablished in the next generation. I intended that as a hopeful thought.

In our world of Mafia capitalism—which works primarily through withholding, threat, and intimidation and includes many heads of business households on the Mafia wave-length—labor law violations are increasing. Naturally the capitalist pressure is toward weakening this very law.

Notes: Annette Berhhardt, Ruth Milkman, Nik Theodore and others, *Broken Laws, Unprotected Workers; Violations of Employment and Labor Laws in America's Cities* is a detailed survey study of 4387 workers. 68% reported at least one violation in the past week. It was supported by the UIC Center for Urban Economic Development, the UCLA Institute for Research on Labor and Employment, and the National Employment Law Project, 2009.

As for the large concentration of day labor see *On the Corner; Day Labor in the United States* by Abel Valenzuela Jr. and others, (UCLA Center for the Study of Urban Poverty, 2006). These men are frequently denied payment for their work; many are subjected to hazardous job sites, and are forced to endure insults and abuses by employers. They contribute further to the rising levels of workers' rights violations described in the above report.

And I mentioned Siobhàn McGrath who compiled *A Survey of Literature Estimating the Prevalence of Employment and Labor Law Violations in the U.S.* (New York: Brennan Center for Justice at New York University School of Law, 2005.)

BUSH

Introduction

This chapter, the longest, gives a set of drawings of the Bush edifice, his unreinforced concrete block Tower of Babel and lies. Over nearly a decade, from before 9/11 through quagmire wars to financial crisis, Bush has been a butt of useless conspiracy theories, jokes and parody. He has been cartooned as the Emperor Nero fiddling while Rome burns, parading himself naked as Godiva his banner reading "Mission Accomplished,"and even as mischief-making Alfred E. Neuman (a *Nation* cover). Humor is good. However, with Neil Postman, I sometimes think that we are amusing ourselves to death.

Bush is not going to be held criminally liable for anything, even as a straw man. He has been labeled "the worst president ever" and let go.

What is missing is attention to Bush policies as the culmination of a generation of Ronald Reagan policies from union busting and deregulation, through our New Poor Law of 1996 which drove down wages, and on to "fixing" facts and public opinion, packing the Supreme Court with reactionaries, cutting taxes on the rich, privatization, and corporate aggrandizement.

Therefore, I felt free to select pieces which focus more on policy and Bush's wars than on the Hollow Man himself. For selective reading you might find "Bush's Gas Bubble," and "Secrets, Secrets," best. For teaching, the pieces on the Supreme Court are pretty good.

∾

War is Hell
(Posted 10/10/2004)

I dreamed last night of two passenger trains. They were small dream versions of the Burlington Zephyr that blew through the small Iowa town where I grew up. These were dream trains packed with munitions, hidden in every available space: explosives, missiles, boxes of shells, grenades, depleted uranium, poison gas canisters, etc. They were dual trains, somewhat like very large dream toys on twin tracks. My job, standing between the twin tracks, was accounting for the munitions and annotating their hiding places on little scraps of paper that I stuffed into chaotic pockets of my jacket and jeans. It was one of those dreams of many repetitions, over and over the same frustrating, unsuccessful sequence of attempted record keeping. At some point, as the tandem trains moved out of sight on their parallel tracks, I woke up.

I have no idea what this means. Clearly, the destruction and slaughter in Iraq is disturbing. That slaughter was most horribly initiated under President Clinton's bombing and punishing embargo. The real equivalent of even an estimated, a mere statistical 500,000 dead children does count and continues to count still. Yes, the news from some parts of Africa is also terrible, but these munitions now being dumped on Iraq is our own current government's personal pocket war, its optional, preemptive, "unauthorized" war. It is solely our responsibility. The only out is not to believe in the existence of a world beyond our borders.

I am not a pacifist. Such things as sending Delta Force guys into the mountains on the border between Afghanistan and Pakistan immediately after 9/11 to kill Taliban and Al Qaeda soldiers did not upset me. I wish they had not been ordered to cease and desist. I wish they had accomplished their mission. Dealing with crime is an honorable job, the greater the crime the more honor. But that is not what happened.

I had been reading Sy Hersh's "Chain of Command" last night. As usual, he interviews hundreds of soldiers, their handlers, and their spooks. They trust Hersh because he has proven that he protects his sources, does not misrepresent, quotes their own real words, and respects them. The whole immediate post-9/11 Bush thing ("We'll get them, dead or alive!")—and I am being very brief here—turned out to be what GIs call a "goat fuck." Completely SNAFU, in Korean War talk. There were delays while the U.S. flew important Pakistanis and who-knows-who out of the target areas to safety. There was totally mindless Defense Department (Rumsfeld) interference. There was a career-threatened chain of command, and professional recommendations ignored, intelligence ignored. A horror show. As usual, many civilians were killed along with their goats. And it was completely ineffectual. I suspect Bush *et al* had pledged not to harm any well-connected Saudi fanatics. History, as written in American universities (where there is no sense of irony) will record the whole thing as a case of "defective intelligence."

As you know Osama is still at large, Al Qaeda is bigger than ever and probably more pious, righteous, and more willing to slaughter the innocent in the name of Allah. Its Saudi sources of funding have never been punished (quite the contrary) nor its Pakistani agents nor any staff college incompetents, nor Rumsfeld, nor lying propagandists, nor and-so-on. A bunch of our guys died, a few. Then (for the splash of a Bush show on the media) the U.S. began bombing Afghan cities to absolute rubble at the cost of thousands of civilian lives, innocent lives. All this celebrated in our media as "Success" with Dept. of Defense color photography, as a Bush "crusade," and Laura Bush talking about "liberating" Afghan women. If you believe a world exists outside our borders, this stuff is insane. Imagine if real cops behaved this way; and 9/11 was a great crime.

Then came Iraq. All I will say now is that perhaps you should read some of Riverbend, a girl blogger from Iraq, or Dahr Jamail, an American journalist from Alaska who also reports from Iraq. These are people who write first-hand about what they see and the people they talk to. They are unembeded, unsupported.

I know them from the Web only, but do not praise the Web excessively. Both Riverbend and Dahr Jamail also appear in the international (although not the U.S.) newspapers. This is not a case of "without the Web innocent lives would fall silently in a forest." These journalists would be having their say, some how or other. They do not have the status or the inclination to write the pounding denunciation of the war and the American occupation that come from John Pilger or Robert Fisk (who also don't do embedded and who also only appear on the Web for Americans) but they let you see things you wouldn't otherwise see. They are the risk prone, first-hand voices, and there are a few others, as precious as other American newspaper correspondents once were.

Reading the above people—honest storytellers however hard the circumstances, however limited the opportunities—I wonder about that other group of professional storytellers, our Protestant ministers. What are they saying, if anything? Their sermons used to be quite a national tradition, awareness and concern expressed in the light of a familiar morality. Why are so few of them against this terrible, evil war? Why don't they speak even in their private conclaves? And why cannot the Catholic orders again release their nuns and priests? After all, this Iraq is the Holy Land of their history, the scene of ancient parables and examples. After all, these ministers and priests desperately need to recover their moral standing and speak as they were speaking in the 1960s.

And the "anti-war movement" for Kerry? What is that about? I know they want to be "strategic" but there is also something to be said for having principles, for at least being against this war. Yes, everyone is exhausted and frightened by the monstrosity of what is going on and has been told that "more than half the nation" doesn't support even their most fundamental Christian values. When did fundamental values become popularity contests and a "strategy" issue?

To have taken the confidence, vigor, and values away from ministers and priests and ordinary anti-war people is quite an accomplishment for Bush and his slavish media empire, quite a crime. It could only be done by terrorizing them, reducing them to walking ciphers, shouting "traitor" in their face, manufacturing "consent" such that their every deacon and functionary quietly suggests "Perhaps you are going too far." The Church in a nation that can no longer produce any Martin Luther Kings is a Church caught in its own "goat fuck." A little identification with the victims and with our soldiers in harm's way is all I am asking for, just a bit of denunciation of this evil war.

And a word for the intellectuals. There is a typical fearful anger expressed in articles about the Iraq War and whatever comes next. Each editorialist writes their take or their own "line" but there are pervasive similarities. Here is Chris Hedges (and I admire him, have read most of his books) writing in the current *NY Review*:

> Only the vanquished know war. They see through the empty jingoism of those who use the abstract words of glory, honor, and patriotism to mask the cries of the wounded, the senseless killing, war profiteering, and chest-pounding grief. They know the lies the victors often do not acknowledge, the lies covered up in stately war memorials and mythic war narratives, filled with stories of courage and comradeship. They know the lies that permeate the thick, self-important memoirs by amoral statesmen who make wars but do not know war. The vanquished know the essence of war—death. They grasp that war is necrophilia. They see that war is a state of almost pure sin with its goals of hatred and destruction.

This is intended to be strong writing. But I swear there is confusion and falseness in it, strong seeming as it is. In actuality, no one invokes "glory" and "honor." That was England's Crimean War in 1854. Yes, national leaders do invoke "freedom" and "democracy," but only as excuses for invasion. How can it be that only the now irrelevant dead know the state of pure sin? No. The smallest participation, well short of death, harms all victims and victimizers. Remember the Winter Soldiers. That is war? No!

What is all this about. Chris Hedges is blaming us. I smell it coming. And he goes on to say: We must grasp the moral corrosiveness of empire or we are Saddam. But we are not Saddam, not on our worse, most dumb and racist day. Chris Hedges is playing Cotton Mather portraying us as sinners in the hands of his angry God. All this is to move us, but to what ineffectual actions? My God, man, who started the Iraq War? Who delivers us to war? It is not our war.

At best this Chris Hedges stuff is "hunter and the squirrel" nonsense (Does the hunter go around the squirrel or does the squirrel go around the tree?). All these implicit "if" things and future warnings are descriptions of present reality. And this vague sense of personal responsibility is supposed to produce what? This is low temperature rhetorical urging to soft activism disguised as passion. It is all pervaded by a dumb faith that "this too will pass," when, in fact, the perpetuators do not intend to let it pass (only to let the lies pass unnoticed). I think the truth is that we will pay for everything that is taking place, or our children will. And not at St. Peter's fanciful gates. What goes around does come around. Hard times are coming and the fact is we are not to blame.

Do not blame your good instincts telling you to "Run! Run!" Instinct is a better guide than liberal blind faith. All the instructors have already fled. Our people cannot do such harm in the world—only for the profits of a few—without paying for the consequences. Therefore, I suggest that you get out of debt, try to own a home somewhere, secure your base among your friends and loved ones. Tell them of your concerns for the future; prepare for worse days; do what you can. But do not be afraid when so many public snakes hiss "Be very afraid." That is my advice. And help me count the ammunition on its way to unjust, aggressive war.

◌◌

Bush's Religion & Bin Laden's
(Posted 04/17/2004)

President Bush's used the words "free" and "freedom" fifty times in his press conference on April 14, 2004. Yes, I know, abuse of language has become unremarkable. Bush, Cheney, Rumsfeld speak the language of low demagogues and unsuccessful CEOs, the language of the Hitlers of this world. That has become unremarkable.

Even "freedom" has become a squeak work, best reserved for spam ads ("free shipping," "free tire rotation"). The Bush handlers wanted a non-religious speech this time so they went with the "free" function. Blinding reiteration of evocative sounds, yet his meaning was clear: he was offering "freedom" to the rest of the world and offering Americans "security." "I feel strongly," he said, "that the course this administration is taking will make America more secure and the world freer."

So that is the offer: security for us, free for you all. Much of American seems to buy it. It is the language of incipient fascism, the promise of trains running on time, cops on the beat, security at home, use of his military to provide leverage over the "Others." Full-spectrum dominance abroad.

A new audio release from Osama bin Laden was transcribed simultaneously on the 14th. This Saudi prince, amoral religious leader, and terrorist also took up the theme of security. "The greatest rule of safety is justice, and stopping injustice and aggression." Addressing Americans, he said: "It is known that security is a pressing necessity for all mankind. We do not agree that you should monopolize it only for yourselves."

Osama said that "Terrorist" is indeed his appropriate description but that it is also a true description of the American administration of George Bush. As a student of religious texts, freely and fulsomely quoted, he noted that "Oppression kills the oppressors." "Reaction comes at the same level as the original action." "Our acts are reaction to your acts which are represented by the destruction and killing of our kinfolk in Afghanistan, Iraq, and Palestine." Any reader of the Old Testament will recognize similar elements from the Koran that Osama bin Laden chooses to quote. It is there throughout the Old Testament also. Just vengeance, or a non-religious saying,"Chickens come home to roost," "What goes around comes around." And he takes responsibility for 9/11 and, in another saying, "he got away with it."

Our media described the tape as Osama offering peace to the Europeans and it did include the message "You want security. Well, we want security also. Let's talk." Our media always finds Osama's speeches to be about something that the media is allowed to talk about and they are not allowed to talk about chickens coming home to roost. The media rule is: enemies only talk schemes, polity advantage, and payoff. We only talk values. What Osama was clearly saying was "Terror for terror."

Thus, both men sheltered their oil and conquest power policies in the security blanket of false language and both promised that God was on his side. Osama's tape was larded with "Almighty Gods." Bush's newly "secular" speech used this bridge: "Freedom is the Almighty's gift to every man and woman in this world." "As the greatest power on the face of the earth, we have an obligation to help the spread of freedom."

God help us all. Bush and Bin Laden sound like vengeful Old Testament prophets saying "Get out of Gods' way," Live free or die.

∞

Bush's Religion II
(Posted 10/14/2004)

The unexpected setbacks in Iraq will cause Bush's press to produce a storm of releases on the theme of his sincerity, seriousness, and commitment. The British press is already doing their round of this with Tony Blair as tragic hero caught up in human blunders, bad intelligence, and so on. The point is that we are not to think of these men as having any responsibility for the deaths they cause.

The national press still repudiates any criticism of the president: We are facing terror; they reiterate. We need Russell Crowe's hand at the tiller of the Ship of State in our George Bush version. The state press implies there is nothing else. The United Nations is a hapless organization, they suggest, compromised by rivalry, full of petty nations who do not like us, and idealist hot air. It is not an agency that works in our national interests.

And then, honest to God, the press mentions the "certainty" provided by Bush's religious convictions, presumably referring to Old Testament ideology which accepts—indeed, cries out for—the slaughter of innocents and teaches that there are those who are beyond the reach of mercy.

The press conflates this imperial religiosity with the Christianity of ordinary people. Our culture's vague religion, to the best of my knowledge, is based on the Sermon on the Mount and is about concrete justice and morality and perhaps about an individual's relationship to a God such that each might live a better life. This may be circular thinking but it has a certain force in people's lives. No sane person's religion is about slaughtering innocent civilians, wasting foreign nations, vengeance, regime change, illegal preemptive wars for fake "security," wiping out evildoers, controlling oil wells, etc., etc. It is not about official lying and misrepresentation. It is not about imposing "freedom" on those who want to make independent decisions free from armed coercion.

They say that Bush became a convert to evangelical Methodism during his tenure as governor of Texas and that he has said that God called him to run for president and that "a sense of divine purpose" informs his response to the challenges of the office. Much is made of his religiosity and his religious "base." If he talked more about his religion—rather than using the few drain-trap slogans about "evil doers" and "crusades" and "divine purpose"—I am sure we would learn that his Christianity has little in common with that of ordinary people, you and I.

However, much more relevant than any religious talk is the language that comes from the Reagan and Bush I and Clinton and Bush/Cheney *Project for the New American Century* (June 1997). That document said, "The history of the 20th Century should have taught us that it is important to shape circumstances before crises emerge, and to meet threats before they become dire." One of its formal principles called for a major increase in defense spending "to carry out our global responsibilities today." Others passages cite the "need to strengthen our ties to democratic allies and to challenge regimes hostile to our interests and values." The document underscored "America's unique role in preserving and extending an international order friendly to our security, our prosperity and our principles." This is rightly called "a Reaganite policy of military strength and moral clarity," more accurately "moral blindness."

43

Among the 25 signatories to the PNAC founding statement were Dick Cheney, Lewis Libby (Cheney's chief of staff), Donald Rumsfeld (who was also defense secretary under President Ford), Paul Wolfowitz (Rumsfeld's No. 2 at the Pentagon who was head of the Pentagon policy team in the first Bush presidency and then defense secretary and now heads the IMF), Richard Perle, Dov Zakheim, and half a dozen Democrats including several from the Clinton Administration who kept Clinton's "sanctions regime" on track and in line with Clinton's Iraq Liberation Act of 1998. Obviously, this fraternity had been marinating their chicken-hawk tough-talk for a long time. Other signers whose names are familiar were Elliot Abrams, Gary Bauer, Jeb Bush, and Norman Podhoretz.

Three years and several aggressive position papers later—in September 2000, just two months before George W. Bush was elected president—the PNAC put military flesh on its statement of principles with a detailed 81-page report titled *Rebuilding America's Defenses*. The report set several "core missions" for U.S. military forces, which included maintaining nuclear superiority, expanding the armed forces by 200,000 active-duty personnel, and "repositioning" those forces "to respond to 21st century strategic realities."

The most startling mission is to "Fight and decisively win multiple, simultaneous major theater wars." The report depicts these potential wars as "large scale" and "spread across [the] globe."

Another escalation proposed for the military by the PNAC is to "perform the 'constabulary' duties associated with shaping the security environment in critical regions."

As for homeland security, the PNAC report says, "Develop and deploy global missile defenses to defend the American homeland and American allies and to provide a secure basis for U.S. power projection around the world. Also the objective of controlling the new 'international commons' of space and 'cyberspace' and "paving the way for the creation of a new military service—U.S. Space Forces—with the mission of space control."

When a president's closest advisers and military planners are patrons (with the usual conflict of interest) of a policy that speaks matter-of-factly of fighting multiple, simultaneous, large-scale wars across the globe, you would think there would be a lot of talk. But only the left liberal opposition to Bush writes about it; and the amateurs among them like me. Most are true liberals and dress their remarks as alarm, as if revealing hidden future threats or ("Ah, ha!") exposing a potential conspiracy. You read it here first, they say. Actually, it is the broad foreign policy orientation inherited from Ronald Reagan and followed to date.

In his new book, *Winning Modern Wars*, retired General Wesley Clark says that serious planning for the Iraq war had already begun only two months after the 9-11 attack. He adds, "As I went back through the Pentagon in November 2001, one of the senior military staff officers had time for a chat. Yes, we were still on track for going against Iraq." This war was being discussed as part of a five-year campaign plan, Clark said, and there were a total of seven countries, beginning with Iraq, then Syria, Lebanon, Libya, Iran, Somalia and Sudan . . . I left the Pentagon that afternoon deeply concerned." Yes, deeply concerned, poor gentleman.

Little wonder the president speaks only in slogans and the language of pep rallies with faint overtones of religiosity. Even so, the hard core of Bush policy is not hidden.

༺༻

John Yoo's Descent to Indecency
(Posted 09/12/2005)

John Yoo dances like a successful young legal professional. In a series of law review articles, lectures at places like the American Enterprise Institute, professor of Law at Berkeley and Chicago, and in *Wall Street Journal* articles he has elaborated on positions he argued under John Ashcroft, Bush's Attorney General from 2001-2004. His arguments supported and sought to provide legal justification for Bush Administration policy, arguments carried forward by Ashcroft's successor Alberto Gonzales. Here is a taste of the positions Yoo defended:

1. The Commander-in-Chief can and should launch pre-emptive strikes
2. Suspected terrorists can and should be assassinated
3. Torture is allowed up to mental harm or pain like that accompanying death or organ failure
4. The Geneva Conventions do not apply to U.S prisoners held as terrorists in the "War on Terror"
5. Secret "renditions,"detention, and interrogation centers are legal
6. Non-public withdrawal from public treaties (including the antiballistic missile treaty) has legal basis
7. U.S. violations of Civil Liberties under the Patriot Act are minor, temporary, and legal

Students at Berkeley have petitioned against Professor Yoo. Human rights organizations have suggested correctly that he is a war criminal. They compare his memos to Nazi legal documents. Amnesty International urged sanctions against him. Powell and others in the State Department have spoken politely against his recommendations. Leaders in the law profession have quietly called him "a dishonor for our profession," one of the men who took us "down the road to Abu Ghraib."

Yoo is arrogantly dismissive of all these critics, calling them "hysterics." His defensive style is that of the very senior academic caught in profound misbehavior: denial, turning accusation against his accusers, suggesting they are irrational: "Must I deal with this raging and screaming? I argue law and history. I cannot be expected to argue against the passion of every low life atheist and leftist partisan with a voice, giving them that credibility."

Yoo was an infant Cold Warrior and has been a life-long evangelical. He was Clarence Thomas's law clerk and was given other soft Texas placements. He makes the argument that "the sword is in the hand of the king" to do with as he sees fit. Yoo has been influential in arguing that the U.S. Constitution and law support the medieval notion of all rights to the king. He has evident influence with prayer-breakfast politicians like Ashcroft, Orrin Hatch, Clarence Thomas, and even Lawrence Silberman (U.S. court of Appeals, Washington), according to the *Journal* article, along with Bolton and Gonzales. Immediately after 9/11/2001, he drafted key documents arguing that the president has broad Constitutional powers above Congressional approval that should be supported by the Judiciary.

You can look up these criticisms of Professor Yoo. The fact is he has never been alone in the Bush Administration, nor even extraordinary. He was a minion of the established fascist emporium, one of many lawyer prostitutes employed by the Justice Department to argue enlargement of presidential powers. Because everyone formally agrees that "the President is not above the law," the task of these reactionaries becomes to change that perception of law or "interpretation" of law so that the President can do as he will. John Yoo made his small contribution. Chief Justice Rehnquist made contributions that are more significant. And I fear the Rehnquist protégé, Chief Justice Roberts, has promised to follow, descending further into that indecency. Still, it would be gratifying to hang at least one calmly pompous minor legal functionary.

ᴄᴡᴏ

Tsunami & Aid
(01/05/2005)

News coverage of the Tsunami disaster is producing outpourings of support for the victims, moving now toward $3 billion, with private, non-institutional aid just beginning to be counted. Our government's aid contribution went quickly from $15 million to $35 million to $350 million in the face of the wide negative publicity. Colin Powell was shameful in his apologetics as the aid ante was raised. "This should not become a contest," he cried. Why not? In both real and per capital contributions most nations (Japan $500 million, for example) far exceed the U.S, contribution.

Jan Egeland, the UN Emergency Relief Coordinator, has played a strong role, calling the initial U.S. offer "stingy." The *NY Times* on Dec. 30 picked this up in an editorial and, as usual, made it into a question: "Are We Stingy? I will be so bold as to answer "Yes" and demand a rewrite.

$35 million remains a miserly drop in the bucket, and is in keeping with the pitiful amount of the United States budget that we allocate for nonmilitary foreign aid. According to a poll, most Americans believe the United States spends 24 percent of its budget on aid to poor countries. It actually spends well under a quarter of 1 percent. Such a level of misconception could arise only in a nation that denies the rest of the world exists.

Remember facts like this when you hear that heartland talk about our giving "too much" aid. Fact is, we do not do aid; we do USAID, a very different animal, guns rather than butter and what you call "interference in internal affairs."

Apologizing for the U.S. stinginess, Powell claimed that the U.S. "has given more aid in the last four years than any other nation or combination of nations in the world." The *Times* did expose this lie, writing, "For development aid, America gave $16.2 billion in 2003; the European Union gave $37.1 billion. In 2002, those numbers were $13.2 billion for America, and $29.9 billion for Europe." The U.S. is not in the top 20 in aid as a percentage of Gross Domestic Product. But never mind the facts, I saw Powell repeating his untrue assertion on all the TV news interviews, building his reputation as U.S. apologist-in-chief.

And the *Times* went on with another well-established fact: "Making things worse, we often pledge more money than we actually deliver. Victims of the earthquake in Bam, Iran, a year ago are still living in tents because aid, including ours, has not materialized in the amounts pledged. And back in 2002, Mr. Bush announced his Millennium Challenge account to give African countries development assistance of up to $5 billion a year, but the account has yet to disburse a single dollar." See globalissues.org if any of this comes as a surprise to you.

So, TV aside (endless photos of GIs distributing packages of food), we should recognize that the Bush administration is still the world's leading thief in the night, the same criminal and conspiratorial bunch who carry out debt plunder, military aggression, and routine interference in the internal affairs of other nations. This same group has killed something like 100,000 Iraqis (plus more than a thousand

G.I. causalities) in their debacle of an oil war. That war is lost and nothing awaits us beyond face-saving fraudulence (plus more death, more casualties).

To be reasonable we must deny that our government has any commitment whatsoever to "disaster relief." There is simply nothing in it for the rich.

Already it appears some "disaster relief" activity is being used to strengthen the brutal Indonesian military government's war on rural insurgents, on enlarging and re-supplying U.S. military bases throughout SE Asia, and on carrying forward the Bush propaganda war against the United Nations. The new theme (as today the press loyally reports) is the claim that our disaster relief will help in the conduct of Bush's "War on Terror." Watch out!

Jan Egeland says that the UN is already "making extraordinary progress in reaching the majority of the people affected in the majority of the areas. We are also experiencing extraordinary obstacles in many, many areas." He emphasizes that the UN is the only organization capable of coordinating such a massive and multi-country relief effort and it has appealed to the U.S. and others to recognize this fact, rather than setting up (as the Bush administration briefly attempted to do) some independent coalition to administer and aid grab. Given our history of terrible and illegal wars, our routine violation of UN resolutions, our historic aid stinginess, and the world poverty sustained and increased by our World Bank/IMF policies, we are best known for the harm we do. Harm not help. We have no right to lead anything other than arms merchandising, at which we excel, champion of the world of arms merchandising.

This Tsunami disaster provides a perfect time for Bush and company to back off, to support rather than exploit the international aid effort, to endorse the UN's leadership in relief and development work. Too bad we do not have any national leadership in Congress willing to say this to him.

Among the huge bureaucracies participating in the relief and reconstruction efforts those of the UN and of the International Red Cross/Red Crescent are deserving of financial support. Of the small organizations I have admired and supported, there is Doctors without Borders. They run low overhead and have the willingness to put themselves in these terrible triage situations where nothing you can do is enough. Above all Doctors without Borders do not make themselves subordinate to American government policy.

There is a good, wide-ranging rundown on what has been reported about this Tsunami disaster on Danny Schecter's web site mediachannel.org and his online *News Dissector* from Jan. 4 on.

∽

William Rehnquist & John Roberts
(Posted 09/15/2005)

William Rehnquist, dead now at 80, served 33 years on the Supreme Court establishing a pretty much consistently reactionary record. He limited the application of the 14th amendment ("due process" and "equal protection" for all Americans), expanded states' rights, limited desegregation, opposed legal abortions, favored school prayer, and supported capital punishment. As Chief Justice for 19 years, he was responsible for determining what issues reached the highest court and used that power to reduce their total by 50% in order to discouraging Civil Rights cases. Often called "a conservative," he is that rare figure that anyone at all may feel secure in calling a reactionary. Under his watch on the court, none of our civil rights extended; many were restricted.

First nominated by Nixon and advanced to Chief Justice by Reagan, Rehnquist's court (1971-2005) turned back the liberal advances of the Warren court (1953-1974). The Warren years included Brown v. Board of Education in 1954 (segregated schools are inherently unequal), for which Warren had secured unanimous consent, and Roe v. Wade 1973 (women's right to choice).

Compared to Warren, Rehnquist was the opposite pole of the law. He was a racist who had supported Plessey v. Ferguson (separate but equal), opposed desegregation, shipwrecked many collegiate affirmative action plans, enshrined "reverse discrimination" in our vocabulary, and did serious harm to the constitutional separation of church and state (upholding the use of government vouchers for parochial school tuition, the right of states to display the Ten Commandments, school prayer, etc.).

When talking eras I often say "Reagan/Bush" to emphasize the duration of the right wing's successful revenge (*revanche*) against the left in America. More properly, we might call it the "Reagan/Rehnquist/Bush era." Retrenchment, retreat, and reaction all down the line. The question is will our times come to be called the "Reagan/Rehnquist/Bush/Roberts era"?

To demonstrate Rehnquist's purely ideological and partisan motivation, I would make two additional points. (1.) Rehnquist used his position to manipulate the Clinton investigations by gaining Kenneth Starr his position and advancing the very partisan impeachment attempt. John Roberts was Starr's chief deputy. (2.) Together Rehnquist and Roberts cited the 14th amendment in ruling for Bush in Bush v. Gore in 2000 (Florida recount issue which disenfranchised many Black voters), a decision so extraordinary that the majority also ruled the judgment a one-off, a ruling so weird that it could never be used as a precedent.

The segregation of urban public schools is a product of "The Rehnquist Years." The recent drop in percentage enrollment of people of color in colleges and professional schools is a Rehnquist effect. Rehnquist diverted innumerable Civil Rights appeals away from the highest court through knowledge that they might be affirmed there. Rehnquist's so-called "states rights" judgments and his decisions sometimes limiting, sometimes extending the application of federal law have been an important element in the rise of the power of modern corporations and their freedom from regulation, their right to influence (if not to control and effectively "own") our elected representatives, and their right to surround us 24/7 with advertising.

Comparing the Warren Years v. the Rehnquist Years—or call it the FDR era v. the Reagan/Rehnquist/Bush era—all of us who think of ourselves as liberals, progressives, leftists, or socialists must admit that we have lost the great battles of the final decades of the twentieth century. We seem aimed at loosing in the twenty-first.

Our efforts during the 70's, 80's, and 90's have failed. We are now further away from social democracy, from internationalism, from social justice, from government accountability than we were at the beginning of the 70's. As a generation, we have failed politically. I believe that is more important to say than any blah-blah-blah you might read in uplifting "left" essays of the Howard Zinn type, essays that replace militancy with hopefulness and offer poetic liberalism and old love stories of "struggle." This attitude was rendered by Horace in a great quip

Why, minded as I am, do I not once again have perfect cheeks.

There is an honor in recognizing defeat, even a kind of potency. The right is dependent on lies and false faith. The right must hide whom they serve. They are crippled in these ways and we need not be. In addition, the admission of failure may let us keep our passion for progress alive while displacing some of our anger (usually called "negativity" or "anti-Americanism," or "cynical criticism"). Our values (equality and a concern for others) are alive, if trampled. Our goals (democracy, the ideals of socialism) are the same even though they now look like the mulch heaped up by the passage of horses along Victorian streets. Defeat can be a temporary thing. Reform movements can come again as they did in England in the 1840's and in the U.S. in the 1930's and again—attenuated, inadequate, misled—in the 1960's and 70's.

Defenders of Rehnquist and his judgments limit themselves to arguing that he "upheld the Constitution." They believe that the quantity and undeniable complexity of judicial decisions will let their soft lies about the constitution stand as truth in the popular mind.

An indicator that John Roberts will be as reactionary as Rehnquist is that he used "following the law" and "upholding the Constitution and precedent" as his main qualifications. As would you or I or any man-on-the-street. His knowledge of Law seems exceptional, but his position with respect to "Law & Society" is obscure and best guess is that he is also a reactionary. He claims he is not "ideological" but that is dishonest word play. He did not descend to us from the skies. As Thomas Mann said, "In our time the destiny of man presents its meanings in political terms." We are all ideological. Roberts will be partisan and ideological, of course he will. He is a Republican, the Party of the Rich, a "conservative," which—proudly announced—means a reactionary. Our most weak hope is that he, like Rehnquist, might once in a while break with the party line.

Although Rehnquist was a consistent supporter of commercial interests (limits on punitive damages, establishing advertising as "free speech," use of states' right to curtail federal regulation, etc.) he did not support the concept of corporations as "persons." He refused to let his court serve corporations as far as the corporations themselves wished. Business page bitching about Rehnquist went on for years. The corporations—whose greed knows no bounds—want judicial activism against class action suits, for a lowered "pleading standard" (how many facts they must present to secure a judgment), against features of the Americans with Disabilities Act, the Securities Exchange Act of 1934, and the Sherman Antitrust Act. They want open access to the court in behalf of their merger and acquisitions grabs, their usury, predatory lending, etc. They want the same quality of access to the courts and the interpretation of law as they have secured to Congresspersons with respect to the making of law.

John Roberts may provide them with that. He has more background in corporate law than any other sitting justice. I can imagine a Roberts who treads a "modest" path on civil rights issues and the precedents of Roe v. Wade and Brown v. Board of Education. He has said as much. And that would be a Roberts who turns energetically toward strengthening the domination of our lives by the great corporations.

On John Robert's confirmation hearings, this much is obvious. The Democrats seem intent only on securing the kind of Senate face-saving vote such as put Rehnquist in his Chief Justice chair (33 against, a record number of opposition votes for a Chief Justice). Not enough to defeat, but a showing. A matter of showing their remnant, dying ideological pride.

The Committee conducting the Roberts hearings learned little beyond that Roberts is a brilliant lawyer. They begged him to nod his respect to Senate prerogatives (with no mention of the undeclared current war) and he complied. They avoided any questions about corrupt and unconstitutional corporate campaign financing, anything on the role of lobbyists in the legislative process, anything on "revolving door" careers in Washington DC, anything about the attacks on Clinton, anything about that peculiar 2000 Florida vote count decision, and, in particular, anything touching on corporate law. And these were supposed to be "investigative" hearings!

I did not listen to every word of the hearings, but I did note a beautifully structured talk from the newly minted Democratic senator from Chicago who explaining that he would not vote to confirm Roberts (in spite, he said, of Roberts' credibility, comportment, temperament, love of the law, adherence to precedent, etc., etc.) because in every crucial decision Roberts had been on the side of the "bullies," for the rich and powerful and against the poor and powerless. I wish that Barack Obama had elaborated on this word play.

The Roberts of record—on rights, entitlement, and education issues—believes in opposition to the weak. They are only a problem. They are disruptive; they stack up as inadequate; they are parasites on the success of others (with their demands for welfare, civil rights, and the right to access and influence that they have done little to deserve). They are "the undeserving poor." Obama implied that this is "his overarching political philosophy," one he shares with those in positions of power.

How can you counter this *revanche* by anti-democratic power brokers like Roberts? What good is strewing flower petal kindness in their path, maintaining collegiality, courtesy, and consideration? Save us from flower petals! Save us from men, seemingly on our side, who are incapable of any visible hatred! That is to say, preserve us from the Democratic Party that allows 22 members to preserve their reputation for liberalism with their ineffectual votes against Roberts. Exactly as those who voted against Rehnquist's confirmation.

We do not want such allies, these FDRs-without-teeth, without real hostility. Even Howard Zinn (who can find beauty in every stumble) cannot justify this flower-strewn path to confirmation. Zinn cannot bring back the past, dates gone into our old rebel and reform chronologies. No progressive should be allowed to touch their cheeks with powder and admire their image in the mirror after they have failed so miserably for so long.

෴

Bush's Gas Bubble
(Posted 09/25/2005)

Imagine the Bush years as a gas bubble. It stays and stays, waiting puncture. The metaphor itself brings some relief. Bush and his co-conspirators live within this gas bubble dimly sensing unwanted pressure from the outside world. Their failures in Afghanistan, Iraq, New Orleans, and many elsewheres swell within. Nowhere to escape. Nothing to relieve the pressure. The frail walls of their bliss are weakening and the only protective coating they enjoy comes from traditional courtesy and respect for an ancient office and from incompetent hacks and hangers-on. It is unstable. Not the best chemistry. A White House renal failure, a blood-pump destroying embolism, terminal cancer, syphilis well advanced.

This is a government in failure. Only the corporations are flourishing. And we, my friends, face three more years witnessing nothing beyond the frantic efforts to find gas-relief for the President while he attempts to stand on his crippled dignity.

A reasonable question: "Why doesn't someone just step forward to puncture this sad balloon?" Do not hold your breath until some Democrat arrives with a sharp pin. If that happens the next president will be, like, Black, Spanish, or Brazilian maid left to clean up the remains of yesterday's Bush birthday bash for the rich. There will be no pleasure in it, little honor, just a job that must be done at $7.50/hour.

Consider the Bush hacks:

1. New chemistry was sought from Norris Alderson of the FDA, from a background in veterinary science, placed to head the Office of Women's Health. That, too, has imploded (Vioxx, defective heart devices, and especially the Administration opposition to Plan B Contraception that was Alderson's real assignment). No one noticed when Susan Wood (former head of that FDA office) resigned in protest. Someday I will chronicle the rain of resignations that the Bush Administration has caused. Those were courageous, career-crippling protest resignations. You have to admire them. Would only some passed-over CIA people, central to the so-called "War on Terror," furnish us with six or twelve major resignations. That might create a stir. Go, people! Anyway, examine any agency, from the CIA or State Department through the Food and Drug Administration on to the Federal Highway Administration. It is the same story.

2. Look at the "Recess Appointment" of John R. Bolton , ambassador to hate the UN, or the Attorney General himself (a very major elevation of a desperate incompetent) or, like John Yoo—a minor figure— one of the vast array of lawyer-prostitutes who have been elevated beyond deserving to justify Administration policy. Consider for a moment the effect on the hundreds of Justice and State and

U.S.-UN staffers—whole careers worth of hard work—as they watch obviously unqualified, fundamentalist dummies placed as head of their agencies.

3. Another is Julie Myers sent to Home Security (that great coagulation of incompetence) to head the $4 billion, 22,000 staff Immigration and Customs Enforcement Agency. However, Julie has no relevant experience. She was one of Chertoff's flunkies earlier, married to his chief of staff, and the niece of Gen. Richard Myers, chairman of the Joint Chiefs. He puts our fate in her hands!

4. Note also David Safavian—White House procurement official for Katrina relief—who was arrested on Monday for lying in the case against Jack Abramoff. Within the bubble, Safavian's wife got him the job for which he had no qualifications whatsoever. She is the top lawyer for the White House whitewash investigation of the blundered Katrina investigation. I thank Maureen Dowd for a couple of these notes.

5. Another is Frances Townsend, appointed to investigation how Homeland Security bungled the Katrina response. Ms. Townsend has extensive credentials as a legal-eagle cover up artist, a fox to investigate the recent raid on the hen house. Ms. Townsend's appointment to an inter-agency investigative task force matches Karl Rove's appointment to supervise the rebuilding effort from Katrina. Neither have disaster or emergency preparedness experience but both know a lot about dispensing favors. The "model" is the way the Defense Department investigated Abu Ghraib and Guantánamo.

6. Add Michael D. Brown, dismissed commissioner for the International Arabian Horses Assoc—he of the fantastically inflated resume—who is now gone as the head of FEMA. The real world FEMA was intended to administer federal disaster relief. Within the Bush Bubble, it seemed to be one of many agencies that could be gutted, incapacitated, and made a haven for incompetent cronies from the 2000 and 2004 election campaigns. You know, folks around the President who make calls, suck up, and make telephone calls hinting at favors to be dispensed. Then came Katrina. So, "Brownie" collapsed to Bush praise and had to go, leaving behind all his friends at FEMA whose incompetence is also the stuff of legend. They have not been fired.

7. Deep into the bureaucracy of two-term Bush are stories of overly promoted incompetents (press secretaries, agency heads, fumbling senior advisers at the head

of passed-over, highly educated teams, deregulation ideologues running regulatory agencies, prestige foreign assignments falling to fundamentalist dunces, etc.).

And the Democratic Party cannot find any sharp objects. They play political minimalism. Perhaps they should also have their respectability punctured before they fall to the floor like Kerry, abject and spent.

Ah, people, I know your plan is simply to wait out these dark toad years. Or deny them. But you will have missed a lesson, ignored the teaching of Lord of the Rings: "There is something strange at work here; the world is changing." Who are we if we do not help relieve the gas of those who oppress us along with the gas of those who fail to defend us?

∞

Secrets, Secrets, More Secrets
(Posted 06/09/2006)

From democratic governments we expect some openness, a degree of honesty, and generous public access to information. Not so this government. Common sense tells us that secrecy is corrupt, masking special privilege and creating opportunities for unfair advantage and crime. Secrecy hides official failures and incompetence and allows unfair blame to go to subordinates. With secrecy comes bonanzas for cronies, corporate boondoggles, and bought loyalty. Given enough secrecy, government becomes a jungle where lions kill and vultures feast on the remains and we hear only the elephantine trumpeting of known lies: The Bush Administration.

I refer you to Bob Perry's *Secrecy & Privilege* on the Bush dynasty's hidden agendas and hidden advantages, Bob Woodward's *Plan of Attack* on the secret plans to attack Iraq well before any public excuses such as the false reports of WMD or false linking of Saddam to 9/11 were offered, John Dean's *Worse than Watergate*, Brisard and Dasquie's *Forbidden Truth*, Daniel Ellsberg's *Secrets*, Dave Lindorff's *This Can't Be Happening!*, and to Jim Bamford's books *The Puzzle Palace*, *Body of Secrets*, and *A Pretext for War*. I refer you to the 90-page minority staff report of the House Committee on Government Reform, the Waxman Staff Report, and to the websites *Sourcewatch*, *BushSecrecy*, *Open the Government*, and *Progressive Regulation*. I refer you to the surprising number of documents by local officials in four states and more than 100 communities that repudiate provisions of that box for secrets called *The Patriot Act I and II*, provisions that flagrantly infringe on local rights and citizen's civil liberties. These books, documents, and sites (only a selection) give us scholars, journalists, local officials, and Democratic Party partisans as they repeat the evidence that the Bush Administration has a fetish for secrets often masked by their scare-tactic "War on Terror."

We call the common sense that secrecy is wrong "an essential value of our culture." However, there is another culture that stands in stark opposition to ours, the culture of very rich.

Who am I talking about? Those whose accumulated personal wealth is on the order of four or five hundred million dollars and up.

Pick out a few dozen individual exceptions if you wish; I will not argue; the fact remains. The culture of those who remain is to hide their excessive wealth behind the walls of compounds; to develop their deals and associations at private clubs, small dinner parties, or closed meetings; to dress down their speech and manner so as to appear acceptably ordinary; to divert their stolen wealth into a spider's web of trusts, fronts, and numbered Swiss accounts or Cayman Island corporations; to hoard gems, precious metals, currencies, and fine art in secret armored places. Like the dog in the manger in Aesop's story, they have seized possession of wealth and resources far beyond anything they could possibly justify as a return for social value rendered. They keep the placid great ox of the public away from their hoarded straw not so much with snarls and biting as with secrecy. Secrecy is the essence of great wealth because inevitably that wealth has been stolen. Naturally, they hide the results and details of the ways in which they shift money from us to themselves.

And so it is with the Bush Administration's mania for secrecy. It exceeds even that of the Reagan Administration, which produced Cheney and Rumsfeld and most of the neo-conservatives. In most respects, the Bush Administration imitates the Reagan Administration. Dave Lindorff wanted to put Reagan's face on the three-dollar bill—emblematic bogus currency for his fraudulent pretense of being democratic—matched by the semi-serious Republican Bills intended to get Reagan on the $10 or $20 bills replacing Alexander Hamilton or Andrew Jackson. But Reagan was comparatively sly while importing the cultural valuelessness of the rich to the Presidency. Bush has boldly overdone it. Bush is a direct descendent of that culture. Reagan was not to the manor born. Bush's membership in the Skull & Bones secret society at Yale was only a playground lesson in how the rich behave. His real playing fields were less Yale and Harvard Business School, more the early corporate deal-making years under the tutelage of his father. And the son remained privy to his father's dark doings as the father became CIA Director in 1976, to his corporate and Middle East shenanigans, his life as Vice President and President (instructive tales of Noriega and Marcos, of doubling the "black budget" for covert ops, of brief but devastating wars, the hostage crisis, Iran/Contra, mining of Nicaraguan harbors, the BCCI scandal, early relations with Enron, the Silverado S&L scandal, and so on). George Bush emerged a full blown and mature secrets junkie. Secrets were "How We Work It."

The inordinately rich are essentially a small tribe of successful criminals. Over his formative years, George Bush, unlike Reagan, had no friends who were not part of that tribe, a sort of higher level of his Delta Epsilon Kappa at Yale. He has always hidden his crimes and lied about them. His private culture, like that of his closest men, is the culture of *omertà*, lies, and subterfuge. His public persona—bluster, repetition, arrogant offhandedness—easily accompanies the private one. You should be able to imagine his private assessment of the slum masses, the undeserving majority. His example describes a good part of how the rich do things.

If we could only have the magic night vision goggles of the class-conscious rich, we too might see how the flow of funds takes place from us to them. As it is we can only grasp the fact as gross statistics leaving us no nearer detailed truth than the Biblical "the rich get richer while the poor get poorer," as if it all was the Lord's curse or some law of nature. Real wages have not improved (discounting one insignificant blip) since the father's heyday.

No more learning, playing, sharing for us now. Now the whole family works when there is work to be had. Social services and the security of pensions are draining away. Meanwhile the significant owners of corporations and property and hoarded wealth (a few thousand families at most) have grown much richer. These are social facts captured in statistics that do not convey much feeling. Gross statistics show nothing of how all the total of political influence has shifted to the very rich and their corporate institutions. Gross statistics convey nothing of the world of pain that lies beneath, among the poor, and defended as "normal" by a blind majority, by my middle class friends who declare, "Surely, you exaggerate."

But statistical facts are better than nothing. Therefore, we should have as much access to information about the very rich as possible. Unfortunately, we are treated to endless news stories about how much trouble the corporations have rubbing two dimes together, how corporate officers are threatened with house arrest for such relatively innocent crimes as insider trading and lying on their tax returns. They are "innocent" as compared to war profiteering that is altogether more common. We are treated to surveys of wealth that obscure the magnitude of the accumulation at the top, surveys that never show how an organized crime wave of theft from us to them takes place, how corporate mafia dons operate, how orders of magnitude of excessive money is accumulated, money beyond all the dreams in all the nation's slumbering prisons.

And President George Bush has bathed the country in secrecy. Today's news describes how a Senator used his "secret hold" powers to block consideration of the "Federal Funding Accountability and Transparency Act" that would give public access to government contracts and expenditures, an Act that will never see the light of day because of many other procedural subterfuges. NSA flat refuses to provide Congress with information about even the total budget for their "black operations," much less the CIA. Homeland Security corrupts our local police by requiring them to investigate immigrants for non-criminal violations of federal immigration law. Local Dept. of Health and Human Services officials stonewall and invent their own "classification" of documents to hide the flaws of bureaucracy. Environmental agencies doctor reports to obscure global warming. And in the world of finance, insider trading in corporate stocks has become as common as dirt (that is, the illegal buying or selling of stock, mainly by brokerages, banks, and institutional investors, based upon secret information not available to the public). The SEC turns a blind eye. Only small players take random walks down Wall Street. They are the ones who step in pot holes and dog shit, who and are hit by taxis, the little people, not the truly rich or their institutions. Cite exceptions if you wish. I will not argue. The fact remains.

It is really pretty bad. Ever broadening definitions of "terrorism" bring more and more legal, public activity—Internet, church and other public meetings, demonstrations, immigrant community social activities, charities, small donations—under the scope of the Patriot Act while major financial transgressions are hidden. Contracts are made—just to give some small illustrations—for bomb disposal containers to be installed in Amtrak passenger trains while train wheels go without inspection; airline employees lose their pensions while shoes and moisturizing lotions are scanned and prohibited; hidden deals with foreign corporations put our ports under supervision by interested strangers; our National Guard is 5800 miles away in hurricane season while bridges, overpasses, and levies go without repair; slush funds flow to political and corporate cronies in safe and placid States for "national security measures." A fiasco of a long war for oil destroys hundreds of thousands of lives while providing barrels of pork for armament, supply, and corrupt construction and private security corporations.

No one would deny the legitimacy of secrecy in defense against real enemies. Justifiable wars are not unknown. We all know that loose lips sink ships. We know the police use secrecy when tracking criminals. However, the endless big and little wars of the last fifty years—along with the war on drugs, war on terror, war on illegals—have little to do with safety or crime prevention and have everything to do with profiteering and terrorizing and rendering helpless the victims of grand theft. Even without magic night vision goggles we are beginning to see in the gross statistics of recent history the criminal enrichment of the very few.

∽

Cheek to Cheek on Iraq
(Posted 01/11/2007)

Listen to the chorus made up of the Administration, Democrats, Republicans, and all the media as they sing the latest Iraq dubba-dubba-dubba in an effort to shift all responsibility for unity, social order, peace, and freedom in Iraq onto "the Iraqi government." Forget the debate over increasing troop strength, called "intense" in *NYTimes*-talk. Measured in 20K increments, Bush and Rumsfeld have already made more then 25 such deployment decisions. The real issue is who is responsible. And, so, it seems that only the Iraqis are responsible.

We are to forget that the Iraqi civil war grew out of an insurgency against Bush's invasion of their country—an invasion based on lies—and out of the corrupting influence of Bremer's and Negroponte's governments there (2003-2005) and the tens of millions of dollars the U.S. and the corporations threw around to buy influence and contracts. In his speech last night announcing escalation of the war, Bush hailed an empty "freedom." He nodded to his God, "the Author of Liberty," threatened Iran and Syria, and issued meaningless commands that the Iraqis must "stand up" and quiet down. Immediately all the respectable voices (Administration, Republican, Democrat, Media) sang the same song: social order is the Iraqis' responsibility. A devastated and corrupted country. Our latest victim. How is that for hypocrisy!

Upon the heads of the Iraqi people—on top of all that our former ally Saddam Hussein's did to them—have come two wars by the world's most expensive military empire. Add the concerted political subversion and interference in Iraqi internal affairs, the deadly American-enforced sanctions, the near endless, near comprehensive bombing, George W. Bush's military occupation, the imposition of a succession of "governments" and a constitution created in London and Washington D.C. Add the deaths, often at random, of more than 655,000 noncombatant Iraqi men, women, and children. Add the major oil, construction, and security corporations, vultures picking over the rich ruins.

Yet now, cheek to cheek, the forces collectively and cooperatively responsible for all of the above are singing about something called "the Iraqi government." In the circumstances, what government is that? It is very like the succession of our puppet governments in South Vietnam—from our North Vietnamese Roman Catholic man Diem through all the rest (Minh, Ky, Theu) who were hailed and then blamed and replaced. Watch as Prime Minister Nuri al-Maliki's wife soon repeats Madam Nhu's comment when she learned of the assassination of her husband Diem: "Whoever has the Americans as allies does not need enemies."

What a sorry spectacle to have Bush still talking of "victory" in Iraq, haltingly reading from the teleprompter, still issuing real threats against Iran and Syria, and adding 20,000 to the 135,000 U.S. troops presently on the ground in Iraq alongside 100,000 or so American private contractor forces (mercenaries). Without specifying, Bush did admit missteps. However, according to him, who is the real culprit? The word "Iraqi" appeared about 60 times in Bush's short (3,000 word) speech last night. At one point—the point where Bush attempts to justify his 20,000 troop escalation and presses the point of Iraqi responsibility—the word "Iraqi" occurs 35 times in just a few paragraphs.

To borrow Barack Obama's proforma expression responding to the Bush speech last night, I do not doubt the sincerity of President Bush's desire for an exit, but he wants to leave without taking any responsibility for the deaths, the sectarian violence, or the civil war. And all who voted for the war or promoted and justified it want to leave on the same terms. *Editor & Publisher* reported that very few national editorials offered any commentary on the escalation. Most will become "critical" of the escalation as that also fails. Nevertheless, they now join the Democratic Party chorus. You can read the chorus:

> I continue to urge a strategy that places pressure on the Iraqi government to resolve the political crisis. [Clinton]

> [We must] force Iraqis to stand up for Iraq [Kerry].

> We have leverage over the Iraqi government . . . the essential problem . . . is the Maliki government [Obama]

Bush is having it all his own way again. The Republicans, the *Times*, the Democrats, and most everyone to the left Joe Lieberman are phrasing their "analysis" around some non-existent "free and independent" Iraqi government. That government, elected in a photo opportunity (the purple fingers), lives under the auspices of an invading military and has been part of the cause—at least by 2005—of a civil war. That government is now used as the dog in the water that everyone is beating. This is hypocrisy, and lies, and fantasy. After conspiring to lay the Iraqi people low, everyone echoes Bush (being careful to disagree on details) and declares, "The Iraqis must stand up." It is like a scene from some cruel play in rural Italy in the 1930s where *He Who Gets Slapped* cowers while everyone gangs up to shout "Stand up! Stand up!."

I did notice that Thomas de Renegotiate echoed me more concisely in a post on the sometimes excellent *Huffingtonpost.com*. On the "craven bankruptcy of the Democratic Party," he writes:

> They are all rushing toward a door marked thusly—blame THEM. The message is: "we did everything we could, especially our heroic troops, now it's up to Iraqis to step up to the plate etc…" And innumerable variations on that theme. What does that amount to? This: the USA invaded this country for no legitimate reason, but the consequences of our invasion are all their fault — those primitive tribal ingrates. That's what it comes down to. You can pretty it up any way you want. But that's what it comes down to.

We will hear little of Mr. de Zengotita in the future. He has transgressed a line accepted journalists must not cross. It is called "Blunt Truth."

૭૦

While Rome Burns
(Posted 01/19/2007)

The cartoon cover of the *New Yorker* (1/22/2007) has Bush as the emperor Nero, fiddling while Rome burns. While sort of funny, the cover in not intended to remind us that Rome was once a republic. Instead it suggests that George Bush is dithered, gone astray, "the poor man."

A similar lack of spirit marks most of our oral and image culture related to the presidency. Nothing is said that recognizes America as an oligarchy—as was Rome—effectively ruled by unelected financial and corporate oligarchs while the titular head, Bush, misspeaks, lies, entertains, repeats himself, and (unlike Nero who died at thirty-two by his own hand) self-perpetuates from Reagan's day to this.

The cartoon does not remind us that we have our circuses on technically vivid television and in glossy advertising, that we have Nero's slaughtered Christians as the poor, the homeless, and the immigrants who seek to avoid the eyes of other citizens, that we have a flourishing capitol and deteriorating provinces. As in Nero's Rome, we have our opportunities to laugh at jokes, including jokes at the President's expense as he carefully reads someone's words on January 11. We "interact" with radio, sass back at TV's personalities, post observations, and make obscene remarks on advertising-laden blogs. We do not organize an opposition.

Nothing in our radio and television culture rises above repetition, or in the "quality text" rises above a careful evasion of exact repetition, or above the reinforcement of what has been repeated. It is the muck that people talk when they are paid to talk or know that their actual knowledge is not wanted and their opinion clearly does not matter. Even Jon Stewart and Steven Cobert have run out of *bel esprit*. The major television news shows are things of poor quality. Cable news with its paltry audience features repetition by personality contestants (Keith Olbermann or whoever is the new Mike Wallace, Bill O'Reilly or whoever is the new Walter Cronkite, Christiane Amanpour or whoever is the new Barbara Walters). Altogether they exist to choke down us once again what we have already been served for lunch. They never speak of or investigate what we all suspect: that the surface is only the scum and that under this scum a vicious oligarchy rules. I you do not read books you are truly dumbfounded.

There is nothing out there in sound bite and image land beyond what has already been adopted and approved. Below literacy swarms a buzzing helplessness, a sense of loss, at best some brief, unsatisfactory titillation. In honesty, I should include a lot of our own private conversations. I do hear some young women interviewed on radio, quick and incisive, but should they become at all radical their voices will be exiled to books. The same if any politician dare speak truth to the powers behind Bush. He or she will be exiled to books, which for a politician is a sentence of death. Even the comedians and the cartoons have betrayed us.

Many thought it odd to see in the newspapers a picture of Hugo Chavez holding up a copy of Noam Chomsky's *Hegemony or Survival* at the podium of the United Nations General Assembly back in September. It was exceptional. That image is all that the oral and image culture provides about hegemony and our hegemonic elites. Chavez then called Bush "the devil"; but that was ridiculed as Latin hyperbole. To a democrat and a socialist, Bush must seem more Mephistopheles than Nero. Nero was weak, silly, and did not govern. Bush does not sing or carouse, but he does govern in behalf of those who rule. They get richer thanks to him. Indeed they do. Moreover, they see that his ambitions are celebrated.

George Bush may have met a dark figure at a crossroads and said he wanted to play trumpet in a famous jazz band. His desire was granted. In return, he blesses foreign wars for oil, packs his administration with arrogant incompetents, pushes tax cuts for the rich, privatizes, deregulates, and ensures plenty of financial dark space providing exemptions from the law for his corporate supporters. The dark figure licks his lips.

All the while, we pour ashes over our heads and await the lions. We are just an ordinary people, exhausted by the failures of our state since early 1976. A generation of exhaustion. Most of us still have our families, our work, and our aspirations, but that is not enough to protect us from decline and fall. We should give up the fiction that our society is temporarily in the hands of some misguided, incompetent Prime Minister, some comic Aberdeen.

Excuse me here while I jump to another, a more appropriate historical analogy. We never completed our declaration of independence from England. We inherited the *Times of London*, House of Lords, and the House of Commons from the bloody English. Our federal administration as well as our language truly derived from our slaver, colonialist, trader, immensely hypocritical, enormously arrogant English antecedents. We are dominated by a corporate oligarchy—call it what you will; I estimate it as about 5,000 unelected men—whom the worst of our English antecedents would immediately embrace as kindred spirits. As for our government, all serve at the pleasure of their underwriters. All treat the head of state with immense courtesy, whatever he does, because they know it is their state. That was the deal.

Since before Reagan took office this oligarchy, not the people, has put every President in place and maintained the House of Lords, or Senate, and the House of Commons, or Representatives. It is like England in 1854 and we are now in the midst of our Crimean War, a war less bloody but more dispiriting and more harmful to the national sap than our Vietnam War. Our Aberdeen government is about to be replaced with another Aberdeen government and we are more demoralized than we have been since 1976. And that was a low point! The day the music died.

In 1976—200 years after our revolution against British rule and our great declaration of independence—we were an especially dispirited people, dispirited over the enormous turmoil because of the Vietnam War, but more than that, over the whole lack of consequence of that enormous turmoil. 55,000 Americans had lost their lives in that war and half a million returned damaged. For what? And the "War at Home" also left some damage. The Vietnamese—horribly victimized by the blind, exquisitely mechanized U.S. aggressor—have been able to recover, as you can see now. But back in the states we remained mired in the disillusion and shallow expediencies of the Nixon and Ford Administration. Famous cartoons then showed a sneering, unshaven Nixon lifting a manhole cover and climbing up out of the sewer. Ford was shown masked with a great bloody axe over one shoulder and holding the bleeding head of the Statue of Liberty. Reagan appeared in an old cowboy hat once worn by Jack Parlance, that exquisite villain.

The Reagan Administration brought back focus and determination, not for the people but for the very, very rich. Within what had all the marks of a dying republic—a common theme then—the Reagan men saw a great opportunity to shift multiples of their already substantial private wealth from the people to themselves. The government would be the essential enabling agency. The Reagan Administration specialized in that service. Huge deficit expenditures paying key corporations billions for armaments and cheap or phony services, a original "War on Terror" to justify any theft from the public purse, privatization, obscurity, bending the law, deregulation, breaking unions, unleashing death squads in Central America and the Caribbean, destroying small, free nations, suppressing Civil Rights, consolidating the oligarchy's interests in the Middle East, etc. And we live now in the Reagan Era.

We are an Oligarchy pretending to be a Republic.

֍

The Next War
(Posted 02/03/2007)

There are yet no major public voices calling for opposition to Bush's next war, the war with Iran. Sentiment against the current Iraq War is near universal, a war so disastrous that only fringe voices—the most extremist of the war-mongering right—now cheer it on. Many progressive journalists have warned against and decried a possible U.S.-Iran war, but public attention stays with the war we have before us. All of Washington claims not to want the next war, but suggests it may be forced upon us. Certainly, the Iranian and American people do not want it. However, these sentiments and claims, the criticism of past lies, fervent hopes, and the warnings provide only hints at future opposition. There is no anti-war movement worth the name.

An Iran War in its probable dimensions will be a human catastrophe exceeding the catastrophe that is the Iraq War with its 650,000 dead, its destroyed national infrastructure, and its civil war.

Iran's population is 70 million, 50% are under 20, and the average longevity is 70. Over the past 30 years, by spending nearly 10% of total government expenditures on health care, Iran has built a health service infrastructure (physicians and nurses per/1000, medical technology, neonatal care, clinic access, etc.) that compares favorably to all countries in the Middle East, some in Southeastern Europe, and above most in Central Asia. [See the WHO and UNICEF State of the

World's Children 2007 websites] Iran has a diverse and widespread manufacturing infrastructure, a strong central government, a selectively socialist economic system, and, under the Nuclear Non-Proliferation Treaty [they are an original signatory nation], Iran is on a path to become the 32nd nation to develop and use nuclear energy.

For many Americans, Iran is an unknown hidden in plain sight. That was true of Iraq once, and other nations. In the past, many pointed out the reality of tiny Nicaragua as Reagan was building steam for his illegal attack on that country in the early 1980s. The World Court found Reagan guilty of war crimes. He wasted tiny Nicaragua. Even now, 30 years later, Nicaragua has hardly recovered its sprit, its remarkable Sandinista fine public art has been painted over by Reagan's Chamorro flunkies. Merely an example.

Anyone who cares to do so can number the dead and damaged children of these 30 years. Again, as with Managua Nicaragua—if you care for another mere example—some people knew the beautiful, diverse city of Sarajevo, its people, and its surrounding nation that was once socialist Yugoslavia. Much the same chronicle of disaster. And for the Middle East, the story is the same, only longer. The extent of killing and destruction by the moral monstrosity that crouches in Washington, D.C. is indescribable, all for the sake of or to "secure" private profits.

The bombing and rocket attacks against Iran, when they commence, will be terrible. Embedded and secured military targets will survive, many tens of thousands of armed and angry men will take to the mountains, the strong central government will survive; but civilians and civilian infrastructure (electricity, water, sanitation, housing, roadways, as well as schools and clinics) will be destroyed or damaged. The progress and accomplishments of a generation will be turned back. That is the drill. We have seen it before.

Now, in building for the next war, our best newspapers, citing no evidence, confidently talk of Iran's "nuclear weapon ambitions" and its "decades of clandestine efforts," and warn of an "accidental war" as if these words described some reality. This is *NY Times* journalism written as if repeated denials, UN evidence, exceptional openness, and very real U.S. warmongering and provocations did not exist. The journalists speak a George Bush reality, reality for which there is no evidence. From Cheney's clandestine war-room in the White House (where Iran War planning was moved away from prying eyes in the Pentagon) comes a flow of questionable tidbits. These are shaped into a story of the "flow of support" from Iran for the insurgents in Iraq (both countries with majority Shiite peoples with a long history of trade, religious celebration, and intermarriage) and of "networks providing advanced weaponry and training to our enemies." Again, this is on the shallowest of Colin Powell-type evidence.

The picture is painted of stubborn and "evil" Iranian leaders with dark intent, wild-eyed, holding lit bombs. Comic book fiction pours out of the White House of Skullduggery. The newspapers and television from Ad Land all do their echo. Then the same news media blandly describe the real deployment of U.S. aircraft carriers, atomic-powered submarines, and missile batteries pointed toward Iran as if this were reasonable, diplomatic, even peace-loving behavior. The Iran War is in the making.

All of Washington seems to accept the Bush doctrine of the U.S.'s right to wage "preemptive" war, a revival of one of the most monstrous and rabid Cold War concepts. Combined with "unlimited offensive force" and the "nuclear option," the concept "preemptive war" frightened even Robert McNamara, and he is a man who cut his teeth on the firebombing of Japanese population centers.

All of Washington seems to accept Bush's "Terrorism," not as something the U.S. has done repeatedly to other countries, but as an endless set of episodes worthy only of television. Bush implies that at any moment those planes may fly again into those towers of American commerce just as they did more than fifty months ago. Or the same with variations. And Bush's trumpeting of 9/11 has resulted in more wide-spread damage that perhaps even a criminal fanatic like Osama could imagine.

Out of every real straw blowing in the chaotic winds in and about destroyed Iraq (which is Bush's great quagmire, his impeachable offense, his grand pay-off to the war and oil merchants), our president and our president's media are building the House of War on Iran. They are strumming the strings of undiscovered, unlikely Iranian weapons of mass destruction, non-existent Nigerian yellow cake, the Saddam-equals-Osama guitar riffs all over again. The song was sold to millions once. "Let's have a sequel!" they cry. Iranian president Ahmadinejad becomes Saddam becomes Hamas becomes Hezbollah becomes Osama. The towers are burning again; block-buster bombs are falling making new and more beautiful explosions. The schools even sell this song to children, and only God knows how the song is affecting the backward, semi-rural cannon fodder and their moms and dads in our enormous nation.

How can the reality underneath all the misrepresentation compare with songs and stories of explosions? Underneath it is a simple reality that is Iranian independence, Iranian disobedience, the "dangerous threat" of the Iranian good example, Iranian principled hostility to Israeli crimes; Iranian support for democratically elected neighbor-country parties; and, yes, the heady experience of agency for a people and its leaders as they undertake the beginnings of uranium ore enrichment like thirty-one other nations in the world.

Ahmadinejad is only one of the foreign national leaders who did not do U.S.'s bidding. Like Noriega, Milosevic, Hussein, and others they are transformed into demons by the magic of the media. Then Iran, like ancient Carthage, must be destroyed. Otherwise Iran may process uranium ore like most of the other advanced countries in the world.

Iran stands rightly accused of support for Hamas (the ruling Palestinian party) and Hezbollah (the de facto leading organization in Lebanon) and of a supportive relationship with the U.S.'s "independent" government in Iraq. Iran also opposes Israel's occupation of Palestinian territories (beyond the borders as settled following the 1967 war). Iran conducts independent international affairs openly in the Middle East and, to a lesser extent, throughout Europe, Asia, and Latin America. Iran prices its oil and gas according to the market and takes payment as it sees fit. It complies with onerous UN sanctions (while objecting to them). It makes speeches at international forums not written in Washington, D.C. As you can see, this is villainy of every sort. And every jack-o-lantern journalist uses whatever witch's brew to build up George Bush's case for war.

Back home all of Washington offers "critical support" for Bush and repeats his position on Iran. John Edwards is a good example. He declares (following Bush exactly): "At the top of the [the security] threats is Iran." "Iran threatens the security of Israel and the entire world. Let me be clear: Under no circumstances can Iran be allowed to have nuclear weapons...We have muddled along for far too long. To ensure that Iran never gets nuclear weapons, we need to keep all options on the table, let me reiterate—all options must remain on the table." "All options," as everybody knows, means bomb them. "All options are open" say all candidates.

Estimates are that 900,000 to 1.7 million Iranian live in the U.S. On average they are more highly educated and slightly wealthier than the average of the U.S. population; nearly half have a college degree and hold managerial/professional jobs. Iran has been one of the world's leading "brain drain" countries. Iran's loss, our gain: in scientists, doctors, and technicians. Most of them in the U.S. speak Farsi at home. They are highly conservative. 400,000 Iranian children have been born in America. Their parents' and grandparents' homeland is about to be destroyed.

All of Washington, following Bush, speaks of "negotiations," but the U.S. has not had diplomatic relations with Iran since 1979 when the U.S. man, the Shah Reza Pahlavi, was overthrown. Claiming to be "open" to diplomacy, Bush says, "And we will seek out and destroy the [Iranian] networks providing advanced weaponry and training to our enemies." And Cheney prompts Rice to reiterate that "all options are open" as she offers war as an act of State Department diplomacy. The war dogs are going to war with Iran and there is little opposition.

Notes:

Early in 2003, investigative journalists began revealing that the Administration-Pentagon Office of Special Plans had been concocting causes and urging war with Iran as well as with Iraq. There was an ongoing FBI investigation of the Zionist AIPAC and then indictments because "Special Plans" had connected Americans who were spying, and urging Iran War, in behalf of Israel. Many knew that Iraq and Iran, as well as Syria, were on the Bush agenda for "regime change." This investigation and some journalism on the insanity of such a war quieted the more public Iran war-mongering from the Administration but it did not shut the major voices (McCain, Edwards, Clinton, Obama). And, within two years, in the midst of the Iraq catastrophe, these Iran war noises were revived. They are almost identical in sum and fraudulent substance to pretexts for war with Iraq. See especially James Bamford's "Iran: The Next War" *Rolling stone* (July 2006).

See James Carroll's *House of War; the Pentagon and the Disastrous Rise of American Power* (2006). McNamara (now 80) did effectively check, for a time, the "strategic air power" war hawks. On the WWII population center firebombing, were he a decent man, McNamara might have said "I still hear the screaming, even now." However, on *The Fog of War* site we hear him blaming the firebombing, and the atomic bombing, on General Curtis Lemma.

❧

Who Are the Dogs of War?
(Posted 02/05/2007)

You think the Dogs of War are the top military brass? Well, sure, in one simple sense. Buying offensive weapons is the primary business of a very large percentage of the Pentagon's top brass. They manage the world's largest arms bazaar. But the total of quasi-civilian sales of arms to third parties abroad are a minor part of total arms sales, less than one quarter. The real money goes to our so-called national defense. The comparison is $450 billion (exclusive of emergency appropriation for the Afghanistan and Iraq Wars) vs. something like $100 billion in civilian sales to third parties.

Additionally, many military officers cycle their careers in military procurement into the private armaments manufacturing industry becoming corporate officers and taking minor ownership positions as well as being sales functionaries.

Very few are like the courageous retired officers who have publicly criticized the Iraq War and President Bush.

Nevertheless, as a class of people, the present and ex-military officers are not the real Dogs of War. They collect only a small part of the harvest from the military orchard. "Defense" procurement generals are only hired gardeners or apple merchants.

Another class of people some call Dogs of War are the authors and publicists who celebrate any war. They were the "War Club" of post WWII, called the "House of War" of the Vietnam era, and the "War Hawks" in the post-Vietnam era. Mostly "neo-conservatives" and "neoliberals," they are paid thinkers, propagandists, and ideologues whose common theme is advancing the interests of U.S. capitalism worldwide via any and every instance of aggressive warfare. Self-interested and fake "national defense" is their basic argument, while their aim is investment super-profits, along with securing raw material wealth and "space" for private corporations. Dogs, indeed, but neither are they the true Dogs of War. And they never name the names of the true Dogs of War.

Many of these publicist-intellectuals give little attention to the underlying aim of war. They prefer to detail how the dogs are fed. That is interesting, but rather like deliberating on "strategy" and "power politics" while never asking "Strategy and politics in whose interest?" The great majority of all our political literature barely touches the Dogs of War. Here is some of the literature related to this question.

A fine, deeply moral book such as James Carroll's *The House of War* (2006)) takes the world as given by the *New York Times* at face value. Andrew Bacevich's *The New American Militarism* (2005) does the same. Seymour Hersh's *Chain of Command* (2004) has the exclusive military focus.

Another important book is Chalmers Johnson's *The Sorrows of Empire*, subtitled *Militarism, Secrecy, and the End of the Republic.* It also focused on the military side of American hegemony especially as it garrisons the earth with bases. Johnson mentions "the spoils of war" from time to time, but primarily he looks at the history of our militarization and at the period after the profit failure of the "Washington Consensus" (around failed World Bank and IMF "globalization") and the consequent turn to today's ever more violent, ever more privatized war profiteering.

These authors personally do not endorse predatory capitalism. However, do we really need to be told, in enormous detail, that the generals are intelligent, well-educated men who play roles in an opera of influence peddling, political calculation, and corporate greed? We do not. Not when the objective of it all—at such human cost—is some specific, unnamed people's wealth accumulation. Why not talk about whose wealth that is?

With many readers, a partial effect of these books is to support one of the great mistakes of the anti-war movement during the Vietnam War: blame the soldiers. Blame the hired killers. Pretend that they hired themselves. Expose their false patriotism, mistaken compliance with the presumed wishes of the majority, their social ignorance and native brutality, or simply blame poor boys in need of jobs and living in awe of uniforms and officialdom, or blame the collective ignorance of their righteous families. These things do exist and they contribute, but "exposing" them is a cheap revelation, acting only on such partial hostility is shallow action.

I recommend less reviewed books. Gregory Elich's *Strange Liberators* (2006) goes over the U.S mayhem and pursuit of profit in Iraq, Korea, Yugoslavia, and Zimbabwe under the guidance of his opening sentence: "U.S. policy is directed at creating conditions that favor the maximization of corporate profit."

And Jeff St. Clair's (2005) *Grand Theft Pentagon* demonstrates the truth of his opening definition:

> War profiteer. It used to be one of the dirtiest slurs in American politics, potent enough to sully the reputations of the rich and powerful. Now it's a calling card, something you might find highlighted in a defense contractor's corporate prospectus as a lure to attract investors looking for bulging profits and escalating dividends.

These authors, like incisive Noam Chomsky, are exiled from popular media. If we look back at 19th century British literature, with its almost automatic disregard of the lower orders, minor gentry, and despised "Indian" families who furnished the leading military functionaries, we come closer to talking about war in terms of whose interests it serves. This old literature exposes how debt holding and redirected investment using leveraged, inflated property value underwriting and state contracts produces profits from conquest and war. More importantly—since these can be dry economic statistics—some of the literature shows how family fortunes are built on war and conquest. It names the families and shows us how patriarchs are able to deliver millions to each child, grandchild, nephew and niece as small family gratuities when the war profits flow.

For a guide to this literature see the opening chapters of *The Decline and Fall of the British Aristocracy* [by David Cannadine, 1990) or, for family portraits, see the research of W. D. Rubinstein in his many studies such as *Elites and the Wealthy in Modern British History* or *Men of Property*. Or see Edward Said's brilliant *Orientalism*

(1978) discovering that even the great Victorian novelists were aware of the war-profiteering basis of upper gentry family wealth.

Closer to our own time, during the vigorous opposition to WWI, the interests of the Morgan banks and other "financiers of Wall Street" and all those profiting from "the capitalist war" was widely exposed. It is a good literature, this progressive era stuff. We have little like it today.

Yes, on the excuse of "national defense," the military buys stuff and destroys it: aircraft carriers, submarines, attack aircraft, fighting vehicles of all sorts, and endless bombs and shells. The Commander-in-chief signs off on the state purchases. Through the magic of media, all this is made to seem justifiable even though it all happens because of and for war profiteers whose wealth and whose media supports that Commander-in-chief.

The hardware has no value outside of aggressive war. We know the names of the corporations (Lockheed Martin, Northrop Grumman, Boeing and its subsidiary McDonnell Douglas, Raytheon, General Dynamics, BAE Systems, Science Applications Intl, Am General, General Electric, L-3, Harris, and a few others), but we do not know the families.

Note that the only major military contracts cancelled during the Bush Administration's tenure have been military defense systems, actual defense: crusader shore artillery, shore air defense system, reconnaissance aircraft, and related products. That is because this stuff has shelf life. This stuff reminds people that actual "defense" exists (such as, once, the National Guard, now doing repeated combat tours in Iraq and Afghanistan, once represented). Also, this defensive hardware is subject to extensive testing and invites fewer cost overruns. For private profit, aggressive war is best. Corporate extortion, the enforcement of unfair trade, sole-source inflated contracts, massive privatization (the essence war's emergencies), trade in lives, hiring private contractors: therein is today's accumulation of identifiable private wealth. We know the corporations but we do not know whose will the corporations, commander-in-chief, and Congress are serving.

Armaments are the ideal product of predatory capitalism. There is one generous buyer, no competition, no marketing costs, and a product that explodes and disappears on use.

Two final points. The great Victorian historians have the good grace not to accused mere labor or small business of the crime of war profiteering, those millions who sacrifice and the thousands who accumulate only local power and minimal holdings and provide extensive services. They concentrate on the truly wealthy whose scope of influence exceeds all imaginable bounds of "gentry." They do not focus on people who make neither policy nor war, on people who cannot own a block of "K" street, own a top-ten D.C. law firm, own a Senator or two or a clutch of Representatives, or own 4.9% and control 40% of Boeing, DynCorp, Fluor, General Dynamics, Halliburton, Northrop Grumman, Raytheon, GE, and the great service corporations, or create private equity funds based on accumulated stock market wealth. No, they look at the few, the top one tenth of one percent. We should do the same. That is where the shame and the lessons are.

And the second point. Note that all the books mentioned above and all the fellow sentiments that motivate them have had no apparent effect on U.S. policy. The lesson from this is the opposite of despair. The lesson is that each shared bit of information about those who lead the war profiteering is precious, just as each small act of opposition is precious. When our massed opinion weighs nothing on the scales of national policy (as with the Iraq War), then certainly those scales are broken and any one added scale weight may be significant. The logic here is that our only insurance is in "what everybody knows" and the growing potency of that knowledge.

Defending our country is the easy issue. We all know what we would do if our homes were attacked, if an enemy attempted to occupy our land. We would risk anything and pay anything. We would sacrifice all of Microsoft, all of Google, all of Broadway, all of the NBA and NASCAR if those resources were needed in defense of our country. For anything that can rightly be called defense we do not need "but what if?" or "ticking bomb," possible scenario arguments and fear mongering.

The Department of War is not about defense at all. It is about consuming product and services bought at public expense and the value of caressing the inevitable public debt that follows. It is about speed and chaos and invisibility where crimes can flourish, about profiting from crisis, and about the iron "Law" that forces—so we are told—the corporation to increase profits for its controlling shareholders as rapidly and extensively as possible. Nothing moves faster than an armaments renewal contract, nothing has such a peppy impact on corporate stock price. The "military-industrial complex" (Eisenhower's phrase) and the "Power Elite" (C Wright Mills' phrase) behind it, account for half of our entire economy (something like $650 billion annually). All of us, all our shops and common products, and our entire infrastructure live on the remainder.

⁂

Death from Above
(Posted 04/14/2007)

The terrible pending war with Iran hangs over us all. While much of the next 22 months may be spent watching the installation of Mrs. Clinton as Democratic candidate and then as President, these are still Bush months. Anything could happen. We have a confused and uncertain Bush (failing to find a "war czar," watching Wolfowitz go down, his Justice Department getting out of hand) and an angry Cheney watching his public reputation as America's Big Man disintegrate.

That may seem more dangerous than it really is. Their private reputations are probably more important to them. They have "done their duty" to the oil and armaments and corporate interests who are now abounding in wealth as a result of the Bush/Cheney Iraq War and their aggressive foreign policy. All the costs of their policies have been shifted onto our broad backs and, consequently, Bush and Cheney are "well thought of" in select, highly discrete circles.

As for Mrs. Clinton, while she has rattled her sword, made it clear that Iran is "an enemy," and pledged that no option is off the table, more recently she is following the advice of Madeleine Albright, certain to be a major foreign policy voice in her administration.

What Albright has been implying for the past year [See her "Iran Action Plan"] is very important. She is a skilled, experienced foreign policy brute—or, as they say, "realist"—able to advance the interests of oil and armaments and American imperial dictatorship without regard to the slaughter of innocents. Clinton/Albright can make that sound like sanity to the Bush-befuddled public. What Albright has been doing is creating (she hopes) better conditions for the Iran War by exaggerating Iran's internal divisions, suggesting these divisions be fomented where possible (i.e., subversion), implying that their government is weak, drawing the line in the sand out more toward 2010 when Iran's non-existent nuclear weapons and so-called aggressive intentions will be a bit more believable, and awaiting the possibility of some sort troop reassignment out of ever-more-dangerous Iraq.

With their (Mrs. Clinton, Madam Albright, President Bush, and Vice President Cheney) formula for profitable war in place, even though different stars will play the lead roles, the formula will proceed. From the president's pulpit, the target nation's leadership is demonized. They are advertised as a great threat to our security. They are said to sponsor (or support or harbor or encourage) "terrorists." They are said to be mythically unpopular, even hated. Then our state media echoes and enlarges upon these themes. We will hear that all or some part of the target nation's people are imprisoned or oppressed and seek "freedom," that the target itself is fragmented, may even "come over" to our side (implying easy victory; implying a lesser harm, implying ourselves as liberators), just as with Iraq. We will hear (although none too specifically) that the target nation has violated some or another sanction or resolution or the norms of the community of nations. Then march forward the parade of provocations; intensify as necessary; find or create "incidents" that galvanize the public. Incidents occur. Fanfare! Announcing "Operation Iranian Freedom!" Curtain! The bombs begin to fall.

This is the way darkly irresponsible men and women will urge our support of their crime and catastrophe. They will win some dark applause. The *New York Times* will display color pictures and present a huge bouquet of roses at the second curtain, then run to write laudatory reviews of the performance. And quizzical editorials. All this—spiritedly and with pictures—duly broadcast over the "public" airways. Authorization will be forthcoming. Authorization, in any event, is clearly irrelevant. Much of Congress already echoes all the war mongering.

The initial massive air campaign will do immense damage to the target nation's infrastructure and—incidentally, unfortunately, inadvertently—to tens of thousands of civilians at once and hundreds of thousands in the wake, as our ship of state "advances." A few military may die, theirs and ours, but war is their profession and defense of the country is their duty. In a mystic way, they volunteered, and they are prepared and protected in ways civilians are not. They tend to accept the fight that is on their dance card. Unfortunately, for them and us, the lords of profitable war have transformed "defense" into offensive war. And they have thoroughly muddied the waters of any understanding of right and wrong.

On the real water, off the coast of Iran, stand the battle groups around the USS Dwight D. Eisenhower and the USS John C. Stennis, with the USS Nimitz group on the way. The marines and sailors are not thinking much of oil, worrying a bit about oily waters is all. Nor are the airmen on the ready at airfields in Central Asia, in Germany, on Diego Garcia, as I read in *Iraq Occupation Times* on ten air bases scattered around Kuwait, Bahrain, Qatar and Jordan, and on the four, led by the Prince Sultan base, in Saudi Arabia, our best-protected ally. The airmen's thoughts are about mission and duty, not oil and profits. They have been given their target specific coordinates, which will be casually described in the newspapers (perhaps even believed by the soldiers and sailors) as "command posts, air fields, radar installations, nuclear plants, missile sites, headquarters locations," etc.

However, other men and women, never at risk, are thinking of oil and profits. These higher "decision makers" know and intend that the entire Iranian population must be hurt to the point of devastation, punished to the point of collapse because of their independence if this next aggressive war is to succeed of even, more likely, if it fails.

And when it fails, as the Iraq War has failed, we should not imagine that it has failed for *everyone*. We should put aside the lies and understand that failure in our terms (since we are not war criminals and brutes) is not failure for those seeking only profits and control of resources and opportunities for commerce. They fully expect the Iran catastrophe to be even more profitable than the Iraq catastrophe.

Ours is a failed nation state awaiting its *terminus ad quem*. In its present form it exercises sufficient control over public opinion and sufficient governmental power to secure compliance with any crime, any obscene action such as the mass bombing of a non-aggressive independent state whose civil society our government has intended to reduce to ashes since about 1979 when "our" obedient Shah was overthrown by a brave coalition of Marxists and follow-on Mullahs.

Great things were planned and initiated in the childhood of our own nation. Many like to thinks back vaguely toward that childhood, quote this and that, and pretend that all is well. However, that child has been left behind. We are the nation that firebombed population centers throughout Germany including Dresden (a bombing Kurt Vonnegut described so vividly in *Slaughterhouse Five*), specific broad neighborhoods housing workers and their families. We are the nation that dropped atomic bombs on the population centers of Hiroshima and Nagasaki. We are the nation that fire-bombed Cambodia and the housing districts of Hanoi for nights without end and made napalm familiar over the whole countryside of Vietnam. We destroyed all civil society in Afghanistan, reducing much of its infrastructure to rubble, and are responsible for the death of more than 655,000 in Iraq just in the last four years. In each case our tiny strata of the very rich (just a small strata at the top, some few hundred families) became richer and more powerful. They rule our government through obvious mechanisms and, of course, rule our mass media.

We are a great people—inventive and diverse—and our labor has created a great economy. But we are an ill-used, ill-led. We could be doing so much that is good in the world. I do not mean to say that there have not been brief times when some leaders attempted to recapture some of the best dreams of the best among us. They may even have been sincere. Ultimately, they capitulated to the few; the Power Elite. They came to lay our heads on the block in behalf of the worse, most crisis prone elements of predatory capitalism. Almost alone in the world, we are sustaining this predatory form of all-powerful capitalism for the very few.

I have not said much here (a prediction or two; some generalizations). However, the amount of reality buried in these predictions and generalizations horrifies me. It would require a Jeremiah to express. Our Iran War will be a great human catastrophe. The powers that be definitely intend to do such a war sooner or later. All their denial of any such intention is one single lie. This is clear and express. It has been their practice in the past. Do not for a moment imagine that they do not intend to profit once again from catastrophe, one of their deliberate making.

I have no advice for them. Much is offered and advice to such as they is a silly activity. I would like to see them facing the threat of being hung for the criminals and murderers they are, but that is not likely to happen. Yet if it should—in Jeremiah's spirit or Madam Deferrer's—I would be there in the front row, knitting a scarf against the winter cold, cackling toothlessly.

∾

Mayday! Mayday!
(Posted 05/02/2007)

On this day, take a look at the layers of the cake baking in the ovens of the powers that be, layers of control and catastrophe.

A. 5/1 U.S. officials released some overall Iraq statistics. In 2006 the number of terrorist incidents almost doubled (rose 91 percent) over 2005. They gave official reassurances about Afghanistan as well as Iraq but admitted that our invasion had become "a rallying cry" for radicalization. The count of our dead in Iraq (not counting our mercenaries) stood at 3,350; and dead Iraqis, as before, stood at "at least 665,000." Now the Iraqis do hate us (as Bush claimed they did in 2002). The rallying cry "Death to U.S. Imperialism!" continues. Their government is a useless puppet. Our government is in the hands of oil and armament billionaires. Congress says, "Its hands are tied," more money is about to be voted for more war.

B. 5/1 Also the State Department released, yet again, its assessment that Iran is "the biggest supporter of terrorism around the world." All presidential candidates have blessed this assessment. In the most recent debate (MSNBC), only Dennis Kucinich and new-on-the-scene Mike Gravel spoke against the idea that we might need to incinerate the Iranian people. After the debate Gravel, looking backs at his fellow candidates, said, "These people frighten me." During the debate, he said, "The military industrial complex not only controls our government, lock, stock and barrel, but they control our culture." For this big media called him "unbalanced" and "flakey."

C. 5/1 The otherwise calm immigration rally in Los Angeles was fired upon with rubber bullets and demonstrators were beaten with batons by LA police. It was one of many rallies involving tens of thousands around the nation. These attacks and the previous week's sudden intensification of arrests of undocumented workers reduced the size of the demonstrations from last year, as was intended.

Concerning conventional shells vs. rubber bullets used against demonstrators, I read a disclosure of an previously unknown tape held by the FBI in which National Guard were given orders to fire on student anti-war demonstrators at Kent state in 1970 (4 killed, 9 wounded). No mention of the killings by state police at a Jackson State demonstration (2 killed, 12 wounded) or the local police killing in 1968 (3 killed, 27 wounded) at South Carolina State, the Orangeburg massacre.

D. 5/1 News on a spike in the number of foreclosures on homes. This foreclosure and fear campaign, as intended, will accelerate the falling housing market making it all the better for profit-taking. Calm assessment is for a "recovery" by mid-2008 (with end-cycle profit-taking). Foreclosures at this rate are exceptional in a generally strong economy.

E. 5/1 There was also the continuing news of the hurried pro-corporate scuttling of environmental regulations at more than one federal agency, this in the face of pending congressional investigations serious enough to result in resignations by senior officials. Beyond the environment—a safe, essentially hot air issue— we hear little but the same is happening in Communications, Education, and Finance. Bush has filled federal agencies with his born-again loyalists and they, like Gonzales, do as they are told regardless of law, civic responsibility, or job description. These religious caterpillars in official positions are crawling all over Washington. There are 150 graduates of Pat Robertson's Regent University in the Bush administration. Who knows how many from Bob Jones University and Jerry Falwell's Liberty University. We face 18 months of this last minute scuttling of regulations.

F. 5/1 Hillary Clinton—our likely next president—dropped her maiden name, Rodham, and leads in all the polls. Her hand shot up at Brian Williams question in last month's debate "Show of hands: Do you believe there is such a thing as a global war on terror?" Her speech at the National Jewish Democratic Council put her squarely in the Bush camp on the issue of Iran. She said that all avenues should be explored (presumably not excepting those proscribed by international law) and "if we do have to take offensive military action [note "offensive"] against Iran, it would be far better if the rest of the world saw it as a position of last resort, not first resort, because the effect and consequences will be global." Note the call for the appearance of reluctance and the recognition that an attack on Iran will ignite global war. Very presidential!

I think of myself as no more than another raisin in the American strudel. You also, no doubt. Deceived by his fake drawl, all of us should have taken George Bush much more seriously. Here he is in a radio address to the nation on March 20, 2004 (my emphasis):

> The war on terror is not a figure of speech. It is *the inescapable calling of our generation*. The terrorists are offended not merely by our

policies. They are offended by our existence as free nations. *No concession* will appease their malice. *No accommodation* will satisfy their endless demands. No course of therapy will cure them of their hatred. *There can be no separate peace* with the terrorist enemy. Whatever it takes we will *seek, and find, and destroy* the terrorists.

The language of fascism.

৵৹

A Constitutional Crisis
(Posted 05/18/2007)

The testimony on May 15 by former Deputy Attorney General James B. Comey to the Senate Judiciary Committee presented a story as good as any scene from a best-selling thriller. That the networks and other major media are avoiding the story, or minimizing it, enhances the drama.

The storyteller, James Comey, is not some serial liar like Alberta Gonzales who is about to resign. Since 2005 Comey has been corporate counsel for Lockheed-Martin, the third largest Aerospace contractor. He was Deputy Attorney General, and acting-AG under John Ashcroft. Gonzales has been Bush's long-time Texas legal flunkey. Gonzales' name will drop like a stone into the waters of obscurity. Comey will remain to facilitate hundreds of millions in contracts and tens of millions in private opportunities as Lockheed-Martin moves up over corrupt, discredited Boeing.

According to Comey's testimony, on the night of March 10, 2004 Attorney General John Ashcroft was in intensive care at George Washington Hospital following major surgery. Rushing toward him in a security town car from the White House were Alberto Gonzales (then White House Counsel, subsequently Attorney General, and, as I say, soon to be driven to resignation) and Andrew Card (then White House Chief of Staff and Bush's "bad cop" resigned March 2006). They were sent to the Ashcroft bedside by Bush to force Ashcroft's signature on documents giving Justice Department authorization for "a particular classified program" (presumably the domestic surveillance executive order) that had been initiated soon after 9/11 and requiring a renewal authorization by March 11th.

Also rushing toward him along Constitution Ave—sirens blaring, calls going out to security and FBI Director Robert Mueller—was Comey. Since Ashcroft's hospitalization a week before Comey was fully-empowered Acting AG, about to be driven over, and he was now on a mission (responding to a call from Ashcroft's wife) to protect Ashcroft from being badgered into signing an illegal authorization. At one point Comey was running up hospital steps to Ashcroft's side, trying to beat out the White House thugs. He had secured Mueller's presence, also racing to the bedside in a separate car. At Comey's behest Mueller had ordered agents in place to, under no circumstances, allow Comey be forced away from Ashcroft's side.

All arrived within minutes of each other. Comey, first to arrive, was at the barely conscious Ashcroft's bed when Gonzales and Card, with the authority of the White House, arrived—envelope in hand—pressing Ashcroft to sign this document. Ashcroft, roused to some alertness by Comey, refused and pointed out that Comey was in fact Acting AG.

Angry conversations followed. Calls and meetings occupying next four hours, from 8:00 PM to 11:00 PM and concluding with private 15 min. phone conversations with Bush for both Comey and Mueller. Bush in fact backed off, telling Comey that the Justice Department could reconstruct the "particular classified program" to their legal satisfaction. And the president secured their agreement not to resign en masse, as they had threatened, in advance of his reelection.

The "rule of law" may sometimes seem a matter of mere form and procedure, but it is the personal and the career loadstone for many in Washington. Some—unlike Bush, Cheney, Rumsfeld, Card, Gonzales, and Wolfowitz—are unwilling to be flagrantly illegal. The legal boy scouts in this story saw the event as a constitutional crisis, another step in a shameful *coup d'etat* by the Bush/Cheney group that must be blocked.

Who are these men? Last week Gonzales again lied under oath to the Senate declaring that there were no disagreements in the highest circles over Patriot Act issues. A set of resignations was already in place over White House insistence that, at very least, NSA warrant-less surveillance be continued. Bush was determined to go to the wall with his obvious assault on the constitution—citing "terror" and 9/11 as usual—to extend his conception of the a presidency free of constitutional checks and balances or congressional oversight, free of formal conformity to the requirement of law and the constitution, a "unitary" presidency. But faced with a "Saturday Night Massacre" (mass resignations such as Nixon experienced) prior to his second term reelection, Bush relented. He was facing men who had built their reputations defending legal formalities.

Both Ashcroft and Comey had previously informed the White House they would not authorize whatever illegality was embodied in the "particular classified program," that the program—whatever it was—had no legal basis. Days before they and their chief aids and FBI Director Mueller had agreed to resign if the program was continued without legal authorization.

We do not know the content of that program. Clearly, the official description is a bit misleading. At very least it included the continuation of warrant-less wiretapping of U.S. citizens. The astonishing thing is that all of these men—both sides of the race to the sick Ashcroft's side—had already authorized torture, extraordinary rendition, and warrant-less surveillance. Both the "good guys" of this story and the White House thugs were instrumental in passage of the Patriot Act, Iraq War authorization, military privatization (a la Rumsfeld), programs of torture, etc., etc. However, there was something more in the documents that Gonzales and Cards carried to Ashcroft's bedside. Signatures had already been refused; resignations already threatened. Clearly, there were career-destroying violations of public law if the documents ever came to light. We can only imagine.

The background of the players is highly relevant. Ashcroft has always been a right-wing extremist, a former Missouri Governor and Senator, famous for dramatic increases in the police forces, number of prisons, and lengthening prison terms in his state. He is a major evangelical personality, enemy of civil liberties (re abortions, gays, protest, etc.), always a warmonger, and now a star at Pat Robertson's Regent's University boasting 150 Christian fundamentalist placements in the Bush Administration. He also has been a major defense industry insider/consultant: a War on Drugs and War on Terror stalwart who finally balked at Bush's extremes.

James Comey has also made his career with the Republican Party and was in on all the above known and subsequent authorizations. His threatened resignation came only after he became convinced that the "program" threatened the very legal credentials on which his career depended.

What was in that package of authorizations? The usual journalists talk as if Bush's terrorist surveillance program is an old story and has been already "modified" and "re-interpreted" to the satisfaction of all. Obviously, that is not the case. Tuesday's Senate testimony—long blocked on "national security" grounds by Gonzales—was both dramatic and significant. Yes, the testimony was structured, vetted, and edited but nevertheless of interest. The scene plays out as an actual constitutional crisis, an element in what is now emerging as Bush's barely under-the-radar *coup d'etat*.

Wikipedia's hard-workers have the full background on the issue. The specific story is also well told in the *Guardian* newspaper. Glenn Greenwald's new book, *A Tragic Legacy: How a Good vs. Evil Mentality Destroyed the Bush Presidency* will be published in June. He and others went over this story on NPR's "Open Source" today. A leading government newspaper brings out Reagan's head of Office of

Legal Counsel, Douglas W. Kmiec to ridicule this testimony as "histrionics" and to dismiss the issue as a mere matter of honest interpretative disagreement.

෮⁓

Memorial Day 2007
(Posted 05/30/2007)

Join me in a few words for this Memorial Day. On Monday (our day of commercial convenience for celebrating May 30, which is Memorial Day) Cindy Sheehan announced her resignation as the leading spokesperson of the anti-war movement. Her son Casey died in Sadr City on April 4, 2004. Within weeks, Sheehan went forth as a speaker for Gold Star Mothers and then as an uncompromising opponent of Bush, Rumsfeld, Cheney and the corporate war system.

With her "Camp Casey" located beside the road outside Bush's Crawford, TX vacation estate; she demanded a personal, presidential answer to her questions "What did my son die for?" She spoke constantly at anti-war rallies and became somewhat well known. Now, three years later, she is clearly exhausted and disappointed:

> The most devastating conclusion that I reached this morning, however, was that Casey did indeed die for nothing. His precious lifeblood drained out in a country far away from his family who loves him, killed by his own country that is beholden to and run by a war machine that even controls what we think. I have tried ever since he died to make his sacrifice meaningful....I failed my boy and that hurts the most.

In 1856, also exhausted and depressed, the Crimean War nurse Florence Nightingale wrote:

> Oh my poor men who endured so patiently. I feel I have been such a bad mother to you to come home & leave you lying in your Crimean grave. 73 percent in eight regiments during six months from disease alone—who thinks of that now? But If I could carry any one point which would prevent any part of the recurrence of this our colossal calamity then I should have been true to the cause of those brave dead.

The sentiment was the same. However, Nightingale had wealth and position, influence and authority. She had her fifteen points of reform and a great deal of determination expressed as "I shall eat straight through England" beginning with Victoria and Prince Albert, the Ministers, the Opposition and the entire House of Commons, "till my last appeal which will be like Cobden's with his Corn Law to the Country."

Sheehan—a commoner, one of us—had only what spirit and energy the Democratic Party had not already sucked out of the broad anti-war movement. She had a plain clear way of speaking and she deserved a broad audience but it was denied. There was no positive press or publicity on the scale, say, of a Nancy Pelosi, who is part of the Democratic Party establishment. Therefore Sheehan was unable to build Gold Star Mothers into a popular mobilization of millions. She was abandoned at the side of the road with only a crippled left to talk to, exposed by its many failed compromises. The corporate media did not treat Sheehan even as well as it had treated Howard Dean.

And, as for that "left," Sheehan writes:

> I have endured a lot of smear and hatred since Casey was killed and especially since I became the so-called "Face" of the American anti-war movement. Especially since I renounced any tie I have remaining with the Democratic Party.
>
> The first conclusion is that I was the darling of the so-called left as long as I limited my protests to George Bush and the Republican Party. Of course, I was slandered and libeled by the right as a "tool" of the Democratic Party. This label was to marginalize me and my message. How could a woman have an original thought, or be working outside of our "two-party" system?
>
> However, when I started to hold the Democratic Party to the same standards that I held the Republican Party, support for my cause started to erode and the "left" started labeling me with the same slurs that the right used. I guess no one paid attention to me when I said that the issue of peace and people dying for no reason is not a matter of "right or left", but "right and wrong."

That is how it goes. Everybody knows. The men at the top are men who commission killings as well as speak at dinners. Then there are their "principal servants." These lead the lambs. And the lambs have been led to believe that those who shear them are "a moral force for good."

Sheehan knew the movement she led was only a fraction left of center; but even that fraction was too much for the Democratic Party who, by and large, are principal servants of the very military industrial complex Sheehan was opposing. And party organizations like MoveOn, tied at birth to Democratic Party apron strings, would naturally reproach and assassinate the character of anyone criticizing Democrats. Every Thanksgiving MoveOn members rejoice that they are not Republicans. That is not nothing; however, it is not much, although the total of what they have to be thankful for and proud of.

Nightingale writes:

> We are tired of hearing of the Crimean catastrophe. We don't want to know anymore about the 'trenches cold & damp', the 'starved & frozen camp', the deficient rations, the stores, which might have saved the 'great Army of the dead', lying unused & undistributed. But was this the real bitterness of that death? Is this all the meaning it has to us? Our men were 'led as sheep to the slaughter & as a lamb before her shearers is dumb, so they opened not their mouths'. The Commander of the Forces was like the drowning Ophelia . . . he let himself & his troops float down to death, unconsciously to himself, with scarcely a struggle against the weeds & the waters which were pulling him down to destruction. As for his principal servants, what shall we say of them? In another age, they would have been tried by court-martial, recalled or disgraced either officially or by opinion. And the least hardened would have become Rapists or retired from life. But what did we see? We came home, with the remains of that lost Army, to see the Throne taking to its bosom the most distinguished of the malefactors, to hear of a Star-chamber farce which had acquitted them—to find them in all the official posts, honors, & drawing-rooms of the kingdom.

Unlike Nightingale, Sheehan on "Democracy Now" speaks vaguely of coming back with another approach, perhaps "appealing directly to humanity." I believe that is what she said. I wish her well. But I do hope she and her sister come up with something better than "appealing directly to humanity." This is the America of silent lambs, of propaganda and advertising deafened ears, the America "led as sheep to the slaughter & as a lamb before her shearers," stunned deaf to such appeals.

◠◡

No End in Sight
(Posted 07/30/2007)

The new film "No End in Sight" makes it clear with insider interviews and documentary clips that the Iraq debacle was made in Washington D.C., a homegrown disaster from the very start.

The documentary was written, directed, and produced by a first-timer, Charles Ferguson and opened July 27 to some significant distribution. Magnolia Pictures also distributed "Who Killed the Electric Car," "Enron: the Smartest Guys in the Room," "The Trials of Henry Kissinger," "Jesus Camp," and about 20 other films. This one has already won a Sundance award. A few million will see it. They are the wrong millions; but nothing we can do about that.

Turns out that the American oligarchy has arranged a wedding between a group of arrogant and incompetent national officials and the most backward sections of our population. The mystery is how so many semi-rural folk from the Heartland, the South, and the West stood up with and even fell in love with this particular set of incompetents. Honestly, I am an ass for not seeing this coming. From that same background myself, I am clearly out of touch with my roots and have overlooked something,, most likely the despicable sick essence of the "opposition" Democratic Party that once honored FDR's name and the unions that once gave us life and income. And long ago I should have seen the incomparable popularity of reactionary "free" television.

George Bush, Jr. had minor corporate experience with Arbusto Energy, Harken Energy, and the Texas Rangers (1978-1994); Cheney brought the interests of Halliburton (1995-2000) and Rumsfeld those of G.D. Searle & Co. (Metamucil, Dramamine, Enovid, NutraSweet) and General Instrument Corp (1977-1985, 1990-1997). They were CEOs in name only, there for the sake of government favors they might woo. We are not talking innovators, entrepreneurs, industry builders here.

Yet these arrogant lobbyists, experts at turning federal dollars their corporations' way, won the hearts and minds and the voting hands of the least corporate, most uneducated, least moneyed, most misinformed of our population.

Thomas Frank's *What's the Matter with Kansas?,* Kevin Phillips' *American Theocracy,* Chris Hedges' *War is a Force that Gives Us Meaning,* and Joe Bageant's *Deer Hunting with Jesus* have all tried to understand this marriage. How could so many fine (if benighted) people act so against their own best interests? The mystery remains. These perplexed authors are not yet ready to see how Bush, Cheney, and Rumsfeld were aided and abetted by the fundamental betrayals of the Democratic Party, most particularly by Clinton's eight years. They do show how the wedding took place, a typical country wedding with shotguns, hardons, passivity, bought lies, and the stolen dowry of the future. They refuse to draw the obvious conclusions.

Thus, we were asked to buy a pre-wrapped wedding package by opportunist cold-warrior pro-business conservative warmongers—led by Bush, Jr. who patented the "faith-based" tax cut good-old-boy gambit in Texas during 1994-2000—and he won the hearts and minds of the ignorant and the pious. Attending the wedding party were enough minor Washington opportunists (Wolfowitz, Bremer, Rice, Chernoff, Brown, Meyers, Gonzales, etc.) to manage two consecutive presidential administrations.

One story would be how they ran the country without opposition. Another would be how they consolidated the Big Five media corporations into a state propaganda agency. Another might be the 1997 *Project for a New American Century*. But the visible story in "No End in Sight" is how they brought us to U.S. foreign policy incompetence and a brazen puffery that staggers the imagination. They brought all the arrogant incompetence of too many minor American CEOs, which they were.

In a "normal" corporate American, there is a combination of law, custom and ever-present fixed costs and wages ("the nut") that constrains CEOs to some rationality and to only moderate incompetence. Most often all that is required of them is figurehead blather or, as it is called, "force of personality," the ability to pretend fatherly affection and high anger at task failure. But give these guys a government to run—as we now see—and they will put into place anti-constitutional devices like pre-emptive war, state secrecy, a unitary executive, immunity from civil and criminal liability, and perversions yet to be identified. They will lend money to friendly dictators as long as they spend it on arms, provide tax breaks for the rich, inflate the profits of the Agra-corporations and Big Pharma, and with the loose change fund religious charlatans and anti-educators to beat up on the squalid masses who voted them into high office.

And, thus, everything goes to hell: a disaster in Iraq, the Taliban flourishing in Afghanistan, a post-Katrina New Orleans, Lebanon and/or Syria about to be attacked again, the two-state solution—or any other—still blocked in Israel-Palestine, a region in near civil war in Pakistan, Africa in deadly fragments, chaos in Gaza and the occupied West Bank, covert destabilizing in Iran. Where does this list stop?

The marriage of the dumbest people in our grand but no longer well-educated nation to desperately incompetent, greedy, slavish "Big Men." Corporate compradors and tyrants worse than in any imagined Africa. It is those who drive and hunt drunk wedded to—what's to say?—those who drive and hunt drunk. It is dim misogynists wedded to condescending misogynists; it is powerless and racist country-fed religious folk married to highly-placed and very rich religious hypocrites, in a wedding celebrated by advertising executives.

∽

Animal Farm
(Posted 08/31/2007)

As you know, the Bush Administration is for privatizing everything: energy policy, social security, health care, pharmaceutical testing, environmental regulation, and even Justice. Have you noticed the effect of privatization in the military?

The winning Republican Party platform program of containing "big government," "starving the beast," and opposing special-interest "hogs at the trough" (weakly echoed by Democratic Party vote-getters, by perpetually confused libertarians, and by liberals seeking quick acceptance around the barbeque grill) has made it possible to turn even the military into an animal farm of private enterprise. Tax revenue billions become mere slop for the private hogs of military contracting. The White House privatizes Iraq and Afghanistan security, reconstruction, servicing, engineering, supply, and even recruitment. With 2000, 2004, and 2006 voter approval, they have turned the reality that capitalism-equals-corruption into the myth that the benefits of making everything a capitalist enterprise trickles down and stimulates the economy.

How could such a myth be sold?

In the boondocks, nobody knows anything about "gov'ment," The only government official they ever met was that asshole Earl at the Farm Bureau office, some uppity Black woman at the license bureau in town, and the folks responsible for the impossibility of getting any question answered on the telephone about their mom's social security payments. They remember every song and story about having the rifle ready against the "revenuers," the pain of annual tax time, and every oppressive hunting & fishing regulation. "Shouldn't we, by God, be an independent country?" This is deep and potent. In the hollow skull, the slogan "Down with Big Government" has always resonated. Thus, Ronald Reagan, and all who followed him to date, have cashed in on semi-rural ignorance, bad education, and backwater prejudices. Privatization keeps "gov'ment" money away from undeserving Blackies, from all the undeserving poor. Thus, more privatization is ahead of us.

Even the military this has become a farmyard to petty capitalist enterprise. Homeland Security is a quasi-military set of privatized rip-offs. Katrina money (that "Heck of a job, Brownie") flowed to the National Guard and sent them far from home and otherwise went to private contractors. Privatized security, supply, and engineering in Iraq and Afghanistan gives up the aroma of manure, low-end rip-offs and the squeal of a few indicted dropout incompetent CEOs and who have gotten caught with their snout in the trough. For a real disaster look at military contracting, a government responsibility if ever there was one.

You know already how these scandals go: the higher-ups skate, one or two big fish Generals are reprimanded and retired, a few small fish are caught in the nets of public interest investigation, and minnows get time. The petty capitalists who have flocked to the risky places of the world with the assistance of their Congresspersons steal public money and go Scott free. Some bribed top brass (or their spouses) have signed off on the out-of-thin-air cost-plus contracts.

Today's report (from David S. Cloud) cites an investigation of 18,000 contracts (each $3 billion plus—could that be a misprint?) that has thus far given up 18 paper companies (plus seven pending) now barred from contracting with the government. ("Oh, that hurts; now we'll have to re-incorporate under another name, promote Fred's wife Shirley to the Board, and redraft all those lobbying contracts!") The Army has given up an additional 22 companies in its investigation.

It works this way: Majors A and B are investigated by the military command immediately above them. They say, "Okay, you caught me; but attempt to do me out of my retirement and I'll drop the dime on you and your higher-up friends." Then a few—pissed off at being charged with doing what everyone is doing— bring law suits in civil court to "clear their good name" and, thus, they become able to go on with their entrepreneurial careers. This is Majors A and B in today's news. Court documents are filed and *Times'* journalist (in a news-weary August) chances to read these documents and writes the story up.

Major A is Gloria Davis (a contracting official in Kuwait). She shot and killed herself the day after admitting her crime and I am sorry about that. Major B is Levonda Selph, a Lt. Col. who was in Commander Petraeus' office. Her case may be related to a separate case that has Major John Cockerham, his wife, and his sister indicted on charges of accepting about $10 million in bribes for contracts in Iraq and Kuwait. No one knows. Anyway, the corporation, Lee Dynamics, "appears to be emblematic of scores of companies formed since the Iraqi government fell to take advantage of billions of dollars in contracts to clothe, feed, and arm American troops in Kuwait and to sustain Iraq security forces in Iraq." According to its own Web site, Lee Dynamics in located in Taji, Umm Qasr, Ramadi, Monsul and Tikrit and "have received, stored and issued a large part of more than a billion dollars worth of materials and equipment that has been ordered for the reconstruction of Iraq." Just guessing, but I doubt if any intrepid reporter could find those warehouses or their content in the above named towns. The classic scam, "steal everything then blow the place up," will have happened more than once.

The pattern is one of total exoneration for Washington and Pentagon mucky-mucks (who, like Caesar, gave the wink & nod) without even a reprimand, retirement for the minor brass who were the paid facilitators, substantial sentences for a few small fish. The pattern is that of Abu Ghraib. Those who get time are rural idiots like Lynda England and Charles Garner. At the military top, suffering well-paid retirement, are like Major General Janis Karpinski and Major General Tagulea of the Abu Ghraib story. In Washington, Caesar's hands are clean. The best we can hope for are some bold quotes such as from Tagulea and Janis Karpinski, who subsequently said, "It was an absolute abandonment by my so-called leaders" or General Tagulea who said, upon being threatened, "I had been in the Army 32 years by then, and it was the first time that I thought I was in the Mafia."

This same day Paul Krugman says that it is "Katrina All the Time." A good line. However, he, poor man, is a loyal liberal Democrat, so we get questions and present-become-future: "Will this be seen as the moment when America remembers the importance of good government?" No, it will not be "seen" that way. Or is it "the moment when neglect and obliviousness to the needs of others became the new American way?" Was this a question? I am disappointed in this liberal softness, which is always in the pattern described. Even the anarchist Orwell and his *Animal Farm* metaphor betray us. "Strident" they called Orwell. I am left to apologize for the weakness of his metaphor, which I borrowed. It is no joke, no barnyard. We need socialism far more than Orwell allowed.

∽

Our Slippery Slope
(Posted 09/19/2007)

That we are sliding down—toward world war, a depression, toward fascism—is a feeling I share with many, only a feeling but that does not mean events are not chasing us.

Before going on with what chases and pushes, I want to look on the bright side. The bright side is that we have a span of attention sufficient to look at the threats and tangle in our schizophrenic news. I mean we are able to care about the horror of aggressive war, economic interests, and about what is happening to social values. Imagine if all we could do was to glance at the snapshot opinions put before us, form impressions on that basis, and conclude either "all is well" or "the end of the world is at hand." From bliss to ignorance they go, the helpless children of network news, talk radio, YouTube, etc. I do not pity them or feel a condescending superiority. I feel something like Wallace Stevens felt. He said, "One must have a mind of winter to regard....the sound of the land full of the same wind that is blowing in the same bare place...and the nothing that is not there and the nothing that is." The full poem is quoted below.

Today's schizophrenia, the most familiar part of it, begins on May Day, 2003 when President Bush—who loves to dress up in military garb—presented himself as a fighter pilot on the deck of the USS Abraham Lincoln to announce the end of combat operations in Iraq, "Mission Accomplished."

His timing was off by years and the USS Lincoln was off San Diego harbor turned to appear to the cameras to be out at sea, as the president, in full fighter pilot regalia, was put down on the deck of the Lincoln by a Navy jet rather than by Presidential helicopter. At the same time, from Baghdad, Defense Secretary Rumsfeld did his parallel announcement of the "end of combat operations" in Afghanistan, also off by years. The thought that Bush's photo-op was designed to coincide with the opening at 4054 theaters of Top Gun Tom Cruse's film "Mission Impossible 3" comes about because FOX and CNN said such shameful, embarrassing things all day long that May Day, all the Mavericky "Top Gun" stupid bravado and jingoism.

The chosen date of the false announcement of "Mission Accomplished" also coincided with traditional international Labor Day (*El Primero de Mayo*) as celebrated throughout the rest of the world.

After the embarrassment settled in there were the usual lies and cover up. All this is documented.

At the same time (on or about May 4, 2003), the Administration in Washington received a remarkable proposal from the highest levels of the government of Iran aimed at resolving all differences. That is, it was received by Karl Rove at the president's office and at the State Department. We would never have heard of it except that it was also relayed to the Administration by Ohio Republican Bob Ney. It came to Ney via a formal visit by Tim Guldimann, the Swiss ambassador in Tehran, the man though whom U.S.-Iranian communications have taken place since diplomatic recognition ended in 1979. Guldimann's cover letter authenticated the proposal and its signatures and Ney publicized what Rove would have scuttled.

The Iranians offered full cooperation on nuclear programs, complete transparency that there were no WMD in development, support for "the establishment of democratic institutions and a non-religious government" in Iraq, the acceptance and complete recognition of Israel, termination of material support for Palestinian militant groups like Hamas, and assistance in fighting the War on Terror (especially against Al-Qaeda).

Perhaps you should reread that last long sentence. That communication should have been real news!

In return, the Iranians wanted to be removed from the U.S. terrorism list and not to be designated part of an "axis of evil" any longer. A religious people, that piece of shameless Bush bravado had always deeply offended the Iranians. They wanted an end to sanctions against food, health products and other non-military trade, access to peaceful nuclear technology, and, in polite diplomatic language, they asked that the U.S., as part of the War on Terror, should also pursue anti-Iranian terrorist groups ("above all" the MEK, a terrorist organization the U.S. had been covertly supporting).

But that was then.

Now, four years later, Iraq has a pro-Iranian Shiite government and has already established many treaties, agreements, and economic plans with Iran. Now the U.S. is four years further into its Iraqi version of Vietnam quagmire (one worthy of its own Westmorland, named David Petraeus, who is presiding over the deaths of yet more, GIs just as General William Westmoreland presided over the death of more than 20,000 final American troops before the U.S. Administration found the political will to extricate itself following the enemy's successful Tet Offensive).

In addition to a pro-Iranian Shiite government ruling in Baghdad, the Middle East has seen the success of Hezbollah against Israel and its consequent mounting prestige and functional social control. Now Syria is stronger and more unified. Now a landslide-elected president of Iran, Ahmadinejad, has made uranium enrichment a centerpiece of Iranian nationalism, which makes it very difficult for the Iranian clerics (who actually hold most power) to again become so conciliatory. Now it almost appears that our Top Gun has lost his taste for theatrical bluster and his stomach for further failure.

An excellent article in the Oct. 11 issue of *The New York Review of Books* has already appeared in *TomDispatch*. Written by former ambassador Peter Galbraith, the article reviews and praises the book *Treacherous Alliance* by Trita Parsi. Galbraith's article makes some of the above points and, best of all, clarifies the stumble-bum ignorance and lack of foresight (especially from flunkey Wolfowitz and powerful Cheney early in this new century (and desperately carried on by Bush, Petraeus and all to date) that has marked U.S. relations with Iran since the ill-advised U.S.-supported coup against the democratically elected, pro-Western, secular Iranian Prime Minister Mossadegh in 1953. It also gives the clearest perspective on the contradiction in Iraq between the Mahdi Army of Moqtada al-Sadr and the pro-Iranian base and history of the current Iraqi government.

This current Iraqi government along with its police, army, and informal militias was created out of the U.S. Coalition Provisional Authority and now is more the product of Iranian initiatives and support than of U.S. intentions, the U.S. having merely supplied troops for pacification and billions of dollars for bribery. Iran now has a pervasive influence in official Iraq, making foolish the idea that Iran has any interest in weakening or overthrowing that government or arming its enemies. The Iraq War has been an enormous strategic victory for Iran and a major strategic loss for the U.S.

Galbraith shows that Shiite-controlled lands now extend to the borders of Kuwait and Saudi Arabia. Please see one of the maps, abounding on the Internet. Bahrain has a Shiite majority (although a Sunni king). The principle U.S. naval base is there. Saudi Arabia's Eastern Province is home of that kingdom's Shiites who are near a majority of the population. That is where Saudi Arabia's oil is located. Iran's Syrian ally, Bashir Asssad, and his Shiite Baathist regime is stronger and more in control than in 2003. In Lebanon, Hezbollah is stronger.

Paul Wolfowitz was entirely wrong about the power of Arab vs. Persian (Iraqi Shiite vs. Iranian Shiite) identify. Many Iraqis have Turcoman, Persian, or Kurdish ancestors. Religious and family identity is strong vs. Wolfowitz's High School concept of Arab against Persian. Galbraith writes, "President Bush has responded to these strategic changes wrought by his own policies by strongly supporting a pro-Iranian government in Baghdad and by arming and training the most pro-Iranian elements in the Iraqi military and police." Not necessarily a bad thing, but the opposite of Bush's intentions. The man and his advisors are simply uninformed.

The Administration should have taken the Iranian 2003 proposal seriously and begun negotiations instead of suppressing, rejecting, and deriding it. They were busy playing Mission Impossible.

However, it is entirely possible that Cheney's independent war office and the Bush voice will simplify everything and call for the bombing of Iran while promoting false explanations along the line of non-existent WMDs and the phony Saddam-9/11 connection. There are indications that this utter simplification is about to take place. Iran—a strong, proud, highly unified, and relatively well-armed though historically non-aggressive country—will be forced to respond to any substantial (beyond provocation) bombing.

I think Cheney/Bush admirers cannot then say that the Administration is acting in America's strategic interests or even in the interest of oil. Nevertheless, they will say exactly that. A lot of oil will go up in smoke in the ensuing war. Their Iran War will compound many times over all the earlier strategic errors and costs, 1953 through 2007.

I have simplifications of my own. If Cheney prevails, I will conclude that he is acting only in behalf of war for war's own sake, that is, war for the sake of the sale of bombs by his private friends to the government he controls. There are many books discussing America's ideology of war and especially the illusions we harbor about WWI, WWII, Korea, and Vietnam. But enough of book recommendations; most simply, we must remember Dwight Eisenhower's warnings about "the military-industrial complex" and remember that bombs are the so-perfect product of capitalism: a single buyer who pays well for tonnage and bells and whistles, no competition, no marketing costs, free distribution. Best of all for war profiteering bombs represent blind aggression rather than complex diplomacy. Upon first use, bombs destroy themselves (as well as surrounding civilians). Then they must be replaced.

That said, I also have a final small story from these sources and from our public schizophrenia. Ambassador Galbraith tells us that Trita Parsi, the author of *Treacherous Alliance; The Secret Dealings of Israel, Iran, and the United States* (Yale UP, 2007), was on Ohio Representative Bob Nay's staff in 2003. Parsi's book documents the Iranian offer and the Bush administration's rejection and why Ney was thought of as a way reach the U.S. government through the thicket thrown up by Karl Rove, who saw himself moving from professional campus young Republican to Henry Kissinger status. Ney was a Republican in Congress for eleven years and he had lived in Iran and spoke Farsi, the only congressperson who did. He was a Republican, but a Republican like Lieberman is a Democrat. Ney supported an array of pro-labor legislation in Congress, he voted against the U.S. Patriot Act, CAFTA, and the Bush Medicaid and after-school program cuts. He had once lobbied for the relaxation of sanctions against Iran. So, for his interference in Affairs of State, Bob Ney was taken down and is now serving 30 months in prison for "bribery" in connection with a role in Texas Tom DeLay's Abramoff Indian Casino scandal. That is a rather severe consequence for a common congressional transgression but a punishment for interfering in the insane Bush war policy.

Note:

The Wallace Stevens poem, quoted above, is "The Snow Man," a beautiful thing dear to my heart and not solely about weather. The full poem reads:

One must have a mind of winter
To regard the frost and the boughs
Of the pine-trees crusted with snow;
And have been cold a long time
To behold the junipers shagged with ice,
The spruces rough in the distant glitter
Of the January sun; and not to think
Of any misery in the sound of the wind,
In the sound of a few leaves,
Which is the sound of the land
Full of the same wind
That is blowing in the same bare place
For the listener, who listens in the snow,
And, nothing himself, beholds
Nothing that is not there and the nothing that is.

ᔕ

Who Is Alan Greenspan?
(Posted 09/20/2007)

Enough is said about Greenspan to make you imagine he is a weapon against global warming.

Not at all. What he did was he served importantly as head of the Federal Reserve Bank from 1987 to January 2006 following, in a more stylish way, the footsteps of lumbering Vulcan Paul Volcker. Together they effectively led U.S. monetary policy for our entire Reagan Era (1976 to date). But the immediately current attention is because of a new Greenspan book supplemented by wide awareness of the looming recession and an entirely natural wicked desire to prick the balloon of his inflated reputation. And perhaps because of Greenspan's bland acknowledgement, for some unknown reason made just now, that the Iraq war was about oil. That has stirred up attention.

I have suspected that Greenspan is so admired in DC because he is both a phrasemaker ("irrational exuberance," "consistent, persistent, grinding, impoverishing inflation," etc.), and one of the masters of evasion, a bit the way the far less worthy Donald Rumsfeld was once admired. Our nation's capital is in many respects like an elite college campus. There is a role for fluency, for word-culture.

There is the same open evidence of segregation, and the same nice infrastructure and dinning facilities. But there is also the way everyone becomes a toady to senior and eccentric professors, gossiping them up, dropping their names, and treating them with Germanic respect. Greenspan was one.

Recognizing the evidence of Greenspan's extremist Republican political bias—indeed, he was a protégé of Ayn Rand, an extremist right-wing anarchist—is not difficult and will be very well documented. That was improper at the head of the Federal Reserve, but perhaps not criminal.

However, given that he was the Fed Chairman sworn to defend the economic interests of all Americans, not just very rich Americans, there are possible criminal charges waiting. Waiting and waiting.

That he provided his authority as a "fiscal conservative" Fed chief in support of Bush's push for tax cuts benefiting primarily the very rich; that he recommending ARMs to ordinary home buyers when mortgage rates were at the bottom (he actually did that!); that he supported cuts in Social Security while recommending that the Bush tax cuts become "permanent" and presented this as an act of "budget balancing." Other changes will emerge, both well and poorly documented, be argued, and then will disappear.

In behalf of all who are faced with at least some of this argument, I want to look at two contrasting opinion articles that can, to my mind, frame the argument. Call them (1) the pro-capitalist or the rich man's sort of article and (2) the timidly socialist or liberal middle class article (this latter, from my point of view, the best we can hope for).

The Pro-Capitalist Rich Man's Argument

Robert J. Samuelson in the *Washington Post* yesterday provides number (1). The theme of his op-ed is the remarkable success of the American economy during Greenspan's reign. Samuelson mentions "two modest recessions" (1990-91 and 2001) but not that they occurred during Bush Administrations. For Greenspan's "astonishing record," Samuelson provides these bullet points:

- The economy (gross domestic product) grew 70 percent from 1987 through 2005.
- The number of nonfarm jobs increased 31.4 million, or 31 percent, with average unemployment of 5.6 percent.
- Annual inflation as measured by the consumer price index averaged 3.1 percent.
- Pretax corporate profits jumped from $369 billion to $1.33 trillion.

- The stock market quadrupled, with the Standard & Poor's 500-stock index rising from 287 (the 1987 average) to 1,207 (the 2005 average).

This is patently the greedy rich man's view of economic success. Today the rich are taxed at a lower rate then at any point in the last fifty years. Essentially they pay the same tax rate as the average wage earner whose wages have actually declined while expenses have increased and whose wages support the life of their families and not—as with the rich—the growth of what the naive call "their savings." These workers also provided more productivity per man/hour of labor but they received none of the benefits of increased productivity. Personal debt for such families has increased while net worth has declined; wives have increased in number in the work force, as have low-paying service jobs; union and better-paying jobs are scarce.

Clearly corporate profits have not "trickled down" and as for the financial market, pensions are more uncertain today than they have ever been. Even Social Security has come under attack by private interests.

Bob Samuelson's is low-level partisan journalism such as you hear in unscripted radio talk shows. Today in Boston—with casino gambling on the state's agenda and gambling tax described as "the last hope for needed state revenue—occasional voices try to raise the question of increasing taxes, especially on the rich. Back at them came State Representative "experts" and others who asserted, without truth and without contradiction, that the rich pay most taxes already (a complete fiction!), that increasing taxes on the rich would remove their "incentive" (contrary to all evidence and history), that the rich might flee (flee where?), and that if state money is going to come from someplace to fix our serious infrastructure problems other than from casino taxes it will have to come from further cuts in social services. At last, the real position of the rich: further cuts in social services.

These false, typical State Rep truisms get endlessly reinforced; real and reasonable options are taken off the table because they are not in the interest of the rich, and false economic pictures are painted by the number. From Alan Greenspan at the Fed, to Robert Samuelson at the *Washington Post*, to whomever it was on whatever network program, opinion is manufactured in the interests of the rich.

The Liberal, Middle Class Argument

This (2) comes from William Greider in *The Nation* blog, "The Lies of Alan Greenspan." The article tells us that Greenspan did endorse Bush's regressive tax cuts, did aggravate American inequality, did cause the housing bubble, did ignore the stock market bubble and, finally, Greenspan—in an honest weak moment, perhaps—did say the Iraq War was "largely about oil," all of which Greenspan denies in his recent book and interviews.

Greenspan, like many, is racing away from the very unpopular George Bush as fast as his long aristocrat legs and a hundred interviews will take him. He does not mind slipping and sliding to do it. The probably is we have not yet seen half the disastrous consequences of "Maestro" Greenspan's tenure at the Fed.

The question, however, remains "A disaster for whom?" Whose interests did Greenspan serve? Whose interests did he harm? The answering details are what we need. In the same way, long ago in 2000 and 2001, we needed to have our liberal journalists ask and answer this precise question rather than to make fun of Bush's cowboy manners and act shocked (Shocked!) at his illiteracy, shocked at the country jingoism and shocked at the inevitable requirement that someone of his background and with his ties and interests constantly told lies to the public.

With blood on their hands, the rich can only tell lies, slink, slide, and hire apologists, can only deny that it is they who are killing our chickens in the henhouse every night.

෬෬

Good for Obama
(Posted 11/02/2007)

Looking stalwart this last Tuesday, the men sailed into Hillary Clinton for her support of Joe Lieberman's initiative, following Bush's lead, declaring the Iranian Revolutionary Guard "a terrorist organization." "What was she thinking of?" they implied.

Obama led off against her and Edwards immediately commented "You gave Ahmadinejad an inch; he will take a mile." Today we find Barack Obama (to be followed by Edwards, I assume) triangulating away from his previous Bush-like position on the need to attack Iran. This is good. It moves us an inch away from an Iran War on top of the Iraq War and Afghanistan War.

Obama now emphasizes that he will "engage in aggressive personal diplomacy" if elected president. I should think! One thing presidents are for in times of a near-war international crisis is to do some personal diplomacy, especially as the new president must face the international mess from two terms of Dick Cheney's favorite cowboy with his "axis of evil", "shock and awe," "with us or against us," "Crusade," "war on terror" tumbleweeds and cowshit. All this cowboy verbiage, this *merde,* is smeared on the nation to obscure grand presidential largesse to the oil and armament corporations.

Obama said "I think it is important for us to send a signal that we are not hell-bent on regime change" by force of arms in their country. A fine statement. After all, it is their country, a distinction Bush does not make and Obama is newly making. Hillary came back at him—foreshadowing the kind of argument we will hear a lot of if she is nominated—questioning his experience, his patriotism. It is called *ad hominem* and is part of her Chenyesque, tough guy, woman-at-war uniform.

Barack Obama's chief weakness is not the literal lack of experience, but his attempt to be the reconciler of all differences, the man of all seasons, and the calm and wise counselor against extremes. He is only three years from the Illinois Senate, that hotbed of calm and wisdom. His has been an amazing rise. He is quite impressive and in no way off-putting. I catch some hints that he has read almost everything and speaks several languages (kept secret, of course, from the education-hostile masses). Of all the contenders, he is the most subtle in argument, not the tangled Yale debating muck of John Kerry's disquisitions but actual fine distinctions. As I remarked earlier ("Edwards on the Issues") Obama made the point that voting for the Revolutionary-Guard-as-terrorists contradicts either our policy of never negotiating with terrorists or our policy of "pursuing negotiation." And yesterday Obama made the point that a major change in our 28-year hostile, indeed bellicose, relationship with Shiite Iran is surely a precondition for a resolution in Iraq—also a Shiite country, one closely tied and substantially dependent on Iran. These are fine points. In a more normal world, a post-Bush world, they should be considered obvious.

As for other issues, the important thing to say right now is that Obama (as has Edwards already) must move to the left. Here is why we may see this happen. In a real sense the very limited and very narrow voter turnout and delegate selection process in the early Party primaries are insignificant. They need not reflect and they may well contradict national voter sentiment. I suspect most people—dependent on TV, a local paper maybe, and talk radio—do not realize how undemocratic this process is. Yes, the process formally will determine who the candidates will be, but unfortunately that will be a decision made beforehand by the most senior party functionaries (who are unelected and represent no one but themselves and their paymasters). That is point one.

Point two is that the opinion of the majority of the nation has been moving away from Republican reaction (see presidential approval ratings, the 2004 vote, adult activism on the rise wherein one union guy on the street is far more effective than 20 oblivious college part-timers, the numerous polls which you may easily consult, the daily news of disorder in the State Department and elsewhere, etc.).

People know that Republican reaction has been too costly in lives and dollars; it has gotten us nowhere (less security not more, hatred not the admiration and affection we are used to, more problems not fewer, and now even the problem of an enormous, unsettled nuclear armed Pakistan, Afghanistan down the drain, Bush's attempt to bribe/bargain proliferation with India falling through, an anti-Yankee Latin America on the move, etc., etc.). People see this (as confirmed by my reading of the Iowa newspapers editorial pages that are online).

The alternative in these circumstances is not someone centrist. All these fine left-moving people have been in fights at one time or another. That is experience. In a fight, centrists are always obstructionists not allies. "Why can't we do away with divisiveness," they cry in the midst of the contention. There is the old Yiddish joke about the Jewish soldier in the midst of battle crying "Stop, stop! Someone might, God forbid, lose an eye!" Centrists do not care much for democracy: so disorderly, so lower-middle class. Anyway, people sense a fight and if the Democrats are going to survive as a Party they must field a fighter, someone who is actually opposed to Bush and opposed to the current ugly drift of things.

Originally, I thought the right centrist Democratic Party leadership (the Clintonian DLC and DNC) would do the usual thing: put up a false flag, anti-war liberal (like Dean) early on just to take the edge off discontent or to mobilize the discontented. Then, after that, they would mobilize everyone behind the candidate chosen by the Party powers (like Kerry), a lesser evil, a new "anybody but Bush." Then they either would loose or would have named and elected someone who is an actual Republican in sheep's clothing like Hillary Clinton or like her husband was. Now I believe the full horror of Bush's misleadership of the country is beginning to dawn on many people, the realities and the increasing number of revelations (rampant financial corruption, State Department disarray, disunity in the military and the intelligence services) are having their effect.

Hence (my third point), the Democratic Party will push further with their experiment (new in this generation) of actually running a non-centrist, a left liberal for President. They will test the waters over the next two months and in the first primaries and then thumbs up or thumbs down, based on the signals they get from their masters (just normal stuff, interests speaking as they have a right to do, no conspiracy at all). They will assess the shape their liberal-leaning candidates are in (energy, skills, commitment, money) and where the Republicans are (like knowing that any warm body can beat a self-indulgent, blow-hard, opportunistic, 9/11 fear-mongering ex-mayor of New York City), and, finally assess the vote outcome of the Party primaries (their 10% to 20% of age-eligible Party organized voter turn-out).

Hillary has powerful interests behind her, in both Parties, many sources of money, and media encouragement. For a new example, the politics of the SEIU vote endorsing Hillary were fascinating, playing on every false flag (a "strong woman," Bill's wife, New York in her pocket (where so many work), and—Can believe this?—"underdog"). In what may turn out to be a decisive factor Hillary has the support of the television media (four conglomerates with very centralized and inbred leadership; actually all one vast pool of very conscious money).

The basis of this loose-seeming generalization, in part, is my reading of a comprehensive analysis of media coverage of the primary titled "The Invisible Primary," by which title they mean a primary determined by Party leadership and correspondingly weighted media coverage. The study does not explain exactly how a two term former First Lady Senator from New York and a first term Black Senator from the Midwest became the unlikely instant "front runners" but it does document that they received twice the press coverage—and more positive coverage—than all other candidates combined (including governors, several 30 year veterans of the Senate, a high-name-recognition former VP candidate, and miscellaneous populists including Dennis Kucinich). Kind of like the press and the Democratic Party doing a parody of itself for the benefit of Republican voters. One suspects they desire a close election. "The Invisible Primary" data nicely summarized it.

Therefore, although I hope not, Hillary may well be the nominee they pick in which case a lot of the organized left liberals (MoveOn, the environmentalist now still basking in Gore's Nobel, many peaceful demonstrators against the war) will go with their pale enthusiasm for her "lesser evil," for her "anybody but a Republican." I do believe America is going to come out ahead in this election.

But the most significant part of the more than year-long run will be these next few months as the Party out-of-power (the Supreme Court is Bush's, Senate Democrats are so compromised they must have more than 60 seats to pass anything, and Bush is still President) decides how it is going to respond to the resurgence of oppositional spirit among the American people.

The Democratic Party leadership may well just say, "Let them go fuck themselves." That has been their general spirit all along. They will go with Hillary regardless. In that case, you will soon see vicious media attacks on Edwards, primarily, and on Obama as a quiet threat. You will see Edwards and Obama standing naked, with no defenders, abandoned by their own Party, swift boated by their own party. Alternatively, on the other hand, the Party leaders may say "Oops!" and make a different decision. They will say "Okay, if it cannot be a Republicrat centrist like Clinton. We have got to start having very major talks, heavy talks with Mr. Obama and/or Mr. Edwards."

A lot is at stake for these party leaders if it appears that the Democratic voters are not going to accept Hillary's absolute centrism, her equivocations, her Bush-nice, her keep-everything-in-place corporatism, then Edwards must continue to move left and Obama must move with him if they intend to contend. If not, Hillary, long since media-christened "front runner," is the final call.

༄

Pakistan, Mukasey, and Torture
(Posted 11/07/2007)

National sentiment against torture remains strong (as reported in two recent presentations by Keith Olbermann on MSNBC). Congress in general does not reflect this national sentiment. Congress approved Alberto Gonzales as Attorney General early in 2005 and, since Gonzales became notorious for his support of the Bush torture policy, Congress has now approved a new Bush Attorney General, Michael Mukasey. He will also not condemn torture, nor hold Bush accountable before the law. He has a reputation of high level judicial opinions that are more reactionary than those of the Texas Bush protégé Gonzales. The Olbermann specials reflect broad U.S. sentiment, so we have this one representative (at least one) at MSNBC but no effective representation in Congress.

Charges of madness, fantasy, and magic thinking abound in Bush criticism these days. They are only metaphors. Bush is not certifiable. He is a classic America folk-speak reactionary absolutely devoted to the interests of the very rich, with whom he is at one, and the conduct of imperial foreign policy in their interests and at whatever cost. They love him, with reservations. The fantasy metaphors originate in the disconnect between what is obviously the case and what is pretended.

1. The current Pakistan mess is one example of this dynamic. The Clinton-Bush strong man, General Pervex Musharraf, is "pro-U.S." What does that mean these days? By the international news that I read and interviews I hear, Pakistan has more sane and honest opinion makers than can be found in Washington D.C. Musharraf is sending them to prison. Bush clings to his and Clinton's puppet dictator, as usual, even though Musharraf is flagrantly beating democracy demonstrators, imprisoning his opposition, putting the entire Pakistani judiciary under arrest, shutting down the free media, etc. Compare freedom today in Pakistan to freedom today in Venezuela, where an anti-Chavez press and TV flourishes, and yet the Chavez's government is always presented by Bush the worst of dictatorships.

Bush says we must have Musharraf because he "helps us in the War on Terror." But Musharraf has contributed nothing to capturing Osama, to cutting off Al-Qaeda bases, to diminishing the Taliban. On the contrary, Musharraf practice against terrorists has always been hesitancy, delay, and finally offering them negotiations and meaningless ceasefires. Last Sunday he freed 25 Islamic fundamentalist militants in exchange for Pakistani army personnel held hostage by the Taliban near the border. Meanwhile his practices against secular, democratic elements (young lawyers, the judiciary, professors, rights activists) has been beatings and jail time under a "Maintenance of Public Order" Act and shutting down the independent media.

Meanwhile our actual war in Iraq continues. Americans and Iraqis die and vast sums are stolen while less and less is being reported. If you remember Vietnam War reportage, you know that there were problems, of course, but the national opposition to that unjust and failed war derived in great part from public journalism and honest photography, from public knowledge of what was actually going on. Not so in Iraq. Reports tell us that 138 journalists have died there, an astonishing number, some probably died at the hands of Americans. Bush continues his failed war and Cheney calls all who oppose it "traitors." And "Homeland Security" is beginning to look more and more like a program for silencing, threatening with prison, "extraordinary rendition," torture, and (in a recently ruling) use of the Army to "maintain public order" within our borders. In other words a program of official denial of law, the constitution, and civil rights; a program of surveillance, official IDs, loyalty oaths, wire taps, Internet tampering, the use of spies and provocateurs, and armed suppression of protest. Just call is fascism.

2. Bush's historically low "approval rating" in another example of this division, this disconnect between the country and Washington, D.C. The current *Nation* gives a valuable summary of eight or so polls all showing that about three quarters of the American public are clearly opposed to Bush and the way things are going.

These low poll approvals are a sharp fall off from the highs of approval that Bush and U.S. policy enjoyed immediately following September 11, 2001. Many noticed how those highs were the product of an amazing media hype around the fall of the twin towers, "Ground Zero," then "Shock and Awe," "Mission Accomplished" and related Bush theater.

Imagine what the ratings would be for Bush's blithering foreign policy if it were not for the fact of Osama bin Laden (still free), his clique of Saudi terrorists called Al Qaeda,(geographically spread, non-state religious fanatics and terrorists), those fundamentalist Taliban leaders in Afghanistan (flourishing and now in process of retaking all of Afghanistan), and a Pakistan leadership that was once rewarded for building up the Taliban and bound in soft relationships with their former protégés.

World opinion is now very hostile to the U.S. Imagine the extremes of that world wide hostility were it not for the existence of some very real and now flourishing groups who do actually sponsor and carry out small terrorist attacks on innocent civilians, small groups of unreachably fanatic Islamists whose objective is to put as much pressure as possible on their "religious enemies."

I say "imagine." Note the coincidence of all this with the panic-like enthusiasm of Bush and his Administration as they continue to talk "9/11" which "changed everything," continue to promote fearfulness, elevate "Threat Levels," talk of "WW III," of "enemies," of nuclear threat and mushroom clouds, and as they publicly celebrate each and every tiny terrorist event, clique, and individual as if these were something much more significant than law-enforcement issues or a lack of cooperation from client governments.

What small acceptance Bush still has (beyond the billionaires) is a contribution of the hidden reality of Osama bin Laden and his ad hoc non-state organization Al Qaeda (once small and only Saudi, now widespread multi-ethnic and flourishing), and the Taliban (now with a new lease on life thanks to the Bush/ Cheney oil war in Iraq). I believe that Bush already would have been impeached but for Osama, Al Qaeda, the Taliban, and because the Middle East is still the long familiar "troubled waters" where oil corporations fish.

Bush is their lease on life.

3. For the third example of disconnect, we go back to the Halls of Congress and note that Charles Schumer, one of the two "liberal Democrats" who made possible the approval of Mukasey as Bush's next Attorney General, had an op-ed in the 11/6/2007 NY Times justifying his vote for Mukasey. Schumer argues—against all experience and reality—that Bush appointed Mukasey because he really wanted to reestablish the rule of law in America and restore the Justice Department to accountability. His new man would undo what Bush's previous Attorney Generals had done, Schumer says. Schumer says he believes Mukasey really would "remove the stench of politics from the Justice Department." If you can believe that.

This nonsense of Schumer's is spun out in the Times in spite of the fact that Mukasey in the confirmation hearings resolutely refused to call water boarding illegal or hold a "war president" (this endless "War on Terror" president) accountable to act within the law. As with the unlawfully called, dishonestly justified, and criminally conducted long set of wars on Iraq, Bush is desperate to make torture legal (as legal as depleted uranium shells, daisy cutters, land mines, air attacks on those who flee, and sanctions, all of which are banned by the UN and practiced by the U.S.).

Probably the order to torture "terrorists"—to "bend forward," "go the extra mile"—originated with Bush-Cheney himself, perhaps as a classic Mafia wink or nod. Mukasey will block that inquiry; and Schumer and Dianne Feinstein (Democratic Party leaders) came forward in Bush's behalf. Like the other Democratic leaders (Pelosi, Emanuel, Dean, etc.), they clearly want to block Bush's impeachment. Very interesting. I wonder if their patrons are whispering in their ears about "social order."

ༀ

The John Roberts Supreme Court
(Posted 12/02/2007)

By way of an article on our Supreme Court, here are notes & quotations from recent e-mails I have sent. Most of it comes because Anthony Lewis reviewed *The Nine: Inside the Secret World of the Supreme Court* by Jeffrey Toobins in *The New York Review of Books* for Dec. 20, 2007. Lewis, a sixties *New York Times* editor and Bill Clinton-era columnist, is an admirable liberal, one of the best on court issues and he even has some early, enlightened pieces on Israel. He is also the author of *Gideon's Trumpet*, which you should have read in school. His wife is Massachusetts' Chief Justice Margaret Marshall. She authored the majority opinion that legalized gay marriage in this state. The Lewis review is not yet available online, so here is a summary:

The current Supreme Court is the product of the conservative Republican ascendancy dating from the mid-1970s. The Republican Party—with its Christian evangelicals, corporate tax cut advocates, and Federalist Society base—has aimed at the following general changes in law:

- Reverse *Roe v. Wade* and allow states to ban abortion.
- Expand executive power.
- End racial preferences intended to assist African Americans.
- Speed executions.
- Welcome religion into the public sphere. (Quotations from Toobin's book)

Initially the conservatives were frustrated by failing to win the above objectives quickly because of Justices Kennedy and O'Connor. These justices were

Reagan appointees but they did not enact the desired Reagan changes. David Souter, appointed by G.H.W. Bush joined them in opposition to the above constitutional changes. These three justices saved Roe v Wade. In doing so, they reflected majority opinion in the US. Lewis cites a 2007 poll showing 62% agreement with the idea that a woman should have the right to an abortion while 32% said women should not have this democratic right.

However, conservatives are not responsive to public opinion (one of the definitions of "conservative") and they persisted in their anti-Roe agitation. Toobin again:

> They organized more, mobilized more, and cared more about the Count than their liberal counterparts. And when their candidate [George W. Bush] won the presidency, these conservatives demanded more–a pair of justices who were precisely to their liking…. With admirable candor, and even greater passion, conservatives have invested in the Court to advance their goals for the country.

Lewis makes the point that liberals were not only outgunned on the issue of appointments to the Supreme Court but also did not fight against the Bush appointments. For supporters of abortion rights and affirmative action it was inescapably obvious that the results of the presidential election of 2000 and 2004 were crucial to the composition (and opinions) of the Supreme Court. And yet the Democratic candidates (Gore/Liebermann in 2000 and Kerry/Edwards in 2004) hardly mentioned the issue.

For conservatives, George Bush was the perfect candidate. He campaigned as "born again," determined to bring Christ to public school children. In Texas, he had refused clemency for all 131 death penalties (Gonzales was his legal counsel). He was firmly for saving the fetus and against rights and protections for women. In addition, he opposed "reverse discrimination" (as conservatives called affirmative action) in any form. His Supreme Count appointments were in accord with these views and Democrats approved his appointments.

Thus, there was a sharp and swift Supreme Court move to the right. Court observers profess surprise. Media liberals were shocked and dismayed (Shock! Dismay!). They fell back on making Bush jokes. Meanwhile a 5 to 4 vote decided many crucial court cases. The conservative five have been Chief Justice Roberts, Scalia, Kennedy, Thomas, and Alito. Thus, after a bit of delay, the Republican Supreme Court is enacting the conservative agenda.

Toobin again:

> The messianic nature of his presidency—Bush's conception of his
> time in office as a moment of dramatic change for the world—
> affected his judicial nominations [in both higher and lower courts
> and in the Justice Department] as it did his decisions on the
> Middle East. Through a combination of the staff he selected, the
> political strategy underlying his reelection, and his own personal
> evolution, Bush now sought transformative appointees, justices
> who would move the Court sharply and immediately to the right.

Chief Justice Roberts' leadership of the court has been the combination of
saying one thing and doing another. He has strongly favored "unanimity" in
words while presiding over a highly divided court. He "upholds" *Brown v. Board of
Education* and the Equal Protection Clause of the 14th Amendment as prohibiting
the use of race in affirmative action programs (which limited use was just recently
confirmed by *Grutter v. Bollinger*). He claims not to be overruling these precedents
(or the forthcoming essential use of race criteria at West Point and Annapolis);
however, the logic of the recent 5-4 decisions in school cases says otherwise. My
impression (from the hearings) of Roberts is that of meeting a thoroughly dishonest man; treat him with decency and courtesy and you will surely loose your point.

Since 1911 (*Leegin Creative Leather Products v. PSKS*) the court has ruled against
price-fixing agreements as violations of the law. But now the Roberts 5-4 court
has ruled that this issue must be ruled on a case-by-case basis. Likewise, (in *Bowles
v. Russell* involving erroneous federal judicial instructions) settled law has been
overruled. Six critical decisions have used what Lewis calls "covert overruling" of
settled law: for instance, in *Gonzales v. Carhart*, the "partial birth abortion" issue,
in overruling the right of the public to challenge measures that assist politically
partisan religious activities, in upholding a lower court judge's right to remove
jurors who oppose the death penalty, in removing employee rights to seek back
pay for discrimination even though they did not immediately upon beginning
work protest the discrimination, and in other instances.

Lewis writes:

> In each of these cases the new majority pointed to particular rea-
> sons for the result it reached. But nobody could miss the overall
> trend: hostile to abortion, affirmative action, the rights of crimi-
> nal defendants, measures against gender discrimination, and
> limits on campaign finance.

Most of the critical decisions of the Supreme Court's October 2006 term have the ring of a conservative manifesto, one dating from Party documents and 1976 fight against controlling campaign financing.

To illustrate how potent the Roberts' court changes are, Lewis includes a discussion of the long-standing feature of Anglo-American law called *stare decisis*, let the decision stand. The example he gives is the famous Miranda decision and the police "Miranda warning" of right to counsel. It became embodied in routine police procedure and, as the previous Chief Justice Rehnquist wrote, became "part of our national culture." Thus, in obedience to *stare decisis*, "Miranda" should not be lightly overruled, and certainly not covertly overruled (on some narrow technical argument).

Stare decisis does not refer to an iron rule of law; however, when the court does change its mind on something of great substance it usually moves in tandem with public feeling and opinion. Thus *Brown v. Board of Education* altered the 1896 *Plessy v. Ferguson* ruling. By 1954—after widespread awareness of what the Nazi's were up to in separating and marking out with yellow stars the Jews in Germany—no law upholding formal racial segregation could stand. Another example is when, by 1986, the country and the court decided not allow individual states to enact criminal punishment for consensual sex.

However—and in spite of Roberts' many words against the court "lurching around because of changes in personnel"—our Supreme Court has been doing a lot of lurching recently. Lewis feels that this endangers our judicially enforced constitutional democracy and damages the enormous respect we have historically shown for the Supreme Court.

In *Bush v Gore* a 5-4 majority gave the election to George W. Bush with a order to stay the recounting of votes in Florida because recounting was "casting a cloud" over the "legitimacy of his election." Toobin, Kennedy and many others do not regard this "casting a cloud" as any example of legal reasoning. In its final decision the court found that because the Florida counties were recounting votes in different ways this denied the constitutional principle of equal protection and, thus, all recounting should stop. Toobin says this was an "inept and unsavory" decision (because the Constitution leaves counting up to the states, as they will, and commits challenges to the judgment of Congress) and sees it as a clear act of political partisanship.

Lewis concludes that, in spite of words to the contrary, Roberts does not value unanimity in the Supreme Court. He is marking himself out as someone determined to read the law and the Constitution in such a way as to achieve reactionary ends. And he is in a hurry. He knows the makeup of the court will change.

The unhappy fact is that George Bush chose his Supreme Court appointees for the historic purpose of "extending his legacy." Both parties approved his choices. That is the way the Constitution is written. A presidential election is our only means of shortening the impact of Bush's court-mandated legacy.

Notes:

Lewis says, "Raids and repression cannot make the Palestinian inhabitants of the West Bank and Gaza content with occupation. They want what Jews struggled so long to get for themselves: a place where they can control their own lives." The rest is blowback from harsh Israeli repression.

Women's right to legal abortion and legal access to contraception has been embodied in practice or in law in many countries since early in the century. Lenin regarded abortion as an elementary democratic right of women and, in 1913, wrote that laws against abortion and contraception reveal nothing but "the hypocrisy of the ruling class."

Souter, Toobin reveals, was so upset by *Bush v. Gore* that he thought of resigning but knew his resignation would hand Bush another appointment that, in all likelihood, the Democrats would approve. And, by the way, Sandra O'Connor, a life-long Republican, voted her party politics in *Bush v. Gore* —the majority opinion, not the dissent like Souter—and subsequently resigned giving Bush the opportunity to make another court appointment. Both acts were conscious and consistent, and still I hear good words from friends about Sandra Day. That she is a woman is no legitimate basis for support, not on something as important as the Supreme Court.

❦

These Endless Wars
(Posted 01/18/2008)

Years of weathering have nearly obliterated the anti-war signs in my neighborhood. And now the two principal war hawks of their respective parties have moved closer to their inevitable nominations this week. Hillary Clinton and John McCain are the most likely to continue the endless wars in Afghanistan and Iraq. They are being crowned "the most electable." The rest of what Clinton and McCain stand for is actually less relevant. Unjust war-making sets the moral orientation. Deaths (ours not theirs) weigh heavily and are the goad toward lesser crime. For the voting public, Democrats will be given their usual lesser evil, decent Republicans will be given their next "compassionate conservative" and the rest of us can bite our thumbs.

The attention of most Americans is going where it is being turned, toward a political campaign, away from the ongoing wars. The statistics from *Projects for Excellence in Journalism* measure this. Coverage of the war has steadily declined over recent quarters. This decline inevitably follows from the Administration's continued (false) announcements of progress, from the government's new cooperation in the news coverage of veteran issues (mostly tragedies), and from the reduction in American causalities. That reduction is largely because the air war over Afghanistan and Iraq has been intensified. The Bush Administration decision-makers—which is to say, Cheney and the war and oil corporatists, their presidential spokesperson in the Oval Office, obedient Defense Secretary Robert Gates, silent CENTCOM head Admiral William Fallon, and politically ambitious Iraq commander General David Petraeus—know that this intensified air war means more civilian casualties in these two ruined countries. They do not care.

Also, the related real purpose of "the surge" is becoming clear. The intention was both our popular sentiment against war back in our face, making it clear that war is the exclusive business of the imperial presidency, and to facilitate the shift to a program of organizing Sunni forces while pacifying and richly rewarding the Shiite militias. That is where most effort is going these days in Iraq.

In Afghanistan, it is less clear. Either serious effort is being made to strengthen the weak Karzai Islamic Government of Afghanistan and its army or to approach a new accommodation with the ever-stronger Taliban Islamic forces. Or both. In both countries, the ground is being prepared for "Civil War," which is by definition "their war" not our occupation. Already "civil war" is replacing "sectarian violence" as the dominant media phrase (again, this is journalism.org counting the words). The Bush Administration knows that the horrendous human cost of civil war—meaning our occupation-induced violence—falls on the civilian population. The political outcome is uncertain, but the State Department will adjust.

As you may have read, the assigned mission now given to some U.S. units is "protecting Iraq's population" along with advancing our counterinsurgency strategy of isolating and controlling the sectarian militias. That announced mission—in addition to being PR—means that American officers, GIs and Marines are working 24/7 and risking their lives to achieve just that mission goal. That is how the army does things. There is an obvious contradiction between the real effect of the Administration's decisions to intensify bombing and consolidate and further arm (or, as it is put, "isolate") the militias and this mission of "protecting Iraq's population." But here, too, the Administration does not care. I see no other possible conclusion concerning the Administration war decisions. They are evil people.

Perpetuating the interests of corporate America is a very big deal. The wars must go on because big corporate America is now entirely dependent on empire, policing, terror, and their control in and around the Middle East oil basins. They require a war hawk and pro-corporate figurehead in the Oval Office even more than they require economic bail-outs, give-aways, "stimulus," interest rate tinkering, and an uninterrupted flow of wealth from all of us to the few of them. Everything the very rich care about hinges on empire, war, and control. If you have a chance read Naomi Klein's *The Shock Doctrine; the Rise of Disaster Capitalism* (Holt, 2007), a swift overall description of what is taking place in the larger context, and readable.

Meanwhile, we are being prepared for eleven months of presidential campaigning on national economic issues. It will be the economy—and secondarily health care, education, cultural issues, etc. In all of this there is much scope for firm blah-blah-blah pronouncements, shallow detail, iffy promises, and stern warnings. Most of the talk will mean nothing in seventeen months. By Super Tuesday (Feb. 5, 2008), we will enter the dog days to decide which warmonger, which friend of the corporations will rule America for the next four years (at least). Neither candidate will give up or significantly set back the unitary presidency Dick Cheney has built. Cheney has worked on this New American Century project steadily since the Ford Administration. On this see "The Cheney Project" by Charlie Savage about his new book *Takeover: The Return of the Imperial Presidency and the Subversion of American Democracy*.

I believe the obviousness of all this has sucked all value from my prediction nearly a year ago that it would be a McCain vs. Clinton election. Knowing that the major media determine public opinion in the collective sense and that they were ignoring the Edwards populist candidacy, I should not have used such hopeful language about Edwards. My only excuse is that I do live in hope, as do we all. In that way we are obedient to the commandment in Matthew 6:19: Lay not up for yourselves treasures upon earth, where moth and rust doth corrupt, and where thieves break through and steal." Or, to put it another way, isn't there some hope in the fact that this is a dying empire, capitalism at its highest and final stage?

Note:

The phrase "Compassionate conservative" is not George Bush's. It dates to 1976, to Ronald Reagan, and to the right-wing motivational books and speeches of Doug Wead.

MEDIA

Introduction

Stranded. You may feel stranded at the edge of the world. I do. A part of what we take to be life beyond family, friends, and neighbors—hopefully these are fine—depends upon the public media. I read newspapers every day, news magazines weekly. I watch the TV news. Even earlier my bench at John Deere and later my desk at various universities were no strangers to our major newspapers. Now, in retirement, these items of secondary life assume greater importance.

Sadly, these few pieces are not the first compilation of reflections on the media I have created. Also I am no stranger to Letters-to-the-Editor, Op-Ed and blog responses, submissions, etc. You are offered this compilation, an inadequate chapter that moves over 2002 to 2008, Bush years, reflecting on the media when Bush was media's pole star.

The curse of those who write about the media is the curse of Heraclites: you cannot step in the same river twice. I admire those who persist, swizzle-toed in that endless flood that has some necessary but no sufficient meaning.

Above, "stranded," is a Van Morrison line. He is Irish and I also thought of the spirit of James Joyce's line: "The Liffey flows the way of all fish," a sad, true reflection on the waters of the media. Perhaps you will pray with me:

Dear Anna Liffey, we have lived on your flesh and we love you.
Please persist. Support our nation, our fishing for meaning.

თ

Manufacturing Consent
(Posted November 24, 2003)

Edward Herman is co-author with Noam Chomsky of *Manufacturing Consent: The Political Economy of the Mass Media* (1988), the single most important book on the American mass media. Noam Chomsky is central to twentieth and twenty-first century cultural literacy and Herman is also important. Here is Herman writing about the famed Thomas Friedman, the *New York Times* senior diplomatic correspondent, author of *Lexis and Olive Tree* and other guides for the lost and unwary:

In sum, the diplomatic correspondent for the *NYT* supports ethnic cleansing and terrorism, but only when done by the United States or one of its clients; he repeatedly supports policies that involve the commission of war crimes, again only when the United States or one of its clients engages in them; he is hostile to real democracy at home and abroad, preferring a plutocracy and sharp market restrictions on popular sovereignty; he assails countries like France for failing to support the United States, always attributing dubious motives to the U.S. opponent, while putting a benevolent and chauvinistic gloss on the objectives and actions of his own country. His analyses of matters such as globalization and the current Iraq crisis are full of rhetoric, contradictions, ideological assumptions, and intellectually they barely make it into the featherweight class. That he is an institution at the NYT, a three-time Pulitzer Prize winner, and is well-regarded elsewhere reflects the degraded state of U.S. mainstream commentary and intellectual life.

Manufacturing Consent is a model in its conclusiveness, methodology, and spiritedness. For an independent reader to miss it, or a teacher fail to introduce it to their students, would be a shame. Herman's latest book is *Degraded Capability: The Media and the Kosovo Crisis*, another fine lesson in method.

∽

Paul Krugman
(Posted 11/30/2003)

For a clear general picture of where our national politics and economics have been going visit Paul Krugman, occasional *NYTimes* columnist and Princeton Economics professor and author of *The Great Unraveling: Losing Our Way In The New Century*.

Krugman identifies the Bush administration as extremely reactionary, seizing upon 9/11 as an opportunity to unleash the dogs of war to control Iraq's oil and to intensify political reaction at home. When comparing Bush to Reagan and to Nixon, Krugman suggests those administrations were at least interested in governing. Bush has no such interest; he is pouring out the federal bathwater to the rich and throwing the baby into the trash, all this under the fog of war and with signature ruthless dishonesty.

Immediate profits go to close friends in the oil, finance, and armaments industries while the lower and middle classes (whose debt is rising while retirement savings and social benefits disappear) pay for it all. Bush's is a "special interests" presidency beyond anything we have seen since Hoover.

The $500 billion deficit of this presidency will remain to face us even after the economy, jobs, etc. recover. At some point soon, we will not be able to pay our debts; the Euro and other currencies will grow even stronger as nations and institutions cease holding their wealth in U.S. notes. We have a trade deficit matching the domestic deficit. In effect, everyone is lending our country money to cover our own slow economic implosion. At some point, as people cease believing that we will get our act together, the practice of propping us up will cease.

Krugman is a liberal Democrat and often his language is that of warning and possibility rather than the blunt "Great Unraveling" of his book title. Undoubtedly he intends to continue as a prominent public voice. He is persistent, topical, and not radical. However, anyone is free to read his many essays and articles on several websites where the total of his views make a much stronger impression than the individual, digestible, "if " and "when" *New York Times* pieces. The *Times* editors clearly impose boundaries. Playing that gig, Krugman will not give broad, radical generalizations about our commonwealth, will not seriously criticize the Democratic Party's complicity with the rich, and will not invoke morality (of the "Thou shalt not kill" sort). Never mind; he is a valuable journalist nevertheless.

According to Krugman, our journalism and the talk on the street is heavily into denial. People cannot believe (or they cannot bring themselves to say) that in dealing with the Bush presidency we are dealing with something completely different. We are dealing with reactionary politics not conservatism, turning the country back to Hoover's time, obliterating everything accomplished in the recovery from the Great Depression, everything accomplished after the victory over fascism in WWII, everything after the building of our successful economic powerhouse with a strong middle class and the world's most trusted currency.

He regards the Bush Administration as extremely dishonest, not merely partisan. He suggests that to claim that this Administration represents one of two broad "sides" in American politics is false. The administration is conspiratorially wedded to a very small set of extremely reactionary interests (old oil, giant armaments, a bought media, a toothless and corrupted Congress, a population terrorized by "Remember 9/11," the idea that Terror can happen to you in Des Moines Iowa, in Atlanta, in Rexburg Idaho.

Krugman says that most (not "some") American journalists are cattle conditioned by the prod to move through the right shoots, into the right cattle cars. "People can't believe that we're dealing with something completely different now, but we are."

Krugman writes clear and popular expository prose, never too literary. His spirit is to say that if Bush has his way,

> "We will all live deep down, now. You'll see. Twenty ways to
> prepare a crayfish. Or, you know, chess. Sanskrit poetry. It will
> hurt like hell, sonny, you'll see." [Alan Furst]

∽

China Beyond the Sunday Papers
(Posted 12/08/ 2003)

The current visit of the Chinese Premier Wen Jiabao may be quite significant. Wen has been in the center of Chinese government for more than two decades, a very centered government. Looked at from the frantic decades of recent U. S. history, Wen's government seems gradualist, careful, and highly successful. Host George Bush's position is not strong. In spite of his near total control over our press, in spite of the power of our economy, Bush is mired in Iraq and Afghanistan, threatened by the strong Euro, successful only in denial and with his lies about our trade deficit, job losses, the disaffection in the military, and his social and environmental attacks on America and its people.

I never want to see the ugliness of a powerful, preemptive, and unilateralist China—or of another imperial Japan or an India of the Hindi fascists, for that matter. None of that is likes when it is the U.S. who is studying war, nuclear threats, attacking international law and the UN, standing on the neck of Latin America, and filling the air with righteous propaganda about freedom and democracy. And it is my U.S. In some way I am, we are, responsible. Therefore, there is some pleasure in this meeting that may add a bit to the exposure of Bush's failures and extremism.

Our journalists will not quote Wen, beyond a phrase or two. The Chinese Premier will be a polite guest; but there is the danger that he may say something cogent about today's world, something that falls outside the bounds of allowable news. Packed around his visit will come lots of U.S. journalistic Styrofoam. Already settled issues between the U.S. and China (Taiwan, trade relations, human rights, intellectual property piracy) will be reiterated in hack blather on TV and in the papers as if they had not been settled. By now this is all boilerplate journalism. Also there will be the usual down-market waste of human-interest anecdotes: the plight of Chinese manufacturing workers, bra prices, and "the sexual revolution sweeping through China's urban young," just to mention those in yesterday's papers. Nevertheless, the main issues of his first major Chinese visit to the U.S. are very important ones.

First is China's "peaceful rise" to a position of greater influence throughout Asia. This is the set of friendly and supportive international initiatives that Wen and President Hu Jintao have been carrying out in Asia while Bush was assaulting the world with his counter-productive "You're either with us or with the terrorists" message and his fake announcement of "Mission Accomplished." I do not know much in detail about these Chinese initiatives in Asia–now also beginning with Africa–but they are intended to strengthen China and secondarily all of Asia (and especially Asia's tens of millions of Han Chinese) economically. Wen will want to reassure the U.S. that this peaceful rise in influence does not bode ill for U.S. corporate and financial interests, the interests Bush represents and the only interests real evidence suggests he cares for.

For example, China has the ability to tame North Korea. Wen has described their willingness to do so. I believe he has reiterated that willingness, although the press missed it every time. I would guess that from here on Bush would let China deal with North Korea while he and Rice will posture like dummies in a storefront window. After labeling North Korea an "Axis of Evil" country, Bush immediately saw them sell their dollars, buy Euros, and begin using Euros for trade. This was not very significant financially, but it came as a shock and a reminder of the dreaded "domino effect." He immediately produced an oil embargo, which immediately killed many poor people in cold North Korea.

Euros for oil is a very sensitive issue. By a U.S.-Saudi agreement, the U.S. dollar has been the exclusive currency used by countries to buy oil, almost without exception, from the WWII period until Saddam Hussein upset this long-standing U.S. advantage converting all of Iraq's reserves to Euros and selling oil for Euros. That act (plus the physical reality of Iraqi oil reserves and their strategic location) made necessary the second Iraq War. That war will not end until Bush (or whoever after) has taken direct control of Iraq's oil reserves (and probably Iraq's government) and returned oil access, oil currency, and oil prices to U.S. control.

This is an issue so sensitive and central it is never mentioned in the U.S. press; you have to read European newspapers and magazines via the Internet to hear it mentioned. Anyway, the North Koreans retaliated against the embargo by reactivating their nuclear program, perhaps in the sure and certain knowledge that the Reagan-model Bush administration will only attack relatively helpless countries.

However, North Korea and China's peaceful rise to influence in Asia will be a topic with reassurances all around. China will reassure that its oil policy (feeding their oil appetite, soon to be as great as ours) is far-flung and diversified, not centered on the Middle East. Bush's press will talk muck about American influence and dominance.

Neither Bush nor Wen will waste any time on the tabloid stories about flight of jobs to China. Even now several in the Bush administration and many additional flacks are pointing out that those three million American jobs were lost to productivity increases or were manufacturing jobs that had already been shipped overseas in Asia and Latin America before China was in a position to win them. Even without the 3 million lost jobs, inventories are up and the product needs a market.

China is an enormous market. The stock market trembles with each hint of trade restrictions. So, "Protecting American jobs" will not be a topic, nor will "China flooding the market with cheap goods." Bush has retreated from his steel tariffs, he has restored the planned agricultural shipments to China, and he will not ban the Chinese bra. It will be a very friendly visit.

The other issue during the visit can be called the trade deficit issue. At the beginning of the Reagan era (or a bit earlier) the U.S. began to run a trade deficit. It was something like $30 billion when Reagan became president and rose to $150 billion early in his second term. It is expected to rise to something like $220 billion in 2004. Those are annual figures. We buy more than we sell with printed money underwritten by Treasury Notes sold to China and Japan for real money. To have the U.S. market as a customer is of great benefit to developing nations. As a consequence of selling to us, China holds a very large stake in the U.S. government Treasury bill and bond market. They hold this form of money—even though the dollar is weakening against the euro—for future purchases of oil or U.S. manufactured goods, especially the more sophisticated and expensive goods.

China's central bank has accumulated $400 billion in currency reserves (mainly in dollar bonds although I suppose with some amount in euros or euro bonds). China is approaching Japan in total accumulation ($650 billion in currency reserves held the same way). Heretofore Japan has been the main underwriter of the U.S. trade deficit. That is to say, once more, the U.S. government can freely print Treasury bonds as long as someone is willing to buy them. Japan has. China's trade with the U.S. began from zero in 1972 and when the Chinese— according to Wen in a UK interview—began to keep good statistics it stood at $2.5 billion. This year it will be $120-$130 billion accounting for a significant part of our deficit. They too are now underwriting our trade deficit.

Our high-consumption economy needs to continue to have the dollar unchallenged in the world, willingly held as the primary reserve currency against future purchases. For Japan and China, oil is the main future purchase. Bush would want the Chinese to be very, very modest in their use of the euro. This even though the euro, over the last few years, was a more profitable way to hold your money. The dollar must continue to be currency used in the purchase of oil, and China is the world's second largest consumer of oil. The financial and manufacturing oligarchy that rules our country does the numbers. If there is any significant swing to the euro as a reserve currency, there will be a depression in the U.S. As China begins to buy more and more from the US, the oligarchy will want the Yuan to buy fewer dollars improving the value of their sold products. This would increase the cost of Chinese products sold to U.S. consumers, dampening that trade; but that is okay as long as it is gradual. Gradual is Chinese for "Go."

It seems plain that oil and arms and expensive industrial and engineering equipment are where our oligarchy lives. There will be more words about the need for the Chinese to accept more "exchange rate flexibility," rather than keeping the Yuan at the level of 8.5 to the dollar. China can pledge not to flirt with the euro and in exchange secure the U.S. agreement to respect their current exchange rate of $1 = 8.5 Yuan or, rather, to except their routine promise to float their currency eventually, someday in the future, when they are ready.

I think I have that about right.

Anyway, China, as I say, appears to have pretty straightforward objectives: to evolve with the U.S. "a mechanism" for mutual trade benefit while not conceding to any U.S. financial manipulations of their currency. Little spats are okay over bras and robes, over corn oil prices, etc., but "trade wars" are loose/loose. Human rights is a non-starter with China, as is regulatory controls (labor, environment) and their central bank. China, while shipping to the world, oddly regards these as "internal affairs."

North Korea and Taiwan will be okay. Bush may even utter some disapproval of the Taiwan separatists. China is 1.3 billion people, a huge market with a special appetite for agricultural product and processing technology. China will be able to carry on their "peaceful rise" of influence in Asia, and perhaps also Africa and Latin America. In exchange, they are probably willing to make no threats against the dollar as long as they are not the last man standing—holding hundreds of billions of devalued dollars—if the U.S. economy has a coronary from overeating.

The Sunday papers will carry China stories, but only those in lime, lilac, scarlet, and yellow.

◌

Year of the Toad
(Posted 12/31/ 2003)

Have you noticed that we are being subjected to a series of big, loudly acclaimed movies on the theme "The Inevitability of Bloody Revenge?" Riding to vengeance in the post-9/11 drama when we bombed impoverished Afghanistan virtually to death and invading already sanctioned, inspected, misled, and impoverished Iraq on the same vengeance and punishment argument, now come the movies. There was "Mystic River," and then "Open Range" and "Kill Bill," and others. The inevitability of bloody revenge is the theme in all of them. We have Hollywood selling inevitability.

The young, who do not judge but only absorb the movies, respond one way: "It's okay, it's a human thing, inescapable, this is a fallen world, perhaps even a meaningless one, and besides, revenge is sweet." We who are older respond a variation on their message: "Folks, this is a world we can best survive by staying out of it. Duck your head! Do not become a player!" Both responses reflect the message of the sell.

Like many people, I though that the U.S. practice of arming and training organizations led by religious fanatics to help defeat the Soviet Union in Afghanistan was a bad idea. I thought sponsoring megalomaniac dictators like Saddam (which we did up to the point where he began to oppose U.S. oil policy in about 2000) was a bad idea. I thought installing a massive U.S. military presence in Saudi Arabia (following the first Gulf War) was a bad idea. You cannot guard some other country's oil wells forever. I even wondered why the go-lightly approach to Al Qaeda, unquestionably terrorist religious fanatics, in spite of the first World Trade Center bombing in 1993, the bombing of the U.S. embassies in Kenya and Tanzania in 1998, and the USS Cole in 2000. Was it because they were Saudis, like the bombers of 9/11?

I thought, like many, that all this had to do with the enormous, high-risk anxiety that afflicts the corporate rulers of America. They have controlled Middle East oil for a half-century's worth of wealth building. But it is slipping, slipping. So they have constantly reinforced our other Middle East land army, Israel, and built further bases. That seemed pretty much part of the same anxiety and a very bad idea.

All these past policies were not only bad, they have now given rise to even worse, quite extremist rogue policy. What previously was done mainly with diplomacy, bribery, and profit sharing was now being done by bombing and the "excuse" of revenge. And all this under an open-ended and illegal policy of "preventive war." "Preventive" war was what the Nazis claimed in their defense at Nuremberg.

President Bush (our bright star for Jesus) led the parade for vengeance and violent forestalling of what he said might happen. He articulated these radical and extremist policies in defense of controlling and dictating the pricing and distribution of the world's greatest supply of petroleum. And, as expected, all the national media reiterated his line, his "War on Terror," his bloody revenge, his whetting of the glittering sword. "You either support the slaughter or you are with the enemy." In addition, the media never mention oil.

Now—here at the end of sad 2003—as it all settles out to a more and more unpopular war and occupation, a quagmire, as the issues begin to become a bit more clear, as a presidential election year yawns before us, we begin to get a barrage of Hollywood movies putting forward the inevitability of bloody revenge in the special, dramatic Hollywood way.

Most concern must go to the extremist policies of the oil president, George Bush. He is our toad in this time of the toad. However, there is little solace in Hollywood with its own snaky way of touting horrible revenge in a fallen world. The real stage is Bush's policy world, Bush's anxious, oil-soaked crimes.

∽

Our Shameful Press
(Posted 01/02/2004)

Censorship is an outrage, a kind of rape. Does it really matter whether the perpetrator is a coward, a pragmatic self-censor, or merely hazy and lazy? Does it matter whether he or she is courting favor with someone more powerful or simply fears loosing his day job? It is the same rape even if the censorship is carried out by government edict? The effects are consistent and the self-interest is one-sided.

> Censorship is never over for those who have experienced it. It is
> a brand on the imagination that affects the individual who has
> suffered it, forever.

In 2003, the national media ignored the biggest domestic terrorist arrest since 1995. 1995 was the year Timothy McVeigh (a right-wing fanatic) killed 168 men, women, and children in the bombing of the Murrah Federal Building in Oklahoma City as an anti-government gesture. Not until late December 2003 (in a *Christian Science Monitor* piece) did I learn of the April 2003 arrest and November indictment of someone named William Krar of Noonday, Texas. The police and FBI recovered dozens of illegal weapons, half a million rounds of ammunition, explosives, and cyanide capable of killing thousands, along with quantities of white supremacist and anti-government pamphlets.

Krar's plot was foiled. Like McVeigh, he was another not-so-isolated criminal fanatic. Same with the plot of the anti-government group who assembled on July 4, 1997 with major weapons and explosives intent on attacking Fort Hood, Texas. That was not reported either. Likewise, there are hints of numerous other stories leaking the aroma of the anti-big-government rhetoric of George W. Bush (six years as Texas governor). The national media has ignored many instances of domestic terrorism.

Domestic terrorism—and its causes—are not on Bush's agenda; therefore, it is not an appropriate subject matter for our media.

Also, it is shameful that the Bush Administration and its press ignores the dead and wounded of Bush's Iraq war, his criminal war. I say "criminal" because the judges in the Nuremberg trial of Nazi leaders rejected the German argument of the "necessity" for pre-emptive attacks against other countries. They ruled:

> To initiate a war of aggression [on the excuse of preemption] is
> not only an international crime; it is the supreme international
> crime differing only from other war crimes in that it contains
> within itself the accumulated evil of the whole.

More than 5000 wounded American soldiers have been flow back to the U.S. and moved silently into Walter Reed Hospital. What little bits of coverage they do receive as reward for their obedience to orders comes from non-press individual initiative. For instance, the singer and actor Cher recently spent a day at Walter Reed talking with some of these wounded soldiers. A friend in the USO had called her requesting she come to see them. In order to give the issue a bit of coverage, Cher called in to a CNN talk show the next day. How else, she had thought, can I give them a little honor when the press pays no attention to them?

Identifying herself to CNN only as "an entertainer," here is what she said:

> Yeah. And I spent the day with—I mean they were great guys.
> . . . They had the most unbelievable courage. It took everything
> that I have as a person to—to not, you know, break down while
> I was talking to these guys. But I just think that if there was no
> reason for this war, this was the most heinous thing I'd ever seen.

And also I wonder why none of Cheney, Wolfowitz, Bremer, the president—why aren't they taking pictures with all these guys? Because I don't understand why these guys are so hidden and why there aren't pictures of them, because you know, talking about the dead and the wounded, that's two different things, but these wounded are so devastatingly wounded. It's unbelievable. It's just unbelievable to me. You know, if you're going to send these people to war, then don't hide them. Have some news coverage where people are sitting and talking to these guys and seeing how they are and seeing their spirit. It's just—I think it's a crime.

Quite a few people recognized her distinctive voice. How deeply is this topic buried when Cher gets no press?

An issue of *Army Times,* which circulates on military bases, did a year-end display of the pictures of the 506 killed in Iraq. Someone sent a copy of that paper to Jimmy Breslin and he did a piece in Long Island's *Newsday* describing the year-end issue. Breslin talked to the *Army Times* managing editor, Robert Hodierne. Hodierne had met Maya Lin who designed the Vietnam Veteran Memorial Wall and he was proud of his unique, special issue. 2003 saw the most U.S. military deaths since 1972 in Vietnam, many of them had died since Bush did his photo-op from the deck of an aircraft carrier, shamefully wearing a flight jacket under a "Mission Accomplished" banner.

Breslin writes:

> The chilling photos [of the dead soldiers in *Army Times*] run at a time when the government tries to describe the war as a civic venture, and nearly all the news industry doesn't know how to object. This probably is the worse failure to inform the public that we have seen. The Pekingese of the Press run clip-clop along the hall to the next government press conference.

There is a consistency in these very different notes. All rape is rape, consistently. The devil is not in the details.

A second quotation from Noam Chomsky—if I had it at hand—would explain this consistency. He says that if some media product (article, Op-Ed, interview, etc.) serves the interest of wealth and power, there will be no censorship. If it serves in any way the interest of the great majority it will be excluded, censored, or otherwise diminished in the major media.

∽

The Hollywood Blacklisting
(Posted 01/06/2004)

Walter Bernstein's *Inside Out; A Memoir of the Blacklist* (1996) is, on many counts, the best book on the subject. I have read it just now. How did this successful screenwriter and his friends deal with the anti-communist hysteria of the 1950s as the House Un-American Activities Committee (HUAC) destroyed their careers? The larger story, which Bernstein does not attempt to tell, is how this episode is a model for today's less crude censorship.

The HUAC hysteria was initiated by the military/industrial complex folks following WWII as a way to keep up the level of military spending and overcome the peace-mindedness of Americans after their victory over fascism in WWII. American peace-mindedness had been their problem since WWI, but they were constantly improving their ability to suppress or distract it. At that time, there was the widespread strike activity as unions fought to regain wage rates that had been voluntarily frozen as part of "the war effort." Factories flew the green "E" (for Effort) flag while the corporate owners did their war profiteering. Also, there was the undeniable attraction of some features of socialism represented by our WWII ally, the USSR. All this worried the corporations and their government. There was also the "threat" of the United Nations with its objective of keeping the peace and its humane internationalism. They would attack that also.

All these were dangers to the rich and powerful and required they and their media shape popular consciousness of a new enemy. Reds and godless Communism became just that. "Paint socialism and the unions black," "Down with civil liberties," "Long live censorship!" "Capitalist power not People power!" Those were the talking points. They dominated the fifties and the following decade and are alive and well today. The "Red Scare," the "McCarthy Era," The "Domino Effect," "Un-American Activities" hunters on the prowl everywhere. All of this got out of hand, destroyed many lives, helped lead us into Vietnam. Yet we live with this model insanity still.

Writers and teachers still routinely insert their little "I am not now and have never been a supporter of the international communist conspiracy" pledges or their antiterrorist assurances into their articles and lectures. Newspapers and the TV are ever ready to hang the next monster, however thin the threat. Now—55 years after WWII, long after Vietnam, after the collapse of the USSR in 1989— new enemies must constantly be found to justify letting our country's social and political health deteriorate while the rich recover everything they believe they lost during the aftermath of the Great Depression, everything they believe they were not able to seize because of the war effort, everything they "needed" in order to "stimulate the economy." Once the next enemy is selected and the hysteria is whipped up, it does not go away but lives on in those whose conformity or consent is needed and who are easily fed on tainted meat.

But back then, in that most painful 1950s, we had a rural demagogue, Joseph McCarthy, who set out to transform traditionally left-favoring rural and working class populations into true believers in the "Conspiracy against America." Joining him were many dozens of opportunists in the House and Senate riding the blood red horse of anticommunist jingoism and winning election victories by accusing the opponent of being "soft on communism," "fellow travelers," and "liberal." Back then, most journalists and academic intellectuals spent part of each day kneeling in prayer to anticommunism and "Americanism." Their old prayers (on record) and the shame of having kneeled shape their idiom even today. Teachers signed "loyalty oaths" as a condition of work (literally) and the fathers of children built shelters against an "Atom bomb attack" that never came. They saw us endangered by falling dominoes that never fell. They worried themselves sick and harsh over an "invasion of our shores" whose tide never came in.

Almost to a man, the professional and academic guardians of reason and once supporters of our four freedoms went into denial. "What freedoms were those?" "I seem to have forgotten the literal meaning of those freedoms." Here is the literal meaning, and a sample of what a progressive president sounded like all those many years ago:

> In the future days, which we seek to make secure, we look forward to a world founded upon four essential human freedoms. The first is freedom of speech and expression -everywhere in the world. The second is freedom of every person to worship God in his own way– everywhere in the world. The third is freedom from want, which, translated into world terms, means economic understandings, which will secure to every nation a healthy peacetime life for its inhabitants –everywhere in the world. The fourth is freedom from fear, which, translated into world terms, means a worldwide reduction of armaments to such a point and in such a thorough fashion that no nation will be in a position to commit an act of physical aggression against any neighbor –anywhere in the world. That is no vision of a distant millennium. It

is a definite basis for a kind of world attainable in our own time and generation. That kind of world is the very antithesis of the so-called "new order" of tyranny, which the dictators seek to create with the crash of a bomb. [FDR, Jan. 6, 1941]

Stirring and important. However, you now know the ease with which absolute control over the mass media and its intellectuals can turn Roosevelt's words—and the underlying practical measures in law, policy, and international agreements—into mere residual liberal rhetoric.

America's anticommunist crusade poisoned the atmosphere of the schools and universities (our institutions previously least responsive to mass media), removed many good men from our public and intellectual life, and left others like shrunken heads. In government corridors, the moral horror of using the atomic bomb became an exercise to "think the unthinkable." Traditional guardians of morality and justice—especially in the churches—went into wholesale denial and literally gave up their former beliefs.

On the ground in Hollywood everyone who had ever attended a progressive meeting or written a progressive article or screenplay came under attach as "red," "a commies" or "a dup" or "fellow traveler." And there were a lot of them. Perhaps they were the majority. The John Waynes, Chariton Hestons, and Ronald Reagans were the minority. Yet most in the industry became willing to protect or enhance their careers by testifying against their industry colleagues.

The FBI and the House Un-American Activity Committee did not need their information; they already knew who attended meetings and who wrote what. What the inquisition needed was the very act of betrayal, this "cooperation." Those who did not "cooperate," who refused to betray their friends and colleagues by testifying to what the Committee already knew, were sanctioned, blacklisted, made unable to work. The Committee spread the word against them among producers and studio owners who were themselves threatened if they did not cooperate. That way everyone was diminished.

The atmosphere of fear, betrayal, distrust, and dependence on lies spread. And this also created the perfect opportunity for the mediocre talents of opportunists and hack propagandists to flourish. Destroy the competition. Take their jobs! Blacklisted progressive Dalton Trumbo ("Papillion," "Spartacus," "Lonely Are the Brave") called it "the Time of the Toad."

And so, Walter Bernstein—the writer/producer of the old John Garfield movies and a good Army journalist and early TV writer—and other blacklisted friends discovered (when he tried to work openly under his own name) that a colleague and his friend Abe Maddow had named names to the Committee, had testified against them, become a stool pigeon before the HUAC. It was devastating for Bernstein. Up to then his friends had survived the black list by writing under assumed names (as did Trumbo), by borrowing from friends, by hiring a "front" to act with executives as if the scripts were their own, by slipping into the screening room after the lights were out, meeting privately in apartments to discuss rewrite, by giving over "authorship" to producers. These are the ways the black-listed—like Bernstein—were forced to piece together some (uncredited) work if they wanted to work in Hollywood.

Following news of Maddow's betrayal, his "naming names," Bernstein called his friend. They talked and Maddow admitted that he had given HUAC seven or eight names, betraying his friends. "Why did you do it?" he was asked. In his answer, Bernstein discovered this:

> It had nothing to do with money or politics or being afraid or not able to work. He simply could no longer stand living in the shadows. Something had broken in him . . . He then said what informers often said: that the names had all been named before anyway, and so he had not really harmed them.

Before his HUAC testimony, Bernstein had seen nothing dark or disloyal in his friend and no hint that he was a broken man. So, he did not feel he could scream or punch or hate him. He had respected Maddow and enjoyed his friendship. Now that no longer existed. "We both understood," he said. A sad, powerful recognition.

I apologize for the lengthy background, but this little story in an excellent book (full of movie stories and politics) is an important one. I believe that something like what happened to Maddow happened in the dominant atmosphere of our country because of the Cold War and the Red Scare. It took awhile to "click" (I date it at 1976). As with Maddow, something broke. I have sat and talked with many broken men, teachers, colleagues, and friends. There is no consolation in saying "But not for me." It does no good to say, "I learned in the struggle against the war in Vietnam to say 'No' to cooperation when the inquisition comes calling." That was then. The break has affected all of us in some way. Something broke inside our culture, our collective heart. State terror does that. It is why we hate fascism so deeply.

Can I measure the fracture? I ask myself how much holding up of "the four freedoms" or their practical expression (the New Deal and the UN Charter) takes place, how much advocacy of socialism takes place, how many meetings and heartfelt conversations and public urgings about our social future take place. How much honest community is left? When I answer, "precious little," I feel I may have exaggerated.

Do we even look for those with answers, or trust the answers we hear if those answers go beyond the bland and general ideas that are current and dominant, ideas that cost us nothing? We both understand.

⸏

Our Unnatural Media
(Posted 08/08/2004)

We all sound like trumpets of truism when talking about our media.

Kay McFadden of the *Seattle Times* writes, "The primary source of mass communication about candidates' policies and voting records has become the campaign commercial." In another article she observes, "If 2004 proves memorable in the annals of campaign coverage, it may well be as the year when advertising and talk shows effectively displaced TV news as the main conduits of information to voters." Right, Kay.

Commercials are income. Talk is cheap. News is costly. You do the math.

Media owners shift from news and news analysis to talking heads to commercials. This is especially noticeable now that a crucial presidential election is about to happen. People feel they should know something about the policies of the candidates, whether they decide to vote or not. Meanwhile, the news is about nothing but the candidate's "shirtsleeve" appearances, their wife's manners, their pets, their sports, and celebrity friends. So bring on the political commercials that are running with amazing frequency in "contested" states.

This displacement of news by commercials, PR releases, infomercials, semi-commercial features, political advertisements, and ever-free political "humor" happened long ago with most newspapers. Asked why they subscribe to a newspaper, a majority of users say they need the advertisements: food on Wednesday, movies and other weekend planning on Thursday, big ticket items on sale announced Friday, furniture on Saturday, over-priced autos everyday, and Sunday for idle curiosity. What's out there?

Eighty percent of Americans say they get what they believe they need to know about our society from television. I suspect every one of them knows that small groups of plutocrats own all the channels, recognize—with the exception of bold Rupert Murdock, once a mere Australian Press Lord—that the plutocrats hide their ugly personages behind a small set of media brands and media corporate names. All recognize that an election via TV is simply another celebrity spectacle.

The major national newspapers, taken all together, reach just over one percent of the American people. So where do Americans learn about public policy? Nowhere.

Robert McChesney, in *Rich Media, Poor Democracy* (1999), says that two dominating principles shape our media: simplification and sensationalism. Commercialism drives both principles, which is to say, private profit is the only motive force. Sensation and simple stuff costs least to produce; ad revenue is at the heart of it all (twenty-something percent of TV time, most pages of newspapers and magazines, nearing the whole of public architecture, and even now running as side-bars on TV and Internet screens). That is a profitable formula. Soon it will take over our phones and those tiny microwave and frig displays.

In his new book, *The Problem of the Media; U.S. Communication Politics in the 21st Century* (2004), McChesney shows how the truisms about our media (commercialism, bias and corporatism, concentration of ownership, shallowness, black holes, censorship, over-simplification, and all the other routine public disserve) arise on a foundation of specific public policy decisions. This is an important point and mainly ignored. The media we have now has been shaped by the undermining of the already inadequate public service requirements of the Communications Act of 1934, by continuous successful lobbying and right-wing court decisions on ownership restriction, and by the transformation of the FCC into what McChesney "a classic 'captured' regulatory agency" run by the corporate interests it supposedly regulates.

The 1996 Telecommunications Act consolidated the victory of the corporations. Moreover, it did so with generous bi-partisan support. That Act removed the requirement that radio and TV present "public interest" programming in return for their free and exclusive use of our airways; it did away with controls on corporate media ownership (single corporations could control all media outlets in a single "major market" community). It eliminated what was once a serious, at least a legal requirement to be "fair and balanced." And, thus, that phrase has become no more than a Murdock, News Corp., FOX advertising slogan.

People are largely unaware of the FCC's corporate-oriented activities. The cartel-like arrangements by Viacom, Sony, News Corporation, Time-Warner, Vivendi, Disney and GE, are mentioned only in the business pages. They collude with each other while competing for shares of the advertising market. The National Association of Broadcasters literally dictates pro-corporate arguments appearing in the speeches that Michael Powell (who heads the FCC) delivers in behalf of media deregulation. These corporations monopolize the public "airways" and the cable and satellite channels (developed with public funds). In exchange for these government handouts—and no longer paying back even so much as public service "announcements"—they create what you see and watch in Cincinnati and Cedar Rapids, a large portion of which is advertising space and time they have sold to corporate advertisers.

Years of propaganda ("deregulation is good," "benevolent market forces," "freedom to choose") has created the illusion that the media is a kind of a natural force, inevitable and immutable. I think this false "natural force" appearance is somewhat like the Iraq quagmire. The Bush administration intended to attack Iraq for reasons of oil, so they made the attack seem necessary and inevitable. All the major media were enthusiastically complicit in the run up to the war (and in the lives lost, the money squandered, the net loss to the war on terror, the undermining of diplomacy and international institutions, etc.).

Now that the proof is in our face, some media (*NY Times*, *Washington Post*) are sort of apologizing for their role in the promotion of the Iraq war; however, we do not see them acting any differently about the rest of the Bush administration's extremism. They are still cheerleading (or explaining or excusing or government press releasing) the aggressive undermining of generations of health, safety, and environmental regulation. They sell an energy policy made by corporate lobbyists, and a Russian Mafia style give-away of public property to friends and campaign contributors. They clarify nothing about inequality and regressive taxation or Bush's Welfare for the Rich. They will never apologize for going along with all of this because, like Bush and Cheney, they, too, believe that, "it is the absolute right of the State to supervise the formation of public opinion." Dr. Joseph Goebbels first established that affective fascist principle.

So, we know all the truisms. Certainly nothing in the current election run-up suggests that the face of the news will change; it is all advertising all the time for the same-old, same-old interests.

⌘

Newspapers: Vehicles of Culture and Democracy
(Posted 01/25/2007)

I had one of those dreams this morning that come as the mind's ploy to keep the body sleeping. In a frozen and empty Alaskan landscape, I was investigating two mysterious stagecoach catastrophes. [I normally dream in the 19th century.] Helping to bury the victims, I discovered papers strewn around the wreckage proving that the victims did in fact own the rights to the intellectual property stolen from them by the unknown marauders. Somehow, this fact was very important. Working feverishly, before rushing off to investigate a second tragic event, gawkers asked me, "Why do you do this?" and "What keeps you going?" Modestly I replied, "A good night's sleep."

Awake now, my subject is the waste made of many of our culture's stage-coaches by corporate marauders and monopolists. They have roamed the land like bandit gangs in the old movies stealing and destroying our great newspaper institutions, in effect destroying culture. The important components of the story have been steadily taking place since 1976. The damage is done. However, let me use the past tense in this brief summary since it is advance warning of worse to come.

Rupert Murdoch has successfully seized pieces of the Tribune Company (Newsday, LA Times, Chicago Tribune, plus TV and Cable holdings). Murdoch was joined in his dismembering of Tribune media by the private equity firm Carlyle Group (who also has a deep and abiding interest in Iraqi oil and reconstruction). Outrider competitors with a special, somewhat protective interest in the City of Los Angeles (they are billionaires from the entertainment, home building and supermarket industries) were forced to stand aside for the bigger dog. It was a brazen ambush on a financially weakened "asset," and Murdoch's invasion adds substantially to his newspaper and other media holdings in America, UK, and Australia, holdings led by the powerful FOX news enterprises. Tribune properties will soon feel the effects of FOX and the "Murdoch Model." Essentially the model is cheap, shallow, and biased news. They will also feel the effect of the private equity speculators like Carlyle who, as usual, will take cash out of their new asset before reselling it, in whole or in parts.

In the 1980's Rupert Murdoch rode successfully into the territory of the "Big Three" (ABC, NBC, CBS), then overwhelmed a competitor (CNN), forcing his model on them all. He is now adding to his influence. Yes, Murdoch's competitors are guilty of imitating his dress code, vulgarity, and sunglasses. Yes, capitulation to Murdoch's "success" is childish, shameful, and all about illusory, hoped-for money. Nevertheless, it is a lesser sin than being a professional Enemy of the People, which is where I would put Murdoch.

Although Murdoch's marauding is legendary and his impact very well recognized, commentators usually describe the above events as no more than business as usual. Occasionally one of them will admit that financial motivations (relatively insignificant by Wall Street standards) explain hardly anything about Murdoch's decisions. Murdoch's notorious history of career reprisals makes them fear to mentions his extremely reactionary—to the point of mad vengeance—and mad corporatist politics as a factor. Nor do they mention the characteristic "dumb it down" effect of his firm dictatorship. Instead, commentators go on about Wall Street pressures and "an orderly transition to new newsbusiness models." They quote without comment Murdoch's lies about "editorial independence." They leave it to scattered, underreported items to tell us of the layoffs at the large metropolitan dailies, the closing of international news bureaus, the steep downturn in hard news staff, the total elimination of investigative journalism, and the negative impact that FOX—putting it bluntly—has on literacy.

Murdoch is only one man like many, I know. He has firmly denied his cultural agenda even as Wall Street praised it as a freedom from "liberal bias." Like Dick Cheney he is a cold man (butter will not melt in his mouth) and so are many of his billionaire peers. All claim no more than responsible right-wing politics (which they define as tax breaks for the rich, continuous cuts in social services, illegal wars and threat-&-bribery diplomacy for the control of resources and markets, an end to restraining regulations on sacred commerce, etc). That does not quite capture the whole picture. Like Murdoch, they claim no cultural agenda (though we can see the dumbing down, the secrecy and censorship, keeping unwanted noses out of the business of business, normal business discretion becoming criminal collusion, and the unchallenged support (which is to say, election) of only those officials who are blood-oath loyal to corporate interests, and their support (to no profit whatsoever) for the growing illiteracy of the subject population).

I am not dreaming this. In trying to envision these men and comprehend the depth of their hatred for a free, vital, and democratic culture, I can only think of Vice President Cheney, who nobody really knows, or the villain in "For a Few Dollars More." That was Gian Maria Volontè, or think of Eli Wallach as Tuco, Marlon Brando as "The Godfather," or Forest Whitaker as "The Last King of Scotland." All of them swathed in money-driven insanity.

Yesterday on NPR Tom Ashbrook gathered some expert commentators who talked about our newspapers' sorry state. They spoke as if the owners and managers of big media were puppets of the Big Board's ups and downs, men who are not political—Oh, no—who had not an adverse thought about our culture. Even Ashbrook's implicit cry from the heart "Will our great newspapers fall into the hands of profiteers?" was hollow, as well as being no question at all. And not a word was said about the effective intent of such ownership to shape opinion into right-wing Jell-O molds and deliberately unenlighten us all. Tom and his commentators (highly regarded every one) have watched FOX and CNN, they have read the *New York Post* and other Murdoch media, surely. They sounded earnest, but I seriously doubt it. To me they seemed frightened of the likes of Gian Maria Volontè and the Godfather. I accuse them of that weakness. No doubt, they are bolder privately among their friends.

And just today two watery journalists from the *New York Times* (Seelye and Fabrikant) give the game of Avoid-the-Obvious away. They describe Rupert Murdoch not as slouching toward his next stagecoach robbery, but as having just now "entered the fray" (for Tribune Company ownership) thereby reviving a "lagging auction" for that asset. They conclude the piece with a long, seemingly innocent quote from Alfonse D'Amato's endorsing the growing Murdoch monopoly, neglecting to mention—which they undoubtedly know—D'Amato's FOX ties, his Verizon ties (interlocked by the ubiquitous "Joint Operating Agreements" with News Corp), or that the Carlyle Group is a client Park Strategies, D'Amato's lobbying firm. Here is a well-known Dean of Services to the billionaires, presented as if he were some detached observer. As educated, professional journalists they know better than I the details of Murdoch's crawl from his first gutter fights for control of culture in Australia to his successful marauding in London and then in the U.S. This polite, pretend-innocent avoidance itself ought to be a crime. Or call it criminal sycophancy.

You can see "State of the News Media 2006" for narrative and statistics. I believe we all know that TV has become almost the sole source of news, with newspapers living off network payments for content (in addition to their declining ad revenue) as old couples in dying small towns live off their Social Security. We know how a substantial part of our population has been dumbed down. We know of declining newspaper readership, declining deeply sourced content, more "soft" content, and more attention paid to powerful institutions. The people behind "State of the News Media" actually count such things (Bless them for that!). They find that TV news does twice the "celebrity" coverage of newspapers, three times the "lifestyle" coverage, twice the "crime" and four times the "accidents." Moreover, TV does the opposite for international coverage and analysis of government policy impact on our society, a small fraction (exclusive of wars) of inadequate newspaper journalism.

This all has to do with the fact that more than half the people believe that Saddam Hussein was responsible for 9/11, cannot say which year the 9/11 attack occurred, believe Blacks and Hispanics are given advantages over others, cannot find Shanghai or Mexico on a map, think raising taxes is always an evil and a waste, and believe the Great Depression was produced by government mismanagement.

Here is the thing. The level of ignorance is deepening, broadening, reaching into the more "educated" portion of the population. An American graduate student in a university class can site a book promotion program by Newt Gingrich on FOX as evidence that our founding fathers were religious fundamentalists (which is the dramatically untrue thesis of Gingrich's new book). Educated Africans and folks from the Middle East, as well as all traveling Europeans, are astonished at the ignorance of history and politics (not to mention Geography and Economics) displayed by Americans. They are polite about it. Otherwise, there would be fights. But tidbits prove nothing.

Here is what does prove: the National Assessment of Adult Literacy (2003) measures a decline in literacy (competence in reading) as you move down the age categories in the U.S.; meanwhile, all U.S. age groups have fallen historically. We do not place in the top ten nations in tests of children's knowledge. Newspaper readership among the educated is close to flat since 1960 although the number of households in the U.S. has more than doubled since that year.

All this makes nonsense of the bland talk that what is now happening to newspapers is "an orderly transition to new business models" or that the FCC regulations governing "cognizable ownership interest" protects us from Murdoch & Co.

It is enough to make me want to go running back to dreamland where I found the coaches ambushed and dreamed I could do something. There have been so many takeovers. Packed up tools (knowledge, skills, and good will) are missing, the men left dead or dying, the women and children raped. The bloody tracks of survivors wander out into the snow until they freeze to death.

All this may seem a bit much, and yet I am going to append here part of another post that is an appreciative review of the anthology edited by Alexander Cockburn and Jeffrey St. Clair titled *End Times*.

If your peace of mind depends on believing in "unintended consequences" or in the fundamental civic mindedness and good intentions of our leading politicians, then this book is not for you. If not you will enjoy the 46 pieces from Cockburn and St. Clair (and a piece each from Ken Silverstein, Ishmael Reed, Bruce Dixon, and Christopher Reed). *End Times: the Death of the Fourth Estate* is an incisive, relevant book, and a pleasure to read.

In addition to wit, this is serious investigative journalism dependent on comprehensive media research, a nose for contradictions and absurdities, considerable literary and library skills, and a potent rolodex. The editors avoid heaping things up in interminable sentences as I tend to do. Often they summarize and extend attention to important additional volumes of investigative journalism. For instance:

1. Dan Baum, *Smoke and Mirrors: The War on Drugs and the Politics of Failure*
2. Lydia Chavez, *The Color Bind: The Campaign to End Affirmative Action*
3. Allan Chase, *The Legacy of Malthus*
4. Gary Webb, *Dark Alliance: The CIA, the Contras, and the Crack Cocaine Explosion*

5. Bruce Page, *The Murdoch Archipelago*
6. Andrew and Patrick Cockburn, *Out of Ashes*

Many books they draw upon are, like Cockburn and St. Clair's *Whiteout*, long books "stuffed with well-documented facts, over which the critics lightly vaulted to charge...'conspiracy-mongering.'" One of the delights of this book is the way they can be pissed off at the agency of power without loosing their good humor.

As per the subtitle, the book is focused on exposing the role of our major media—*New York Times*, *Washington Post*, television (which is the advertiser-funded derivative of print journalism), and all the others. This media, our media, just normally reinforces the efforts to discount official crimes. It charges "conspiracy theory" when obvious truth is pointed out, demands "smoking gun" documentation, and demands never-forthcoming formal admissions of guilt. This media nit-picks every criticism of power and swallows official lies whole.

It is no wonder Cockburn and St. Claire have been hostile to the 9/11 speculators ("Bush did it," "Cheney was behind it," and so on) who pose as investigative journalists while tilting with windmills. 9/11 conspiracy theory, as George Monbiot has said, is a displacement activity, as when a squirrel sees a larger squirrel stealing its hoard of nuts and, instead of attacking its rival, it sinks its teeth into a tree and starts ripping bark to pieces.

If that is not clear to you read the final sentence of a preeminent 9/11 conspiracy theorist, David Ray Griffin, as he tries to reply to Monbiot. "We [the 9/11 Truthers] focus on the 9/11 myth because, until it is exposed, getting our governments to focus wholeheartedly on the truly urgent issues of our time will be impossible." Raise you hand if the government's "wholehearted focus on urgent issues" does not inspire you with confidence, if waiting until all myth is exposed does not thrill.

The final section of *End Times* is 16 pieces mainly by Cockburn, titled "CounterPunch's Side of the Story." It is worth the price of admission. I read their excellent newsletter, *Counterpunch*, but for these 2006 pieces Cockburn enhances the stories, including facts about Reagan, Clinton and Gore, John Kerry, the late Billy Graham that do not change the picture but are certainly eye-catching.

My favorite piece is the one on Rupert Murdoch, composed of Cockburn's questions to Bruce Page (author of *The Murdoch Archipelago*) and Page's smart replies. Page's book is available only in an expensive UK edition thus far. His core thesis (and he takes Murdoch's move into Chinese media very seriously) is that "Murdoch offers his target governments a privatized version of a state propaganda service, manipulated without scruple and with no regard for truth."

◌

Cracks in the Media Filter
(Posted 11/11/2007)

An unpopular war, a liar leadership in its seventh year, an approaching presidential election: these are enough to create some vigorous political talk. I am not suggesting any zeitgeist shift nor singing anthem lines, "the times they are a-changing," but there is some good news. Cracks are appearing in the media filter.

I have mentioned Keith Olbermann's MSNBC broadcasts and I hope you listened. Then there are more than one thousand "Impeach Bush" videos on *YouTube* totaling many millions of hits. The House has twenty-two sponsors for Resolution 333 (to impeach Cheney). Dennis Kucinich is getting the most press on this (and not doing much with it) and we hear little from the Black Caucus Democrats, CodePink (like Danny Davis from Chicago who was an early sponsor of impeaching Bush), or from the cowed Progressive Caucus. However, on the other hand, there were 100,000 at the September anti-war/impeach Bush demonstration in D.C. and another 100,000 collectively in demonstrations in October, including some militant civil disobedience from CodePink.

Traditional tear-up-the-administration comedy (the tradition of Lenny Bruce and Mort Saul in my generation) flourishes and now reaches well beyond the comedy clubs. Jon Stewart (leading all), Steven Colbert, SNL and the like have significant televison audiences. Club comics themselves have gotten more political and more oppositional. There is George Carlin recently, obscene as usual, being very pointed and angry. The spirit is "We're fed up and we're not going to take this any more,"sounding not half so hollow as the film in which that expression first appeared.

Also, I believe, the grammar of editorialists and op-ed writers has changed a bit. There has been a broad editorial switch in many papers away from exclusive reliance on the liberal "If only" and "I hope that" tone that is so pathetic, so terribly common. Editorially, the *New York Times*, is trying to come up to the partisan level of the *Wall Street Journal* even though the news pages remain in the vice grip of Bush Administration press releases. Frank Rich, Paul Krugman, and Bob Herbert continue to be oppositional Op-Ed voices. Noam Chomsky also writes for the New York Time Syndicate, although his decisive 1,000-word Op-Eds have only appeared in a few regional papers and in Europe. As well as this change in tone, regional and local papers are accepting more stories on Vietnam and

Afghanistan-Iraq veterans and soldiers (health care, PTSD, homelessness, record suicides, alcoholism). A few stories from veterans and families against the war are beginning to appear. True, this only follows behind the national polls where Bush's approval rating is a historic low but now *Army Times* reports record disapproval of Bush even among soldiers, down to 50% from 83% following March 2003. A few books by veterans are being noticed and that is a very healthy thing.

Many books of substance giving more than sound bite denunciations of these Years of Bush have appeared. They now get some reviews. This is in progressive publishing from small firms (Verso, CounterPunch, CityLights, Haymarket, Common Courage, or Parry's Media Consortium, alongside important critical titles from Crown's Owl subsidiary and from Basic Books and others). Books seldom reach national attention. Events like an Oprah endorsement or Hugo Chavez holding up Noam Chomsky's *Hegemony or Survival before* the General Assembly, or Al Gore's *An Inconvenient Truth* and *Assault on Reason* enjoying his Nobel Prize are rare events; but, remember, every progressive book produces a book tour and speaking engagements and a resource of panelists and radio interview subjects even though book sales figures are minimal.

The bad new is that right wing extremists still have their voices all over the media. They are easily recognizable as those who would pursue "victory" in Iraq, bomb Iran, privatize social security, eliminate Medicare, limit the regulation of corporations, and open public land to "development." They are racist, anti-immigrant, and hostile to everything international, and oppose all civil rights except those of the fetus. To a man, they are "on message" and so it is easy to make accurate lists their position on everything. To those who passionately consume these reactionary, anti-people positions, the whole main stream media seems "liberal." It is "liberal" only because by law our media cannot be flagrantly racist, it must in some small way seem to serve "the public interest," and because the media (other than FOX and News Corp) somewhat bows toward the tradition of "fair and balanced." Only for these reasons do these people of the right condemn it as "liberal." But never mind that. Such folks are not as emboldened by Bush as they once were. There are alternatives showing though cracks in the pro-corporate media filter.

Cracks aside, the bad news is that most numbers are not good. We are three hundred million people and most get their news from television. FOX is the dominant news channel. It has nine of the top ten news programs (only Olbermann and Larry King compete). News viewership in total, even on Fox, is not large. An estimated 30 million are permanently tuned to Fox but none of the top network news shows, including those of FOX, top 11-12 million. Olbermann—a tendentious open liberal—captured 800,000. Bill O'Reilly who leads FOX in bluster and distortions (a letter-perfect, right wing extremist as described above) regularly secures two million. No news show appears in any top 20 list for viewership. 75% of Americans over 65 say television is getting worse, but the average time spent watching it keeps going up. They are escaping to ultra-cheap "reality" shows, fake contests, and ball games. They are not watching the news.

While "alternative media" and NPR are gaining listeners and viewers (many through *YouTube* and podcasts) against the trend of all news media, the number are still woefully small: two million a day for NPR's "Mourning Edition" according to Arbitron although that goes against the trend of turning off the news. NPR is recorded gaining 2% over the recent past in all their efforts.

For news magazines, the story is desperate. *U.S. News and World Report*, on the right, can announce "A National Crisis of Confidence" in the most recent issue. On the left *The Nation* exclaims "A Time to Choose" in their most recent issue. But *U.S. News* continues to run Republican propaganda exclusively and *Nation* is wedded to the installed leadership of the Democratic Party. In between, we have conservatives of all varieties and press release coverage as usual. Ah, well.

In its decline, the current *Time* magazine does now give us some statistics: Overall, rich and poor together, "average income has grown 26.5% since 1980. However, most Americans are not feeling it. For 99% of taxpayers, incomes have been nearly flat." The top one tenth of one percent saw their income grow 408% since 1980. And, thus, in a small back page item, *Time* struggles for relevance. They just did a "Century of Wealth" piece showing the astonishing average annual income growth of the top one tenth of one percent from 1910 (including capital gains). In 2005, that group consisted of 14,488 taxpayers. The accumulated wealth-holding of this top 0.1% would have shown a much steeper line (off the chart actually) if *Time* did not include the value of homes, which is a small part to great wealth's wealth but the great part what the rest of us can claim as "wealth."

In an earlier post, I noted that magazine readership has been in decline since the turn of the century. The current top 100 magazines declined by 3% last year. Single purchases decline was 1.4% overall and 3.4% for *Time* magazine, a flagship of patriotic publicity and the leading newsmagazine for many decades.

Newspapers, as with book publishers, they have become the cheapest of assets for acquisition. Really cheap. The total newspaper circulation of the top 100 U.S. newspapers is thirty six million and single paper sales (the best indicator of actual readership) have been declining annually. The Internet is definitely not picking up this slack while estimates are that 80% of Internet news content originates with the print papers that have been cutting away investigative and other quality journalism while frantically selling their space to advertisers.

In "Goodbye to Newspapers?" the fine journalist Russell Baker explains what has happened to them. First, long ago, newspapers became financially dependent on advertising sales. At first, it was supplemental income; then it became their primary source of revenue and of profit to the owners. Major national papers and many regional papers remained for some time in the hands of independently wealthy families. These controlling families enjoyed a somewhat justified high-minded sense that their papers were public institutions, the backbone of democracy and all that. Some profit was essential but was not the primary purpose of their ownership. This high-mindedness lasted only until owning a newspaper actually cost money; high-mindedness vanished in a New York minute.

Forty years ago, the local (family) owners began selling their papers to corporations and reorganizing them as public (stock for sale) corporations. Owners, once identifiable human beings, became anonymous corporations accountable to managers, investors, and to the bottom line. The cuts began. Then came the "post-corporate phase of ownership" as these quasi-independent corporations sold themselves off, like sides of beef, to financial conglomerates. Thus the *Los Angeles Times* became aggregated into a financial package that included *Newsday*, the *Baltimore Sun*, the *Hartford Courant*, and other papers, media, and non-news enterprises. These aggregations were purchased with the inflated stock market dollars of the conglomerates. Then, with the collapse of the 1999-2002 stock market bubble, cost cutting began in earnest.

This is an acute simplification of the dramatic stories of each of our great papers, but we each of us have seen it in our own geography: LA, Seattle, Louisville, Boston, Des Moines and so on. Right now, the two-tier stock structure that preserved family ownership of the *New York Times* and the *Washington Post* is under attack from Morgan Stanley. The two-tier arrangement somewhat shielded the key owners from the pressure of the financial market. But for the *Wall Street Journal* and many others, the shield was shattered.

Rupert Murdoch now owns the *Wall Street Journal*. There are two main things about Murdoch. The first is "deference to power." His practice has been to cut deals with governments (Australia, Great Britain, the U.S, China), their regulatory agencies, and their Internal Revenue Services to secure financial advantages (direct subsidies, exemptions, blows against competitors, benefits for his subsidiaries in other media, etc.) in return for which he provides a loyal and on-call news slant and all-out support for those with their hands on the wheel of power. That is half of his successful "non-ideological" business plan. In this way, our Federal Communications Commission, a regulatory agency, becomes an enemy of diversity, free programming, and public service.

The second part of his business plan is his flagrant exploitation of all that is worse in an irresponsible media. Murdoch is a bottom feeder and at the bottom are sensationalism, pornography, shallow celebrity, dumbing down, and a vomiting hypocrisy. This has been part two of his "winning formula" from his first tabloids in Australia through breaking down the British media market to coming to America where he is now a citizen Press Lord. He makes massive use of flagrant bias and sexual imagery together and—like the pimp he is—selling drugs on the side accompanied by his tamed ladies. MediaChannel has covered this well. Bill O'Reilly in attack-dog mode against anything progressive, blind to the Iraq War tragedies and lying about it, alongside hypocritical denunciations of "moral decline in America" illustrates everything with continuous salacious clips of those he clearly regards as Whores of Babylon. For instance, he reports on a random murder in Miami shot not against the slums, not against the usual Miami bank architecture, but against hot bikini beach dancing. Or a long denunciation of normal civil liberties, which O'Reilly shoots against lengthy segments of lesbian kissing. It is hours and days and months and now years of that kind of "news." The Murdoch formula.

On another front, *Google* and *Yahoo*, touted for their billions in surely inflated stock value, run automated news sites and contribute nothing into the creation of serious journalism. They field no news staff, underwrite no desks or stringers, provide no independent coverage, and—since they are flagrant "new media" opportunists—hate investigative journalism like sin. It is too expensive and much too long. Meanwhile the cuts continue.

It is good news (perhaps) that media news consumption among Black Americans and Hispanic Americans is increasing and goes against the national trend of decline? Here is the historic America story of bringing outsiders into the American mainstream via education and readership. It is slight but significant. Hispanic population news consumption has climbed for the eighth straight year. Hispanics are 14.8% of overall U.S. population (from 11.2% in 1998) and Black population stands at 12.8 percent. The reported up ticks in consumption of Black and Hispanic papers and radio news matches the percentage of their growing population. This growing minority listening to News/Talk/Information radio [no such data on newspapers] is divided about equally between genders and the educational and income level, which is rising in these audiences. Thirty percent of Black listeners are from households in the S75, 000+ income level; the nearly two million Hispanic listeners are 36% college graduates. It is too much for me to make break down the complex Arbitron numbers, but I am confident of the fact of growing minority news consumption against the declining overall national trend. Welcome to the show! You may figure it all out more quickly then we did.

However, in sum and all, very little news content reaches our 300,000,000 total population. Those like me, White non-Hispanic, are a declining 70%. Overt racism is still common and conventional news-shaping means that a continuing slight majority would approve of bombing Iran and believe Iraq had something to do with 9/11. This ignorance, and the marked inequality of income in our country, creates a dance cards for any fascist populist who follows behind Bush.

Well-reported, tendentious but fair-minded news, and especially news with some international orientation, is the antidote to fascism. Ignorance is its hot bed. Thus, it is sad to see the decline in newspaper readership, the cancer within that is corporate television, and the weak numbers for progressive, alternative, public news, in spite of the good news of a few cracks in the media filter.

◦◦

Step Carefully
(Posted 11/18/2007)

Step carefully around journalism when the word "epidemic" appears. Even the popular scientific articles and books can get your shoes dirty. I have in mind "the AIDS epidemic in Africa," the "epidemic" of heart disease in India, the Staph epidemic that strikes wherever groups of people interact, and Cancer. The pharmaceutical companies or their publicists sponsor epidemic fears. Now, with a presidential campaign underway, we have a veritable epidemic of epidemics.

Rudy Giuliani leads the epidemic sweepstakes touting his response to the "heroin epidemic," the "crack cocaine epidemic," and the "tuberculosis epidemic" as mayor of New York City. Now he has added the "obesity epidemic," along with his special contribution, 9/11 in epidemic proportions. Romney has an "influenza epidemic" victory as Governor. Hillary Clinton as Senator fought the "lead poisoning epidemic." We are in for a season of fear-mongering, special interest, bad science self-promotion as candidates race to see who best wears the banner "Fighting Epidemics at Home and Abroad."

Likewise, there are problems with the work "fascist." Using the word yourself—never mine how appropriate—will get you accused of conflating the horrors of Nazi Germany (SA, SS, Hitler Youth, Crystal Night, Gestapo, Heil Hitler himself, Reichsfuhrer Himmler, the Holocaust, and the Winterschlacht in the USSR) with our thirty years of swollen private corporate power and political reaction. You might get away with calling this "growing fascism," following FDR and Eisenhower, but probably not.

On the other hand, the neo-conservative invention "Islamo-Fascism" is welcomed in the press. Here also Giuliani leads all candidates making "Fighting Islamo-Fascism" his link with the extremist Bush-trained wing of the Republican

Party while his advisers (Norman—"I pray Bush will bomb Iran"—Podhoretz, Michael Rubin and David Frum) provide reinforcement and suggest that Democrat "Big Government" equates to fascism. These nasty gentlemen see in Giuliani the second coming of Dick Cheney. They could care less that our current blend of a "unitary presidency" and a reliquary Congress actually defines fascism.

Another topic to tread carefully around during this season is "global warming," actually, "global" anything, a somehow sacred abstract noun. The Library of Congress records over five thousand books employing "global" in the title, only a small fraction are math or computer programming books. Most titles intend to suggest a thing of awesome significance beyond what the word "international" can convey. "International" in this Reagan era carries the taint of "United Nations" and respect for other people's culture, history, and territorial integrity. "International" has been replaced with the more exploitation-friendly term "Global;" it invokes empty space.

"Global warming" already appears on the candidates' banners along with its related sacred phrases: "alternative energy," "independence from foreign oil," "renewable resources," and "Save the Planet." We should beware of cheering too loudly under these leaky and suspect balloon slogans.

Take, for instance, ethanol as an alternative renewable resource used to fight "global warming" and "dependence on foreign" anything. There are now over 200 ethanol plants—essentially stills, distilleries—operating or being built in the Midwest with Iowa and its corn at the epicenter. Lobbyists such as the Renewable Fuels Association and easy-issue politicians have raised the hue and cry for ethanol. Policy and legislation follows. Ethanol distillery loans and contracts were let to those with friends in high places. Plants were located where once were farms. Initially people applauded (as intended) with only a few voices pointing out that this was not an energy efficient way of stretching out our petroleum consumption.

And the plants? Yes, they stink. Of course, their emissions taint milk products. Naturally, land prices go up again, the water table takes a hit, feed prices rise, corn prices enjoy a brief upsurge until an ethanol glut and an absence of pipelines to the coasts force the value down. There is even the suspicion that the ethanol stills have something to do with rising food prices and the odd coincidence of impoverished towns, rampant amphetamine addiction, and a growing number of prisons dotting that same Iowa landscape. Statistically real, not merely a tendentious points or "coincidences."

Certainly ethanol production, as with the massive Cargill corn sugar plants that preceded them, has something to do with the declining quality of rural life. People are now meeting the new ethanol plants with lawsuits, petitions, and protests. As Anne Yoder of rural Kansas said, "This isn't as pretty a picture as everyone wants to make it out to be" ("In Farm Belt, Ethanol Plants Hit Resistance," *NYTimes*).

A few of these distilleries are substantial, ten million gallons a year or more, and have been around for a while. Most are petty enterprises employing few workers—nothing the size of the massive Cargill plant in Eddyville, Iowa that produces sugars from that same corn. Ethanol stills grew like Topsy over the last few years. They were contract opportunities for small capitalists under the "independence from foreign oil" and "global warming" slogans. Corn-based ethanol product is not an energy efficient oil substitute (in exactly the same way small-scale solar panel profusion and the small wind energy enterprises are not), but they fit a Small Cap business model called "entrepreneurial," a small capitalist private profit opportunity that can be facilitated by government subsidy and tax exemptions fitted to political contributions and to the current epidemic of "global warming" slogans, a sort of mini-dot com boom that, of course, will bust at tax-payer expense.

I would love to tell you the whole story of the destruction of the family farm in the Midwest, of Agriculture Secretary Ezra Taft Benson who once declared all farm aid and price supports were "socialism" and his successor Earl Butz who declared "Get big or get out," and the subsequent policies (essentially socialism for corporations) facilitating giant food product outfits like ConAgra, Cargill, and Archer Daniels Midland.

We are now a nation where some 65% of farm acreage is on corporate-sized farms of 1,000 to over 10,000 acres and where subsidy money flows to these corporate farms making them ever richer. You might see the government publication *Growing Farm Size and Distribution of Farm Payments*. Higher income farm "Households" (as they are now deceptively called in government literature; those in the 90th percentile of all national income) have enjoyed a greater than 80 percent increase in their percentage of subsidy income since 1989.

This would be a long story involving economies of scale, increases in land productivity, an emerging "global" food market, the domination of the large corporate food producers, and, above all, this shift of federal commodity payments to ever-larger farm corporations. One way or another, this is actually an anti-capitalist story, a story of corporate socialism. The story also has a lot to do with our unrepresentative Senate in which about 10 percent of the voting population (small population, largely rural states) dominate the Senate.

For another anti-capitalist or corporate-socialist story, examine epidemics and the role of the pharmaceutical corporations. And, as I suggest, yet another story unfolds as you examine the flourishing of petty capital contracts for ethanol, wind, and solar alternative energy while other alternatives (those requiring "Big

Government" such as tidal, hydrogen conversion, sunlight concentrators, etc.) remain undeveloped.

The story that most needs telling is that of our genuine epidemics and the role of Big Pharma, the Medical Establishment, the Hospital Industry, and the regressive for-profit direction in all matters effecting health that our government has brought about over the last decades. I will leave that story, forced by the reality of inadequate modern media reporting, to the likes of Devra Davis in her *The Secret History of the War on Cancer* and the other few, fine watchdogs. She and others do enormously laborious work, but they are a small a part of the total media sound. Step carefully!

∽

Pressed against the Glass
(Posted 12/08/2007)

The *New York Times* has been throwing repeated one-two punches toward Hugo Chavez this past week. Robert Cohen (11/29, 12/03 and 12/06) writes the Op-Eds, full of slander and hatred, while Rimon Romero backs them up with front page "news" articles (11/30, 12/04, 12/06) mostly cribbed from the opposition press in Caracas. It is a *Times* three-syllable version of FOX and CNN declaring Chavez a "dictator," a "tyrant," and "menace." The nation's leading newspaper—but not FOX—falls just short of labeling Chavez a terrorist and calling for his assassination.

"Fascist" is the first word out of Cohen's mouth on 11/30, "the cult of soil, blood and savagery." Chavez of Venezuela is moving toward "dictatorial absolutism," "centered in the armed forces," and "a huge nomenklatura." Chavez is "a wily barracks-bred buffoon whose leftist rhetoric is just a veneer" and his "grab for socialist-emperor status" is as "grotesque and dangerous as Fascism was."

Wow! Beautiful Venezuela, you folk had better run into Bush's mothering arms!

Cohen has a command of sentences as well as vituperation. He ranges (often within one paragraph) over broadly untrue economic generalizations and misrepresented issues of governmental structure and constitution. He dismisses "socialist" ideals (Socialism died in 1989, he tells us, and asks how could ideals possibly motivate a buffoon?), dismisses Chavez's "chumminess" with other demonized leaders, his "trademark verbal diarrhea," and (not to leave anything out) his Christianity. All in the same breath.

And this prelude to an assassination is what innocent Americans people read!

We learn nothing from Romero's lengthy reports in this *Times* tradecraft, just as we learn nothing about the Venezuelan constitution or the Chavez social programs; but the anti-Chavez blitz and identical content from FOX and CNN should remind us of the demonization practiced by the major media prior to other U.S. government sanctions, blockades, assassinations, subversions, bombings, and invasions. It should remind us of America's crimes in Allende's Chile and Sandinista Nicaragua, in El Salvador and from the skies over Serbia, and, for years now, over and on the ground of Iraq. It should remind us of how our presidents have lied to us (tiny Nicaragua "threatening invasion," "exporting terrorism," "weapons of mass destructions," "ethnic cleansing" met with "humanitarian" bombing) and how the major media has consistently amplified their lies and lent them credence.

The *New York Times* on Venezuela is so very extreme I am thinking that within the glass tower on 8th Ave. housing the *Times*—pretend as they may—they hate Hugo Chavez for his virtues rather than his faults.

What are his crimes? They are independence of mind; the threat of a good example; being a man of the people, winner of repeated, strongly contested elections by substantial majority? Imagine having a president like that! More realistically, imagine working for the *Times* and constantly having to publicize the wonder and the majesty of George W. Bush's foreign policy. Shame and envy must run deep within the denizens of that glass tower.

Gore Vidal observed that Bush has committed acts that would mean impeachment in a proper country. You do not lie to a country, get it into a war, waste a trillion dollars and kill a lot of people all because of your vanity, your lust, and your adoration of the rich. Not in a proper country.

I believe that some significant part of the *New York Times* staff has a special relationship with George W. Bush.

Harold Pinter, 2005 Nobel laureate in literature, described this "Special Relationship":

> The bombs go off
> The legs go off
> The heads go off
>
> The arms go off
> The feet go off
> The light goes out

The heads go off
The legs go off
The lust is up

The dead are dirt
The lights go out
The dead are dust

A man bows down before another man
And sucks his lust

Early on, anti-Chavez slanders and racism in the *Times* were mostly delivered at second hand from Venezuela's flourishing anti-Chavez press, all about his "warmed over fascism," the "incoherent policies" of a disgusting *pardo* with oriental eyes and vulgar songs. A bit nasty, certainly, but not first hand opinion. Likewise the introduction of talk of assassination was only reporting the facts, ma'am, only "news." If the *Times* succeeds in supporting the murder of Chavez then its pages will surely be available to wipe up the blood.

Editorially, these days, the *Times* can appear genuinely upset by Bush, the Iraq War, the Military Commission Act, etc. But that is *ex post facto*. Their distress comes after Bush's political and military failure in Iraq. It is as if Bush has betrayed the grand illusions of empire that flourish within the *Times'* glass tower. Prior to the failures in Afghanistan and Iraq, the leading newspaper was just one more media voice calling "off with their head," front paging Saddam's imagined atomic weapons and poison gas, and declaring the wonders of Bush's own awesome and humanitarian war that would deliver "freedom" and "democracy" to the Iraqi people. You have lived through this and I need not elaborate.

So what are we to make of this Cold War, Red Scare terroristic blitz against Hugo Chavez now? This *Times* propaganda—literally unfit to print—is aimed at the same people who were persuaded by the *Times* that the Sandinistas were terrorists bent on invading Texas and deserved blockade, floating explosives in their harbor, starvation, and the tender mercies of an illegal death squad Contra army trained by the Western Hemisphere Institute for Security Cooperation at Fort Benning, Georgia. These are the same people who were persuaded that Tito's socialist inheritors were doing genocide and therefore deserved genocide in turn, or at very least seven weeks of NATO bombing with cluster bombs and incendiaries; the same people who are persuaded that the leaders of Iraq and Iran aimed to create mushroom clouds over American cities and they should be murdered, along with hundreds of thousands of their people.

Cohen and Romero and all the *Times*men have always known that this propaganda was all a lying and dangerous sham. Nevertheless, when the president
speaks they fall to their knees and suck his lust. They are now paid to talk about
Chavez "receding into dictatorship." Chavez can make no disrespectful remark
while pointing northward without this and his every joke about "the smell of sul-
fur" and "the devil's doing" being reported as if they were threats of another 9/11.

One more *Times* quotation:

> When the rule of law is absent, when opposition TV stations are
> curtailed, when birth certificates and national identity cards are
> bought for a few hundred dollars, when tens of billions go miss-
> ing in the national budget, when the judiciary is subservient and
> corruption is a way of life, democracy and despotism begin to
> overlap.

This is odd thinking—aside from the misrepresentation and plagiarism out of
the opposition Caracas press as the only evidence. Most dangerously, it is a denial
of the obvious markers of actual democracy. It is warped thinking made common
by Bush and the media; and now, as a consequence, we have all the presidential
candidates—who have supported Bush's foreign policy in most respects—talking as if democracy is impossible without the exercise of imperial power. They,
too, have become advocates of "preemptive democracy" running to replace Bush's
specific lies but still with "regime change" as foreign policy and bombing as
"humanitarian," and purple-fingered, military occupied puppet states as examples
of "democracy." They are going to end by making democracy a dirty word.

Therefore, we owe a debt to Hugo Chavez while he lasts. He is a practical and
effective socialist who believes in democracy. With the vigorous assistance of the
New York Times, Chavez may go down. Many good things will go with him. It will
be a loss for all of Latin America. But, like Fidel Castro, he has lit another socialist
and democratic fire in this hemisphere making the flame less likely, in the long
run, to be altogether put out. The man is a hero.

No doubt, this "Indian from Baninas" is an offense to some. He laughs at the
racists. He holds up a copy of Chomsky's *Hegemony or Survival* at the UN General
Assembly. He enjoys the liberation murals all over the barrio walls featuring Che
and Castro. He enjoys speaking in the open streets at length and with enthusiasm, greeting the people flowing in and out of the free medical clinics with their
children, and christening the new high-speed commuter train running south, not
to the wealthy suburban enclosures but into the poorest countryside. There will
be setbacks and mistakes and, as always, poorly trained officials. However, all the

votes and all I have seen in one trip to Venezuela and all I have read in the alternative press smacks of democracy. Meanwhile, we at home have George Bush and those whose faces are pressed against the glass of that 8th Avenue *Times* tower.

Our major media belittles all of us. One set of Op-Eds and news stories from the *Times* hardly captures how desperately bad our press can be.

I believe I will write to Harold Pinter asking for another poem. "Do something with the image the *Times* presents, Pinter. Earn that Nobel Prize yet again. Please."

What Next from the Media?
(Posted 03/01/2008)

What next from the media that urged so many to support the Iraq War? In a dramatic compilation the Center for Public Integrity offers—in one place and searchable—all documents containing all the lies behind all the news that took us to war in Iraq. They call their compilation *The War Card*. It is a 380,000 word database of major public statements by Bush, Cheney, Rumsfeld, Rice, Wolfowitz, McClellan, Powell, and others demonstrating that these officials together made nearly a thousand false statements about the existence of weapons of mass destruction in Iraq and Iraqi-Al Qaeda ties in order to create public opinion for the March 19, 2003 invasion and occupation of Iraq.

You can search for "WMD," "yellowcake," "mushroom cloud," "aluminum tubes," "nuclear blackmail" and "arsenals." None of these existed in the real world. All the fictions were amplified by the corporate news media to terrorize a population into support for war.

These lies have no further news interest. Support for the deed was secured. The dirty deed is done. Other investigative journalists also have made lists of the lies and have examined each and the each later justifications (usually officials and their sycophants blame the lies "poor intelligence" provided by subordinates). By now, I suspect, the lies reside in school textbooks that will be read by children for many years to come.

The War Card is important because it allows easy access to the general argument that accompanied the specific lies. Here is the line of that argument.

> If there is "a volatile region" and a country in the region has "a bad regime" and there are signs of something called "an ideology

of hatred" (meaning, strongly expressed disagreement), then there is "a serious threat" to our "national interest" that "must be stopped" dead in its tracks.

The argument gives war-makers *carte blanche*.

If evidence is lacking, one of Colin Powell's "exploitation teams" can always be sent into that country to the "volatile region" to dredge up evidence of wrong-doing. Perhaps, as with Iraq, they will find nothing. Even so, hold on to your hats because this argument, by itself, calls for another round of carnage and catastrophe; thinking of like the million Iraqi lives lost, refugees by the millions, thousands of American casualties, $1 trillion blown on armaments and contractors, as well as the long-range consequences (growth of terrorist groups, second life for bin Laden, sustained damage in world opinion, reemergence of the Taliban in Afghanistan, Pakistan going ballistic, new war-mongers in office, etc.).

All the necessary ingredients exist in many locations. Spin the globe. We have been taught to believe in the ideology of military power. The ideology of military power is our state religion. For any president or presidential candidate the "national security" ghost story is sacred.

Look at the history of how this came about. John Marshall (Chief Justice 1801-1835) declared the president "the sole organ of the nation in its external relations." The U.S. Supreme Court has relied on this Marshall judgment to confirm that the president has "plenary and exclusive power [that does] not require as a basis for its exercise an act of Congress" (multiple decisions from 1936 onward). Recent presidents read this as a license to go anywhere and kill people or, if you prefer the phrase, conduct "preemptive war." The license was by no means George W. Bush's invention.

All that is required is allowing the news media to persuade us with lies and ghost stories. It is a given that the national defense commander-in-chief must be supported; war mongering is his bully pulpit and military power his big stick. Most people are persuaded in advance. They believe that WWII was a "good" war, the Korean War was necessary, that our mighty arms prevented the dominoes of socialism from crushing "freedom" in South East Asia, that we "won" the Cold War, and that military arms are now defending us against Weapons of Mass Destruction in an ever-present "War on Terror." Evidence to the contrary notwithstanding.

Already arms cost half the national budget, going on two thirds and that is a big part of whole objective. Establishing the rightness of all this falseness is the work of our popular media. For an aggressive national administration bent on war, there will always be plenty of Judith Millers and Bill O'Reillys, essentially propaganda slaveys. No Obama-promised "Office of Public Integrity" can make such sycophants vanish.

Morton Mintz, for *Nieman Watch*, has a discussion of the media attention not given to the January 28, 2008 *War Card* compilation. His concern is not with the facts (that is, the fact of lies aplenty) but with the media reception for this latest report on the volume of lies. ABC, NBC, CBS and on down the line ignored *The War Card*. The *New York Times* gave it a few inches on a buried page. The *Boston Globe* and a scattering of other city papers mentioned it. Very few gave a link to the compilation.

Mainly the news media responds to lies by broadcasting them. Then they ignore the consequence of their work. The news media ignored *The War Card* and that is only one example. For other see how the media totally ignored Ward Churchill's *A Government of Laws? -US Obstructions, Subversions, Violations and Refusals of International Legality since World War II,* another systematic compilation of facts. They also ignored Charlie Savage in *The Boston Globe* on April 30, 2006 detailing how Bush claimed authority to disobey more than 750 laws enacted since he took office. Rather than his constitutionally mandated right to veto legislation that he opposed, he entered "signing statements" taking some exception to the law, and then claiming that the existence of these signing statements licensed him to violate the law. The subjects were military rules and regs, affirmative-action provisions, whistle-blower protection, various safeguards against interference with research, required corporate regulation, and immigration programs, etc. In this way, his word is law. The news media almost never reports signing statements. It never reports on their consequences.

The news media also ignored, more or less, Colbert King in the *Seattle Post-Intelligencer* (June 9, 2007) reporting in his column on the "Downing Street Memo" revealing that our government "fixed the intelligence" around the plan to go to war in Iraq. There are numerous other examples. Another press watchdog organization publishes the top unreported stories in *Hidden in Plain Sight*. Mintz makes the point that some journalists do take notice of these realities and publish them, others do not; and that while the news departments often take no notice, the editorial departments sometimes do. Often real news appears first in the op-ed or editorial columns. Mostly there is nothing on TV, nothing in the major papers in most of the states, nothing in *Newsweek, Time,* or *U.S. News.* The operation of the media as an agency of state propaganda does not depend on "silencing" anything in the absolute sense. It depends now on "Jamming" but on comprehensively diminishing the amount of exposure, tuning the volume down below the public threshold.

None of this is news. Main stream media complicity is a yawn topic. But my illustration here do underline that we are dependent on alternative sources of information if we wish to remain any sense a free people. Ours is an ignorant nation, poorly educated, easily distracted, and massively entertained. Media corporations manufacture our consent. As Jefferson explained long ago, this being so, we are, therefore, not a free country.

No one has any excuse for helping along this ignorance. That stretches the boundaries of "being nice" too far. That builds toward the dead end of freedom— as when we allow those we talk with to imagine that what they hear and see on TV represents all that can and should be known. Such nice allowance is no better than agreeing with lies. We are much closer to our forefathers than usually imagined. They depended upon talking to each other for knowledge of what was going on. And trust in each other. The difference is that they were not silent and could tell the difference between an issue and a distraction.

No leader has yet come along who talks in such a way that the truth he speaks cannot be hidden. Certainly Obama (the winner of Super Tuesday) is not that leader. He talks a very tiny fraction of what he knows. He allows the implication of what he does not say to remain hidden. No Office of Public Integrity can deal with that kind of expedient sophistication, that "tactical" silence, that halting at mere transactions. It leaves all real transformation to some distant future and to far bolder American leaders.

What next from the media? I think we had better become aware of alternative sources of information.

Sorry to go on so, but in further illustration of the last point consider the succession of speculative financial bubbles. All have been costly and falsely called "unexpected." These bubbles (inevitably, predictably bursting) diminished wages, government benefits and services, and acted as an indirect form of taxation on the general population.

One bubble was the stock market from 1984-1987 involving financial deregulation, "junk bonds," program trading, and betting on "futures." None of us did these things, but in October 1987 the stock market fell 20% in one day. The Federal Reserve—at taxpayer's expense—guaranteed the solvency of the market makers the day after, making each dollar we possessed or earned worth less.

Next came the technology or "dot com" bubble. When that one burst, with some stocks falling 60% in a few weeks, every mom & pop IRA, 401K, and pension fund paid the price. They are paying for it still in the reduced quality of their retirement, in weakened financial security. These bubbles are mechanisms for shifting our wealth (earnings, savings, and options) toward the top wealth-holding tiny segment (especially the top one tenth of one percent) of the population and further increasing financial inequality in America. These were their bubbles of media-celebrated cost to us.

Then came the speculative housing bubble. We can see that one more clearly. As Keynes wrote, enterprises ride on these bubbles (a "bubble," he noted, is no longer a light and not very costly aberration riding on be back of substantial enterprises). The housing bubble costs are being paid for by ordinary Americans as loss of property value—almost our sole form of savings or wealth—and by the foreclosures, elevated rents (to be shortly witnessed), homelessness, and, as always, diminishing of government services as corporate government rushes to save its financial family gods from a flood of their own making.

The likelihood is that the next financial bubble to be blown (and has been inflating for some time) may be a vast shifting of public funds to armaments and national security spending with a deliberate inflation of all the fears and fantasies necessary to support it. Our tax dollars will go increasingly to unneeded armaments and unneeded "security" in an atmosphere of artificial fears sponsored by the lies of corporate government and broadcast by the news media.

Okay then: given the allegiance of our national media, matters of great importance are lied about, hidden, or ignored. Anything can still be hidden from most of us. Therefore, we have some obligation to learn and circulate stories that tell the truth. Inevitably, that means alternative media. The class war will not appear on television.

༄

Presidential Campaign Media
(Posted 01/15/2008)

The leading national pattern is to give right-wing, reactionary populism news coverage along with photographs while progressive populism is gets a bit of editorial space. That is "balance." Here are some recent Op-Ed quotations concerning John Edwards.

Paul Krugman writes today in *The New York Times*:

> On the Democratic side, John Edwards, although never the front-runner, has been driving his party's policy agenda. He's done it again on economic stimulus: last month, before the economic

consensus turned as negative as it now has, he proposed a stimulus package including aid to unemployed workers, aid to cash-strapped state and local governments, public investment in alternative energy, and other measures.

Christopher Hayes writes in *The Nation*:

The fact remains that the Edwards campaign has set the domestic policy agenda for the entire field. He was the first with a bold universal health care plan, the first with an ambitious climate change proposal that called for cap-and-trade, and the leader on reforming predatory lending practices and raising the minimum wage to a level where it regains its lost purchasing power.

Ezra Klein writes in *The American Prospect*:

Much more so than Obama, it was Edwards who forced a new style of politics, unfettered by the fear and timidity of the 90s, adamant that liberalism was an electoral boon and economic justice a popular sentiment. Knowing they had to defend against his challenge, both Hillary and Obama edged closer to his appeal. It left the Democrats in a much stronger position overall, and forced them to argue for, and commit to, a much broader and more inspiring agenda than we otherwise might have seen.

Kevin Drawbaugh reports for *Reuters*:

Ask corporate lobbyists which presidential contender is most feared by their clients and the answer is almost always the same — Democrat John Edwards. One business lobbyist said an Edwards presidency would be a 'disaster' for his well-heeled industrialist clients. 'I think Hillary is approachable. She knows where a lot of her funding has come from to be blunt,' said Greg Valliere, chief political strategist at Stanford Group Co., a market and policy analysis group.

Much as I would like to see a full John Edwards national campaign against the Republicans—who are a bunch of love-the-rich, war-mongering troglodytes each with their own particular ugliness—we are not likely to hear much substantive left populism after the Democratic National Convention nominates Hillary on August 25-28, 2008.

First off, issues do not play much of a role in presidential campaigns. The national focus is media-created, media-dominated and is on personality, likeability, minor gaffs, and "electability." That is cheap and easy journalism. The standard run of journalist does not have a reach that exceeds his bent elbow. "Facts," even if they are trivial or subjective are in demand and most journalists are not willing to do the work required to present issues to the public in a coherent way. The dominant inexpensive model now followed in national journalism—the interview—directs them away from issues and challenges and toward sound bites, stump-speech simplifications, speculation, and tidbits. No one interviewed is allowed more than a few seconds lest they overwhelm the network's paid "personality" and the advertising-obligation time.

Finally, because Edwards is not advocating for the rich, the word is out in the corporate media to ignore his campaign. In the usual corporate fashion, national journalists are all "safe hires" who obey the boss. Ultimately, the boss these days is Rupert Murdoch or his parody. None of Murdoch's top-level colleagues at the other news corporations will take him on or attack his FOX model of schlock, sexsation, lies, and bluster.

And, really, I am being too kind to the press. Just to hear a piety such as "democracies rely on a vibrant, probing, and trusted press" is to remind you that the only real journalism in America is alternative journalism, out of the mainstream.

The *Times*, without endorsement, is accepting Hillary, Hillary, Hillary—the Republican Choice and the Democrat's Lady Godiva as in the cartoon that accompanied Frank Rich's column in Sunday's *Times*. And yet these editors will do nothing in opposition, *Times* editorial page editors seem to deplore the idea of another four years of slick Clinton conservatism and fighting wars for Money's empire, but they cannot oppose. Someone higher than they are imposing on them.

And even on the left, organizers lack the will to contradict the Democratic Dukes of Patronage who control the Democratic Party's many machines. Imagine if you ran a progressive NGO, Institute, or publication, or if you were salaried in some grass-roots social organization, or even if you hoped for a public job in a decent city. You would not bite the Democrat hand that feeds you. Therefore, only financially independent progressive celebrity individuals are endorsing Edwards, not organizations or publications. And celebrity voices are not loud enough to break through the nearly comprehensive media silence.

Obama and his $100,000,000 campaign chest will be played for the inspiring run he is making and for the ad revenue it represents. All the senior party hacks know that Obama carries much more questionable fund-raising baggage than Hillary. The Republicans will use all of that and make up more. Stop. Perhaps not. Given their own feeding at the corporate troff. In any event, they will run a racist campaign to the 87% of the U.S. population that is not Black. And, then, a woman and a Black man make for easy personality journalism. Therefore, the media are trying to hurry Edwards out. From Idaho, Iowa and Ohio (to the Eastern nation that is "Ohidaho") the people vote their TV-derived preferences. Coverage and money spent translate directly into votes.

To break the media silence, Edwards would require a major effort from all the loyalists to a more progressive America. But he is not getting that effort. Cynicism plays some role (or they may know more about Edwards than I do) and there is not much basis for trust. But general passivity and a tired habituation to disaster capitalism (when the train wreck has not yet occurred) plays a greater role. I see no sense of excitement among liberal journalists or single-issue progressive people. Among many journalists there is a lot of arrogant "ho hum," dismissing the election "yada, yada, yada."

Part of the reason is that the *Times*, just for the leading instance, has a rule against columnists openly endorsing anything too progressive. They may hope and wish for "change," criticize the past, say anything they wish in passive voice, and expose things here and there. They may imply but seldom advocate. And that is the Op-Ed columnists! Imagine the position of some senior editor's dogs-body news journalist who hears Edwards and feels that what he is saying about inequality, corruption, and empire is important to report. He would be a fool even to try to get his copy in.

Note:

A troglodyte is a cave-dwelling bone-gnawer (used to indicate one with outmoded or reactionary attitudes). In this current Republican Party of the Rich case, the bones they gnaw on are ours.

 ᕼᕤ

Winter Soldiers, 2008
(Posted 03/22/2008)

Once again the alternative media has reported and the major media has ignored the "Winter Soldier: Iraq and Afghanistan" hearings held March 13-16 in Silver Spring, Maryland, the testimony of dozens of veterans about atrocities allowed and encouraged by the military command while conducting Bush's wars. In the nature of such testimony—and much similar testimony has appeared before in bits and pieces—the guys take personal responsibility for their actions. After all, they are once again civilians and individuals, these former reservists and economic draftees, these veterans. I admire them very much.

Iraq Veterans against the War sponsored these new Winter Soldiers in taking up another duty as had *Vietnam Veterans against the War* in the original 1971 Winter Soldier testimonies. *Democracy Now* broadcast much of the testimony. Also, the veteran's organization I am with, Smedley D. Butler Brigade, Chapter 9, of *Veterans for Peace* has good links to this Winter Soldier testimony, as have many other places in the alternative Internet media.

You can construct from the testimony the nature of the training and the command atmosphere in which the "atrocity producing situations" were acted out: the stories of check-point murders, of "dead-checking" the wounded, of routine "clearing" of rooms before entering with fragmentation grenades, of the endless, horrible pleasure of "shooting stuff up."

The U.S. military command is not held accountable even for Abu Ghraib, for Falugia, for Haditha—for a thousand Hadithas–although there are ample videos of colonels and majors shouting at young reservists in Iraq about "fucking Hadjis," "rag heads," and putting their raw troops through exercises where normal human responses to a child or an older woman is condemned as a fatal weakness (as, at the end of a faked up training video, the woman opens her burkha to expose a belt of explosives). Suddenly, on shipment over, all the obscenities and diminishment you were subjected to in normal stateside training are transferred to "the enemy." And "the enemy" turns out to be the whole civilian population of the invaded country. Just as in Vietnam.

Some magic how, a few guys glimmer that this war is about a deeply corrupted American politics. They glimpse that they are living a life without honor that has little to do with service and duty. The Commander-in-Chief's words had become mother's milk ("Axis of Evil") but mom has again turned out to be a lying sociopath who leads her children to commit atrocities else they be thrown from the tit, thrown from the fellowship with her other children. You come to see, as one put it, that "the war itself is the atrocity," and that there needs to be some accounting. None is likely. That is why we were given our second round of Winter Soldier hearings where young men and women try to recover their moral center by speaking of their individual crimes.

It is a terrible hard thing to get your head around, how they can say "Well, you know, we just did it; we fucking killed them all," and thereby, with those words in the Winter Soldier context, reclaim some moral honesty. We are not taught to understand that aggressive war is murder, plain and simple. Teachers now deny that right is on the side of those who defend their homes. They and the church ministers all become sycophants of power while we are taught to be mute employees not citizens and yet we must risk our lives for shit wages. And the Boss-Criminal, the *capo di capi*, trains us with his endless racist repetition of "Us against Them."

> See, in my line of work you got to keep repeating things over and
> over and over again for the truth to sink in, to kind of catapult
> the propaganda. — George W. Bush, New York," May 24, 2005.

That is what our politics has come to, the sort of politics celebrated by Boards of Directors and major media. Its opposite, citizenship, is damned or ignored exactly as the Winter Soldier investigations are now ignored and will be damned. Instead, we are led before pompous Cheneys, O'Reillys, and McCains to be admonished like children, damned, whipped, and then ignored. Cheney replied "So what" to a journalist's point about "overwhelming" U.S. disapproval of the war.

However, nothing should diminish the words spoken by the Winter Soldiers earlier this month in Silver Spring. They know directly that the war in Iraq is largely about murder. They have come to see the war in human terms, not in Bush terms. And many see the politics of it. Their testimony is part of their recovered honor and a step closer to holding our leaders responsible for these atrocities. Chris Hedges says it well:

> The battered wrecks of men and women who return from Iraq
> and speak the halting words we do not want to hear, words that
> we must listen to and need to know ourselves. They tell us war
> is a soulless void. They have seen and tasted how war plunges us
> to barbarity, perversion, pain and an unchecked orgy of death.

Hedges has reported our every war since El Salvador in 1983, twenty-five years focused on what he calls our most powerful narcotic. He is an honest journalists pulling "human interest" up by the bootstraps of context and what used to be called "values" from the muck into which it has fallen.

In better times, Hedges would have been made an icon or leader of the movement against the war in Iraq because of his dramatic early opposition to the war (he was shouted off college platforms back when he was truly a lone voice); however, our movement against the war has been a movement undermined by its slavishness to the Democratic Party. That Party is simply another deeply compromised advocate of "preemptive war" along with its bed partner, the Republican Party. Chris Hedges' recent and forthcoming books are *War is a Forge That Gives Us Meaning* (2002), *What Every Person Should Know about War* (2003), *Loosing Moses on the Freeway* (2005), *American Fascists* (2007) and *I Don't Believe in Atheists* (2008).

Mainly I want to recommend his essay on the current Winter Soldier testimony.

There will be other testimony, products of the Iraq and Afghanistan war, and books that compare to Michael Herr's *Dispatches* or Stan Goff's *Hideous Dream* and *Full Spectrum Disorder* if we are lucky. If this testimony and these books weaken our "potent and lethal addiction" to the drug of war, they will be healing. And there will be healers on both sides. Just as with Vietnam.

The central issue, I insist, is our aggression and our injustice and the politics that leads them. In Iraq, over these years, the scale of the death of innocents surpasses the Rwanda genocide. The level of leukemia among Iraqi children is as high as that of Japanese children after Hiroshima. Lancet puts the direct death toll among Iraqis at 1.2 million. And yet it seems hard to frame what we have done in the Middle East while the major media is in full avoidance mode. Even friends, who have become habituated to repetition, look at me strangely when I say something they have not heard before. "Not even on NPR or MSNBC." The general word we should use is "crime," but a crime without punishment for the initiating criminals.

We have lost in Iraq, as in Vietnam. Yet private enterprise national security still pens us in and offers again its swine's Win-Win. I fatten you up and then I eat you. Private American energy and armament corporations publicly announce profit margin, avoid taxes, and flourish. Now here is a "Win-Win" as insane as private enterprise nation health care while we stand so low in all world measures of national health,

OPPOSITION

Rhetoric or Opposition?
(Posted 10/21/2004)

The Democratic National Committee has groups and individuals whose business it is to develop leads toward revelations, investigations, lines-of-argument, and buzz that can harm the Bush run for a second term. The Bush administration itself will create conditions for this good work, as when CIA operative Valerie (Palme) Wilson was outed in order to punish her husband, former ambassador Joseph Wilson, for his criticism of Bush. The DNC, it seems, is beginning to use some of this material in selected ads and initiatives.

Also, there is a tone of "I've been driven to extremities" in some of our respectable public voices in addressing President Bush. Granted, most of them are, as Bush would say, "liberals," or as Ashcroft would say "terrorists" and their criticism is indeed liberal and limited.

William Safire in the *Atlantic*, upset over Bush's military tribunals, says that Bush is "replacing the American rule of law and 225 years of judicial tradition." Safire remarks, "On what meat doth this our Caesar feed." The quote is from Shakespeare's Cassius talking up Brutus toward the assassination of Caesar to save the Republic.

> Why, man, he doth bestride the narrow world
> Like a Colossus, and we petty men
> Walk under his huge legs and peep about
> To find ourselves dishonorable graves.
> Men at some time are masters of their fates:
> The fault, dear Brutus, is not in our stars,
> But in ourselves, that we are underlings.
> Brutus and Caesar: what should be in that 'Caesar'?
> Why should that name be sounded more than yours?
> Write them together, yours is as fair a name;
> Sound them, it doth become the mouth as well;
> Weigh them, it is as heavy; conjure with 'em,
> Brutus will start a spirit as soon as Caesar.
> Now, in the names of all the gods at once,
> Upon what meat doth this our Caesar feed,
> That he is grown so great?
> Age, thou art shamed!

In the same magazine, Jack Beatty says that Bush "calculated that the future does not exist." Seemingly strong language.

And Senators Robert Byrd and Edward Kennedy, along with Dennis Kucinich and others in the House, have roundly criticized Bush recently. Kennedy's words were the strongest: It has been "lie after lie after lie," he said.

All the administration's rationalizations as they prepared to go to war now stand revealed as double-talk. The American people were told Saddam Hussein was building nuclear weapons. He was not. We were told he had stockpiles of other weapons of mass destruction. He did not. We were told Saddam was involved in 9/11. He was not. We were told Iraq was attracting and supporting terrorists from Al Qaeda. It was not. We were told our soldiers would be viewed as liberators. They are not. We were told Iraq could pay for its own reconstruction. It cannot. We were told the war would make America safer. It has not.

These oppositional speeches pretty much remain buried in the *Congressional Record*. What is reported is the Bush team "lashing back," calling Kennedy's attack "a new low," "a hate speech" and—most cutting of all—"uncivil."

Bush's extremism calls up Safire's and Kennedy's strong language: "Upon what meat doth is our Caesar feed that he has grown so great?" Bush is guided by his evil slogan "You're either with us or with the terrorists" and his broadened evocation of the "axis of evil." Yes, it is warmed over Reagan, but nowadays people are subject more than ever to the rhetoric of the presidency and to media echoing the Republican president.

Bush's press conference back in March mentioned 9/11 eight times along with his motif "the oceans no longer protect us." Sowing fear and threats has continued. In *Brave New World,* Huxley explained that tyrants do usually use propaganda techniques like this: catchwords, suppressing and distorting facts, sowing fear. Hitler's *Mein Kampf* is his example. The theory is that the masses run on instinct and emotion and are easily manipulated; fear can be conjured out of catchphrases and repetition, requiring only that lying propaganda confines itself to the bare necessities. After Bush's repetition and simplification we have Donald Rumsfeld speaking in support of the $86 billion in war funds saying that the terrorists take heart from any criticism of Bush, that criticism "leads to more money going into these [terrorist] activities or that leads to more recruits or that leads to more encouragement or that leads to more staying power." [From reporters traveling with Rumsfeld, via Reuters.]

The test of quality of oppositional language is in transgressing boundaries not in mere rhetoric and counter-repetition. The fact is that the U.S. government—in behalf of the major finance groups and corporations that dictate its underlying policy—occupies center stage and "news" is stage publicity. Election year opposition language becomes a bit stronger; but is unlikely to match the extremism of the Bush Administration. We can be certain that no one will challenge the central dogmas: Bush will say that America is just and justly dominant; America is moral (the citadel of democracy, etc.); anything done in the name of American security or "interests" is justified before the fact, Israel is our precious client and, likewise, can do no wrong; control of the Middle East and its oil at the right price is American's right; any threat (and threats are everywhere) is terrorism and evil. Opposition language must challenge all that, all the central dogmas.

You know the factual story: Overlords ("the few, the powerful, and the connected") have charged the U.S. government with responsibility for maintaining control over the world's major energy resources. That charge, as usual, is delivered government "leaders" privately and emphatically. Our heads of state know that the Overlords will stop at nothing to enforce their will. They live as in the pages of a John le Carré novel. For instance, over the past 40 years our heads of state and all our media have supported Israel as a well-armed pro-Western power against any Palestinian independence and against any dictator-led Arab state (and much of Arab state weakness is also our doing) and against Arab nationalism. It is all somewhat similar to the African and Latin American acts in this Global Power drama starring corporate Overlords: the U.S. government fought the independence movements and Third World nationalism using anti-communist slogans. We overthrew democratically elected governments, subverted national movements, installed fascist dictatorships and, as needed, we bombed and send troops. In this performance, Israel (with some assist from Turkey and Saudi Arabia) became an important mercenary insuring that the U.S. corporations control the world's major energy resources. In return, Israel, a client state, is allowed to carry out its own program of ethnic cleansing and land seizures. That is a sub-plot perhaps, adjusted from time to time, while the main arc of the story continues.

Undercurrents of the act: Christians and Jews stand off against Muslims; English and Hebrew against Arabic; imports and high-tech education stand off against agriculture and Islamic religious extremism; oasis against desert; tanks and explosive shells against personal weapons and packages of hand-carried explosives, and so on. There has been over 40 years of this, with the U.S. government supporting Israeli repression of the Palestinians, integration of the occupied territories into Israel via settlements, various Apartheid-like projects, flow of arms and money for this occupation by force, state terror, resistance, more settlement, etc.

In line with the normal manufacturing of consent in the U.S., stories and analysis are constantly delivered to the American population in all media over these 40 years endorsing Israeli violence and deploring Palestinian violence. Policy and opinion on Israel is made uniform over all parties and all politicians over all this time. The Palestinians "attack" and the Israelis only "retaliate." The U.S "mediates peace" or a cease-fire while strengthening Israeli armaments. It does not matter that for decades the Palestinians assert and act on the assertion that they accept Israel's right to exist within the 1967 borders just as any other country within its borders, and to possess the same self-determination as any other state under international law. It does not matter. The media reports only that the Palestinians do not accept this principle and that becomes a false given. The media view is that it is Israel that is "struggling for survival" and occupying Palestinian territories as part of that struggle. The media boycotts any mention of US-Israeli violation of Security Council Resolutions and other signed agreements and core principles of international law. The media boycotts maps. They would make clear what is happening. They also boycott reporting of Israeli internal opposition.

The official boundaries of opinion are not crossed. In spite of the Safire touch of drama, drawing on Shakespeare, there no oppositional language, no thorough transgressing of the boundaries of public talk as is required by real political opposition.

◞◦

Howard Dean's New Mimicry
(Posted 01/04/2004)

Howard Dean, surrounded by Democratic Party pallbearers, is abandoning any independent position. Some ask, "Why vote?" The Democratic National Committee's question is "Who doesn't love a mimic?" But, as Dean begins to mimic Bush, where is the Opposition now?

In the beginning, the thought was that Governor Dean was in Opposition. He had a somewhat populist manner, spoke with vigor, and was not bought and paid for by the oil industry and the military/industrial complex. So it seemed. At very least he seemed to oppose Bush's criminal wars.

These were wars without Congressional legitimacy, in violation of international law, supported by lies and misrepresentation. These were wars that slaughtered—or wounded and dismembered—thousands of silenced young Americans (to date) along with uncounted hundreds of thousands of Iraqis and Afghani civilians. All for oil and corporation profits.

Dean opposed the wars and seemed willing to put forward some acceptable plans for revitalizing American education, our decaying local infrastructure, our riddled excuse for public healthcare, our punished environment, etc.

You might rightly say, "Anybody can say that, it is only platitudes." However, Howard Dean also showed a willingness to accuse the Bush administration of its extremism.

Bush's collection of old cold warriors, corporate criminals, Zionists, liars, and Christian fundamentalist hypocrites have attacked all our public institutions, our environment, our checks and balances, international institutions, and international law. They exposed us to greater terrorism. Why not hold Bush accountable for the consequences of his provocative belligerence, for his "God is with us" hypocrisy, for his lying, for his crusade against Islam? Why not? Dean showed some signs of willingness, speaking as a voice of the American people.

However, as this sorry presidential campaign proceeds, all reason for hope evaporates. Dean, as a hope for unseating Bush and his reactionaries, is rushing to the embrace the same reactionary national postures for which Bush is the standard-bearer. Why vote for a mimic?

Dean now pretends to offer himself as the "security" president, making us feel safer. He offers himself as Dean the Christian soldier, Dean the World Policeman. But George Bush has already preempted those theatrical roles. And George Bush is the incumbent, no lame duck. Why change horses asses in the middle of a "War on Terror"?

If Dean cannot bring himself to become an Opposition Candidate—which we all desire as a real hope or just for the fun of a change from our diet of media pap—then all he can run on are promises of health care reform and a balanced budget. He will loose miserably. No matter how you lick that lollypop still retains the same colors, the same swirl of the candy letters spelling "Reform, Fiscal Responsibility, and Defense."

As Dean runs from his initial anti-war position, runs to embrace the American God Security, runs to the sidelines, his pallbearers wait to carry him to his well-deserved grave. All the while Americans keep dying for unmentioned oil profits (along with countless others: civilian women and children mainly). All the while, other nations continue to reformulate us as the New Nazi Germany. Our rap sheet gets longer.

I have been reading Dean's web site regularly. It is a sorry spectacle to see him run from the initial anti-war position that activated so many fine young people. Most of Dean's troops will fall way in disappointment and await the next confidence trickster. A small set of future political farmers of America, hoping to learn how it is all done, will stay around for the lessons. In the same lack of spirit, they will pick up on the next Democrat ready, for a moment, to fill their bottle with *Eau de Opposition*.

Note:

This was written before Dean came in third (After Kerry and Edwards) in the 2004 Iowa caucus vote (Jan. 19) and before the "Dean Scream." That was a notorious media-made incident that caught Dean shouting "Yeah!" to his supporters while their own constant shouting was suppressed by a special microphone. His loud and seeming awkward and isolated scream was rebroadcast many hundreds of times over the next days to Dean's great disadvantage, as was clearly intended. He had been running as a left populist and, what seemed to most, an anti-war campaign while raising massive grass-roots funds and building an organization of young supporters prior to these events. He had been endorsed by SEIU and AFSCME but by a relative few in his Party. He appeared to be the clear front-runner before the Iowa caucus votes. My point in the above effusion, all this aside, was that as soon as Dean appeared to be emerging from the pack he had begun moving to the right especially on national security policy.

૭∿

Trampled in the Mud
(Posted 02/21/2005)

A simple admission: I am discouraged. Yet I continue reading my liberal press with its hope-springs-eternal pieties and its lesser-evil Democratic Party loyalty. On top of the *New York Times*, *The Nation*, and all that, I listen without objection to the self-denying righteousness of my folks in Kansas/Iowa/Nebraska whom I love. All they seem to ask for is some king—or Bank president or even the head of the Junior Chamber of Commerce—who is careful of his persona (Clinton was not, Bush is), as if civilization hangs by a thread as thin as personal decency. "Until it breaks," they tell me in their country logic, "it is as strong as any rope." I would feel embarrassment except that gives me too much credit. A better admission is that I am discouraged. Even depressed. Depression is the state of being trampled in the public mud.

With recovery in mind, I think to spend the summer months summarizing, covering the main national political points succinctly: Where have we been? Where are we now? Where are we going? And "Is there any difference?" Perhaps it is all "The Inevitable Path," our Karma. "Oh, spare me," she says.

Depression, as you may know, is when your life becomes a stranger to you. You are assailed by a foreign condition (like Iraq by the U.S.) and have lost your ownership of "You." It is mild Alzheimer's. You look in the mirror and cannot remember who that is. There is nothing for which you can take responsibility other than blessedly simple routines, those by which mankind survives the worst catastrophes. Yet it is still difficult to move from one room to another.

With recovery in mind, I thought to find "focus" by ignoring the entire Bush legislative agenda and concentrating on the little things that Congress does, the talk shop small personal "Bills" with which Congressmen attempt to burnish their local reputations, pork barrel amendments, ear marks, the trivia of a session's agenda, and the sorry "grab the limelight" legislative Acts and acts.

These are so far removed from the central concerns of the imperial presidential agenda that Bush and Cheney and their media allow them to tweak the nation's attention. It is a deal struck between the Main Man and his minions, Democrat or Republican, to save their face, to localize them, to neuter the sometimes obstreperous (although that is much too great a word) Senate, and to put a few small chips on the table just to keep the game going.

In this way, ours is the Roman Senate under Caesar as when, on occasion, Caesar would turn a blind eye on minor opposition, would say "He is a dreamer; let us leave him pass." Or he might pretend exhaustion and cry "Help me, or I sink." Or he might act quietly, helping the little ones find their dishonorable graves. Such is Caesar's largess, according to William Shakespeare.

The mud of current political life is depressing. I have read some about depression. I will mention only William Styron's fine *Darkness Visible* (a title from Milton, no less) and avoid mentioning all the poets and their biographers who have explored this subject like vampire Freuds. Styron had a determination to survive, survive with never a whine. He only wanted us to understand his affliction. And I must mention again the writing of Ayi Kwei Armah, beginning with *The Beautiful Ones Are Not Yet Born*. Everything he writes is to respect disappointment as legitimate and to depart from the depressed "Man." "Man" is the only name he gives his lead character in *The Beautiful Ones Are Not Yet Born*. His fine title is what he once saw painted on the side a small bus in Senegal. An African kind of optimism for you.

Concerning depression, repetition is a thing to watch out for. The circular dreams that repeat or daydreaming over and over the same ground. Those oddities of sleep—in the depressive forms of sleeplessness or that sort of undergraduate lying in bed throughout the hours—is also something to be considered. Lying dormant is always a bad sign among humans. It never works. Lying dormant within our immense corporate prison system (where lives the greatest national percentage of per capita incarcerations) totally fails to "improve" society. "Improvement" is a prison's stated justification while it does its massive social harm. It is modeled on the death penalty, the final sleep, given in daily doses.

The historian Gordon Wood identifies an important radical in our early Republic before the era of regal presidential Caesars. That was Abraham Bishop of Connecticut, who said that "dormant acquiescence" and the habit of following great men (as with my Kansas/Iowa/Nebraska self-denying folk) sums up American culture and describes its greatest weakness. "Dormant," because all of this sheep-like acquiescence is to live in a state of subordination to fantasy, unreality, and mere inventions. Bishop was very thoughtful. Nothing makes Bush sacred or even credible, not even the office he continues to hold. It is an invented office that may not function and that may be on the way to replacement by some Nazi corporate corporal. What else does Bush foreshadow?

"The application of all this to my depression?" you may ask. Beware of what you acquiesce to and note the health that may exist in a studied refusal to accept what seems necessary to accept.

Her most powerful childhood nurse had told Florence Nightingale that she was a "monster." As children do, she came to believe this. She then put away childish things, put them far away. And yet some version of that image of the monster "I" did sometime haunt her, usually putting her in the grip of dread suffering dreams or equally dread ambitious "dreaming." Some days she could not find the energy to get out of bed. And even when functioning these dreams might seize her while walking for exercise, at a dinner party, touring somewhere, visiting family. She had a hard time forgiving herself for this dreaming and the underlying "beating herself up." She uses the words "slavery," "sin" and "the long moral death" to describe it. She calls it a thing more loathsome than the use of opium.

She knew fully how hard it is for women to recover from the lies and hypocrisy taught them as children. Chinese women's feet or any women's feet remain small even after the binding is removed. How easy to become stuck in the incapacitated and depressed I who is "hateful," and "a Monster" even though the thought has no more basis that an irritated parental slander.

If you want to discover what Nightingale did about this condition you might start by reading her "Cassandra." And also there is the sensitive and perceptive treatment of her depression (this woman of such force and accomplishment!) in Gillian Gill's new biography *Nightingales; The Extraordinary Upbringing and Curious Life of Miss Florence Nightingale"*

In a true summary, I will tell you that what Florence Nightingale did was to switch from the first person singular to the first person plural. She says God taught her that. "The poor beast"—as she calls God at one point—"carrying all our load and his own as well" taught us to switch to the first person plural. Make what you will of that, my loves. The important thing is to compensate your way out of personal accusations of being "a Monster." Somehow.

༄

How Bush Won
(Posted 02/22/2005)

There is quite a literature on "Why Bush Won." I will push the view that Bush won his first and his second term as president because the political contests were uncontested. Yes, formally, there was a party running against him; but that was an illusion of opposition. The Democratic Party as opposition (the "vital opposition" that yesterday Bush arrogantly demanded of the Russians) is an American fiction no longer sustainable. Except for those who have some role as "a player" in Party politics, few deny that we have two collusive party syndicates each in their own way acting in behalf of a ruling corporate oligarchy that pays their bills.

Full of illusion and sad at heart, I read back over some of John Kerry's statements. They are limp and incoherent (just compare them to Nader's statements to see what I mean). Even now he does not attack Bush: not for lying; not for his additional harm to our reputation among nations; not for the slaughter in Iraq; not for endorsing torture or ignoring our homeland security; not for rewarding the most thieving of corporations; not for playing wink-wink with the rich while he guts social services and makes a joke of federal regulation; not for corrupting our press; and, worst of all, not for the next pre-election war he is so obviously planning.

In *Harper's Magazine*, Editor Lewis Lapham tried to describe this fraud of opposition. He takes some days to do a gallery audit of the first days of the 109th Congress and comments, "In the greatest deliberative body in the world all of them look very much like one another. No diversity visible to the naked eye."

Over the next days, he observed:

> Nothing in their manner suggested a shred of difference in their preconceptions and modus operandi. Red state, blue state; Old Testament, New Testament, popular assembly, oligarchic junta—why argue the details as long as everybody knows how and when to count the money.

I have also watched CSPAN. The first days of the 109th were a song by T. Bone Walker: "Blues on Monday, Tuesdays just as bad, Wednesday's worse, and Thursday's twice as sad." Henry Waxman, a bit outspoken, commented, "It's truly amazing that so many people still think that this place is on the level." Nancy

Pelosi, Ed Markey, and a few other Democrats express an awareness that they are being fucked over. Yet not one of them seems to believe in serious opposition.

Obvious forms of opposition are not tried: a sneak attack; a walk out when faced with the Republican's disabling parliamentary rule changes; getting behind one of their own number—say honorable old Senator Byrd—and delivering a week's worth of praise quoting on and on this stern octogenarian words about Bush's destruction of the American constitution (they must now amount to volumns); a rabble-rouse or rebel yell (surely one of their number can do that); appear present but refuse to be seated; launch a few Senate floor attacks on the whole press (not just corrupt, right-wing FOX and sold-out CNN). How about impeachment proceedings or even trying to pass an unconstitutional "bill of attainer" against Bush for lying the American people into a hopeless war. Or how about pouring scorn and ridicule or a few speeches that go back over Bush nominees now that they are abusing the offices they occupy? Pass what are called "movements to revoke" against them. None of that happens. Give the talk shop show a little vitality, how about?

Lapham would choose Gonzales, the Attorney General soon to be Supreme Court justice, for renewed attack:

> The nominee showed himself to be a man of little principle and less integrity, a clever eunuch in a corporate harem, grinning and self-satisfied, unwilling to give a straight answer to questions, dodging behind the phrases 'I don't recall . . . I don't remember.'

This, the Attorney General! No, the Democrats do not hold anyone—and especially not our simple, well-focused and vicious president—accountable. Lapham writes, "I couldn't have guessed at the scale of the defeat until I came to Washington in the hope of proving it a dismal rumor."

Yet other major opinion-makers are working to suggest that the collapse of the Democratic Party is really its opposite. Not to worry, come 2006, we will "Get Out the Vote," they say. *The Nation* continues to call the faithful to rally round the Democrats and offers up, once a week, shameless articles touting the fighting spirit of one or several liberal Democrats. We are given—obviously from congressional staff or the politician himself—cute insider tidbits and told that they are "bad-ass" and setting Republicans tails on fire. This week they are hailing Howard Dean's appointment to head the DNC. No mention (although many newspapers do mention) that Dean got the job by abandoning his former anti-Iraq war stand and else wise moving to the right. No, they say, with Dean the Democratic Party "has become something it has not been for a long time, exciting." Note the tense; an accomplished fact made of a fiction.

Likewise, the current issue of *The New York Review* (once more) addresses "How Bush Won?" And again (Mark Danner) says it was all about emotions and attitudes (especially about our supposed fear and our supposed respect for cowboys) and nothing about Bush winning over a record of crimes through lack of opposition.

There is no mystery to opposition. Simple opposition would have been to do against Bush and for Kerry what the Bush team did to Kerry and for Bush. Attack and enhancement. Policy is another matter altogether, both Parties have abandoned that touchy subject. Presumably there are still liberal Democrats whose staff can write good legislation, but they do not fight to get the floor because actual votes might embarrass their colleague Republicans. And the magazines, the ones I read, are all about persuading us to support the Democrats in their run in 2006—on the simple principle of unexplained lesser-evilism—because it would be "divisive" to be principled.

All this defines what Walter Karp (*Indispensable Enemies; The Politics of Misrule in America*, 1993) called the collusion of the party syndicates at work in support of a single corporate oligarchy.

◦∕◦

Poetic Opposition: First We Take Manhattan
(Posted 02/23/2005)

When Leonard Cohen's album "The Future" appeared in 1992 a lot of people, millions of us, saw how the lyrics of a song could go beyond entertainment and perfectly express our disappointed hopes. There was that sense of apocalypse in the title song:

Give me back the Berlin Wall
give me Stalin and St Paul
I've seen the future, brother
it is murder.

The sense of rebellion in "First We Take Manhattan":

They sentenced me to twenty years of boredom
For trying to change the system from within

Opposition

> I'm coming now I'm coming to reward them
> First we take Manhattan, then we take Berlin.

Cohen is a fine lyric poet who, in addition, had the wit and moxie to give us songs to sing. There was "Suzanne" and "A Singer Must Die" and "Like a bird on a wire / Like a drunk in a midnight choir / I have tried in my way to be free."

In "The Tower of Song" Cohen sang:

> I said to Hank Williams: how lonely does it get?
> Hank Williams hasn't answered yet
> But I hear him coughing all night long
> A hundred floors above me
> In the Tower of Song

And he provided, also, lovely translations, this one from Lorca:

> There's a concert hall in Vienna
> where your mouth had a thousand reviews.
> There's a bar where the boys have stopped talking,
> they've been sentenced to death by the blues.
> Ah, but who is it climbs to your picture
> with a garland of freshly cut tears?
>
> Ay, ay, ay, ay
> Take this waltz, take this waltz,
> take this waltz, it's been dying for years.

Now he has a new album, steeped in death, and with other of the old qualities as well:

> That men shall know the commonwealth again
> From bitter searching of the heart.

His is beautiful stuff, all his songs about failure and the consolations of love. If you want to stretch a point, they are about acceptance. The fabled Sixties just did not go where Cohen wanted them to go. Yet he saw a small hope in the grand fault in American's triumphal Liberty Bell.

Ring the bells that still can ring
Forget your perfect offering.
There is a crack in everything
That's how the light gets in.

Try as they might, no one can quite turn Cohen's strange Buddhism into "accept-ance is all." He never consented "to call the darkness poetry."

Any system you contrive without us
will be brought down.

"At times," he would admit, "I cannot bring my butchered mind to bear upon the facts" but clarity would return as when "A heavy burden lifted from my soul / I heard that love was out of my control." The final spirit, much as in his first small collections of Canadian poems, remains:

From bitter searching of the heart,
Quickened with passion and with pain
We rise to play a greater part.
This is the faith from which we start:
Men shall know commonwealth again
From bitter searching of the heart.

And here I am, more or less thrumming my finger tips impatiently on the kitchen table top, trying to find a way to say that those Sixties (like 1964-1976) were more about an angry demand for change and about opposition to what we saw coming than about acceptance and different strokes for different folks. How do we revivify that anger and opposition now? Too bad if we end without even a memory of hav-ing fought, a memory of Cohen's fraught songs.

ം

Howard Dean Again
(Posted 06/10/2005)

Living in this empire as it decays from within; people cry, "What's wrong?" Well, for one thing, look at what passes for opposition leadership. Look at Howard Dean, ex-presidential candidate now four months into his leadership of the Democratic National Committee.

The last few days in the press, Dean has been doing obligatory, "make news," against the Republicans. I am assuming that the *Boston Globe* (owned by the *NY Times*) and the *Times* itself have the choice bits. Here they are. Republicans "have not made an honest living in their lives," "pretty much a party of white Christian conservatives," "the average American doesn't care," the Republicans are "despicable." These statements served on the "Today Show" as another excuse to interview Republicans declaring yet again that Dean has "gone off the deep end" and Democrats who declare yet again that Dean is doing harm to Democratic Party fund-raising with his excessive talk. Ask not what excesses those were. Thus far nothing he has said is at all excessive.

This is diaper politics. Even the most incompetent Caesar would say "Pass by" exactly as Bush has. Who cares what Howard Dean says? Certainly not Bush. Of the disastrous Iraq War (become the rotting body of a shot albatross handing round Bush's neck), Dean now says "We must have a strong national defense." Dean is firmly in the war camp where he was headed all along.

The worn fiction is that Dean is a "maverick," an overexposed "loose cannon" that might—at any minute, folks–actually become relevant. Forget it. Dean is a piece of obedient bluster. Once a right center, fiscal conservative governor from impoverished Vermont with a bit of a mouth, he was brought into the presidential primaries to steal away the anti-war, anti-Bush anger from Ralph Nader, Dennis Kucinich and Al Sharpton back in the days. That was back in the days when the Democratic Party leadership was terrorized by the specter that the nation might actually want an oppositional candidate. Who better to co-opt that sentiment than an ex-executive from Morgan Stanley Dean Witter? And so Howard Dean emerged as "anti-war," then segued into support for John Kerry, and eventually into support for Bush's war in Iraq. And it was an easy sell.

Dean is the Park Avenue raised, prep schooled son of a major Wall Street broker. After Yale he graduated to Dean Witter where he made a bundle. Then, becoming bored, he did Med School, married a real doctor, became bored again, and went into Vermont politics, into the "Politics of Deceit" as Joshua Frank calls it in his collection of articles from *CounterPunch* in the excellent book *Left Out* just published by Common Courage Press.

But let us not rag on Dean's endorsement of our colonial occupation of Iraq as if it were solely Bush's War. Lament the human cost certainly—especially now that the occupation is in such incompetent hands—but do not deny that this war was in the making well before Bush became president twice.

Here is Hillary Clinton in October, 2002:

In the four years since the inspectors left, intelligence reports show that Saddam Hussein has worked to rebuild his chemical and biological weapons stock ... his missile deliver capability, and his nuclear program. He has also given aid, comfort, and sanctuary to terrorist, including Al Qaeda members. It is clear, however, that if left unchecked, Saddam Hussein will continue to increase his capacity to wage biological and chemical warfare, and will keep trying to develop nuclear weapons.

There is no real evidence for any of this. And here is Bill Clinton, who is actually the architect of this whole argument for "sending a message" to the terrorists by relentlessly bombing Iraq, missiles raining on Baghdad in February 1991, with the "collateral damage" (half a million children killed!), the embargo, the 1998 Iraq Liberation Act, and in late 1998 another massive and cruel bombing. Here is President Bill:

Earlier today, I ordered America's armed forces to strike military and security targets in Iraq. They are joined by British force. Their mission is to attack Iraq's nuclear, chemical and biological weapons programs and its military capacity to threaten it neighbors.... Their purpose is to protect the national interest of the United States, and indeed the interests of people throughout the Middle East and around the world.

On September 11, 2001 inevitable chickens from Clinton's "message" and actions came home to roost.

As you read in the library of articles and books denouncing Bush's lies and his "Pretext for War," realize that much of this journalism originated in the 2004 electoral campaign when Democratic Party guardians of liberty spoke truth to power by pretending that the quagmire and the great shame that is the Iraq War was solely Bush's doing. Bush inherited from Clinton. It was a Democratic/Republican venture, as all subsequent coy dancing around the issue of "opposing the war" and Dean's career, in its coyness, shows.

We do not have two parties. It is completely silly to distinguish between them. War criminals are war criminals. You can identify a hawk by its feathers, even if they are not pressed into a book of published, well-documented crimes. Howard Dean, a minor tail feather, had a small walk-on part in this show. He arrived crying "Tennis, anyone?" and MoveOn stepped forward to play temporary anti-war tennis with him.

༺

John Kerry: Sunshine Patriot
(Posted 06/24/2006)

On the 22nd of this month, John Kerry gave a major speech in Boston's historic Faneuil Hall. The occasion was the 35th anniversary of his dramatic Senate testimony in behalf of the "Winter Soldiers" of Vietnam and their organization, the Vietnam Veterans against the War (VVAW).

Kerry's political opponents will dismiss the speech as opportunism. Kerry, they will say, sensing the tide is turning against the Iraq War and beginning his run for President in 2008 now names the war "a deceit and a failure." Still, the speech is a welcome addition to the array of retired generals, former Administration figures, Senators, and Representative who have finally joined the rest of us in doing something, anything, against this criminal and lost war.

The Bush Administration, Kerry said, "cannot let go of the myths and outright lies that it broadcast in the rush to war in Iraq." They are "imprisoned in a failed policy," and he mentions the torturing of prisoners, "negligence and incompetence," "stubbornness and pride," unwarranted secrecy and illegal spying, their "blindness and cynicism" while they continue to send "brave young American to be killed or maimed for a mission the leaders themselves no longer believed in." Right on!

However, he does not call for impeachment or censure (as some of his colleagues in Congress are now doing). Instead, he calls for a schedule for withdrawing American combat forces by year's end. Kerry gives a good general denunciation of "the Bush-Cheney Doctrine" but he does not name it "Fascism."

Kerry is—as T.S. Elliot describes in "The Hollow Men"—"cautious, politic, meticulous, full of high sentence but a bit obtuse, at times, indeed, almost ridiculous" as he moves quickly on to toast and tea. His theme was the necessity and "our right to dissent" and he gave it a fine textbook outline and presentation on that hallowed and familiar subject. However, Kerry chose not to remind people of real dissent, on its very anniversary. He did not mention the "Winter Soldiers" or their sponsor organization, Vietnam Veterans against the War.

By not mentioning the Winter Soldiers then or Iraq Veterans against the War now, Kerry allows Bush, Cheney, Rumsfeld, and minions to compound their original crimes by flaunting a war they know is already lost.

In 1971, back in 1971, when Kerry talked to the Senate Committee as the spokesman for VVAW, he said:

It was clear to me that hundreds of thousands of soldiers, sailors, marines and airmen—disproportionately poor and minority Americans—were being sent into the valley of the shadow of death for an illusion privately abandoned by the very men who kept sending them there.

Yes! And the majority of American deaths and injuries in Vietnam, and additional hundreds of thousands of Vietnamese causalities, came after 1971 when it was clear the war was lost. Like Bush now, Nixon said on tape that he was not going to be the first American president in office when a war was lost. No matter to him how many were sacrificed before he left office. Likewise, hundreds will be sacrificed to Bush's "reputation." This year Kerry eulogized our "right to dissent" while not dissenting in real time.

Kerry speaks seeking "moral authority" and he no longer speaks effectively. 35 years ago, he spoke in behalf of the Winter Soldiers whose moral authority came from their confessions and their opposition to the war. At Faneuil Hall on June 22, 2006, Kerry chose not to remind his audience that his 1971 Senate testimony was for the purpose of bringing public attention to the "Winter Soldier Investigation" of VVAW that had taken place in Detroit earlier that year. More than 150 honorably discharged and often decorated Vietnam vets had testified in Detroit—as Kerry said back then—"to war crimes committed in Southeast Asia. These were not isolated incidents but crimes committed on a day-to-day basis with the full awareness of officers at all levels of command." These were atrocities of the most wholesale, criminal, and racist kind.

In 1971, 35 years ago, Kerry was brave enough to describe them before the Senate. He reported from the Detroit investigations:

They [the Winter Soldiers] told the stories at times they had personally raped, cut off ears, cut off heads, taped wires from portable telephones to human genitals and turned up the power, cut off limbs, blown up bodies, randomly shot at civilians, razed villages in fashion reminiscent of Genghis Khan, shot cattle and dogs for fun, poisoned food stocks, and generally ravaged the countryside of South Vietnam in addition to the normal ravage of war, and the normal and very particular ravaging which is done by the applied bombing power of this country.

All this the veterans admitted, witnessed to, and talked of in order to awaken the American people to what their leaders had led them into. No "sunshine patriots," these Winter Soldiers testified to their guilt, took their responsibility, and wept over the crimes they had committed and witnessed.

You can read the Winter Soldier testimony published in the *Congressional Record*, "Extensions and Remarks," April 7, 1971: 2825-2900, 2903-2936; and it is available online under "Winter Soldier Testimony."

The Winter Soldiers and VVAW spoke in behalf of a desperately needed rule-based international society. Yes, they wanted peace and reconciliation; but especially they wanted law and decency. They had thought that was what they were fighting for. We have now savaged the international law these men believed in: the Geneva Conventions, the Court of International Justice in The Hague, the Charter of the United Nations, the Universal Declaration of Human Rights, the ICC, and the much similar U.S. law, similar U.S. conventions and treaties. This is the "Vietnam Era" Bush and his patrons want us to forget. The Bush Administration sets all this truth aside, ignores evidence and testimony, preaches lawlessness, and teaches disrespect for the international legal system and international institutions. The Bush Administration has done this for their ideology of "preemption" and for Bush's own armament industry and oil sponsors. He has done it just at the point we most need respect for law. He has practiced terrorism and emboldened the terrorism of others, that is practices by men as ignorant, fanatical, or as "sold" as he. He has increased terrorism, genocide-as-policy, preemptive and criminal violence from the air and from boots on the ground.

Let's remember the Winter Soldiers because John Kerry, once their effective spokesman, chose not to mention them nor even mention the name of their organization on what is their anniversary, not his.

Note:

The phrase "sunshine patriots" is from Tom Paine's famous essay early in the American Revolution when the outcome was very uncertain. Paine wrote:

> These are the times that try men's souls: The summer soldier and the sunshine patriot will, in this crisis, shrink from the service of his country; but he that stands it now, deserves the love and thanks of man and woman.

Thus, we have the powerful image of the Winter Soldier, who willingly fights in defense of country but comes to speak out against unnecessary war, unjust war, and against war profiteering. They speak in behalf of humanity and the ideals codified in the United Nations Charter and the Universal Declaration of Human Rights. If you do read the Winter Soldier documents, remember that these are young men and women who had read the Declaration of Independence and the great UN documents back in grade school, back when they were posted on every public school classroom wall. They are gone from those walls now. Literally gone.

༄

Changing Guard at the Talk Shop
(Posted 11/08/2006)

Later this morning the mid-term election circus will strike its tents. The losing performers will begin thinking about other jobs as private consultants or lobbyists or returning to private law practice. The Republican Party, who has lost the House and perhaps the Senate, will worry about money for 2008, money for the next circus, but also the money promised to its connected contractors and for earmark funding, not to mention their profits from bought legislation, regulatory exemptions, and other corrupt legislative intent. And might the tax cuts for the very rich now be challenged? That is another worry. They are the Grand Old Party of the Moneyed. Losing control of the House and Senate may be costly.

Also, in losing this election, Republicans lose the cover of George Bush, now a very lame duck. Bush had pitched his and his party's mansion in extreme right field. The lame administrative Vulcans (Bush, Cheney, Rumsfeld) made it possible for all of Congress to be viewed, at least to some extent, as legislators giving patriotic consent to a "War President." Now everything has turned out badly: the invasion of Iraq become a fiasco; a lost election; an exposed false flag of "war on terror"; a failed disaster recovery in New Orleans; off-shored jobs by the millions; welfare only for the rich; health, education, science, and the environment all degraded; national debt up; the dollar down; colleagues ousted or exposed. Then, also, there were the lies, crimes, and fear mongering that was essential to Bush politics and to his whole tent pitched that far into right field.

Republicans will loose something like 30 seats. Consider that Rick Santorum (R-PA) and James Talent (R-MO) both lost. Together these two have received over $48 million in corporate contributions, corporate lobbying contributions, and corporate PAC money (2001-2006) while serving on the Agriculture Nutrition and Forestry, Armed Services, Banking, Energy and Natural Resources, and Finance committees of the Senate. They were lead recipients of the Republican Party's $112 million from corporations in the agriculture, armament, finance, and energy industries.

We can speak with certainty only of this $48 million in campaign circus money. This is the fraction publicly disclosed by law. If the Republicans are to win back seats in 2008, win back lost governorships, and state legislatures gone Democratic Party, if they are to get Senator John McCain elected president (or some other acceptable representative of the rich), they will have to show the promise of a return on future corporate investment, the ROI, investment in political hacks and slaveys.

Even if the Democrats conduct the nation's business as usual for the next two years—and I have no doubt that it will be—the Republicans will be thinking hard about winning in 2008. In order to defeat the Democrats in 2008 all remaining Republican legislative influence and voice will be devoted to making the Democrats look bad, poisoning their new-born status, crippling any initiative they dare to advance—hesitant though it will be—and chopping at the knees of any genuinely popular presidential candidate that might appear against them. That will be their sole objective; the public be damned. They will hope to face Senator Clinton or Senator Obama or Senator Kerry in 2008—since it appears that none can win—or hope for an actual or virtual third party candidate to split the vote against them. However, more than reliance on hope, they will be proactive. They will attack any true words spoken by any Democratic contender who sounds like he might continue the slight Democratic revival that took place on November 7, 2006.

By "true words" I mean to say any words that express political objectives to the left of center such as some redistribution of wealth from the top one tenths of one percent to the middle and the poor, a significant reigning in of the corporate hegemony in Washington, a program for national health insurance, making quality education available to all, seriously regulating the corrupt monopolies in energy, drugs, and media, support for international law and the humane objectives of the United Nations, etc., etc. No such things will come from Clinton, Obama, or Kerry.

The seeming Democratic revival happened because so many people used this election to voice their opposition to the Bush Administration on account of its ugliness (lies and crimes) and the above listed failures. However, as you know, opposition to the Bush Administration and to Republicanism is where the Democratic Party is weakest. Any Democratic contender in 2008 (such as a good man of "true words," whoever he/she may be) will seem to be a lonely voice, hardly heard, easily attacked. The Republicans and the corporate media will see to that.

As for legislation, that also is a downside to the seeming Democratic victories. Bush has already proven that he can legislate around any legislature, declare war at will, amend the constitution in the name of "security," legislate by "findings," by Executive Orders, and with presidential, "signing notes," etc. He is already immensely secretive. He is surrounded by those wishing to push him further to the right. The more rabid ideologues of the Bush presidency—Richard Perle and associates—are already declaring that Middle East policy failed because Bush lacked commitment and decisiveness, like the line they use that says we did not lose but "gave up" in Vietnam. These thug public intellectuals advocate "nuke Iran," "limit civil rights," "assassinate Fidel, Chavez, Morales, and Ortega." They will continue their war-mongering, fear-mongering themes and the lay in wait to trash anything progressive, this Death Squad for the rich. Meanwhile the professional politicians will play it cool, renew their promises, their commitment to the corporations, and keep the lid on things.

As for the beloved-on-NPR "public debate," the framework of the Democrats' compromise and "reasonableness" is already set. Spokesperson Pelosi declared, "We are prepared to govern, working together with the Administration and Republicans in Congress in partnership." That was the theme of every broadcast victory speeches I heard. Absolutely no one will hold anyone responsible for anything. What is past is past.

A secondary Democratic Party theme is coming from the handful of traditional or "left" Democrats. They attribute their mandate to grass roots activism, to popular participation in "getting out the vote," and to "traditional Democratic values." In response to this "pressure", they will see to it that any ethics reform is only for show and will continue private party organizing, massive TV campaign advertisements, and automated phone calls. They will all cry "cooperation!"

The last time any prominent Democrats participated in a demonstration, Martin Luther King was leading it.

No party functionary, Democrat or Republican, wants a populist uprising to come from Bush's extremism, naked imperialism, and massive shifting of wealth to the already obscenely wealthy. Without their temporizing and obstruction that is where it would be headed. Our 2006 fed-up-with-Bush vote is interpreted by the Democratic Party as a mandate not to let there be any uprising. We really blew that one!

This is the meaning of their making nice, cooperation, "reasonableness" and bipartisanship. In fact, as Jon Steward suggested tonight, after the Democrats' substantial victory—which fools took to be a show of opposition—they will now "slowly back out of the room while their brother gets yelled at for burning down the garage." This was a brilliant aside.

I see no significant turn as the result of this election, no turn on any of the true issues mentioned above, nor on "Free trade," maintaining armed control of oil resources, our close alliances with criminal states (Saudi Arabia, Pakistan, Turkey), on preventing socialist dominoes from falling in Africa and Latin America (if that can be prevented by hook and crook), no turn on the free ride offered the major corporations, nor even a turn toward slowing the shift of more wealth to the already wealthy. This Reagan Era will continue.

After all, the Democratic Party has been in control of the Senate for half the 30 years since 1976, including eight years with their charming former governor from AK as President securing major Republican political objectives (NAFTA, cutting Welfare, adventures in Haiti, Bosnia, and Kosovo) and including 2001-2002 when all the cats were herded toward support for illegal, immoral, and now failed war in Iraq. They launched no counterattack against Bush-led social reaction. They met the Republican squeak victories in 2000 and 2004 passively. Now—on the night of November 7, 2006—they are even refusing their mandate to oppose Bush, are prepared to scuttle instead on ragged claws to new meetings with corporate lobbyists.

Nor should we have illusions about what any mildly progressive Democrat for 2008 (say, just to the left of Hillary Clinton) is in for. One look at what Bush's best neo-cons are saying now about Bush himself is an eye opener (the thugs whose policy papers called for the Iraq War even before 9/11). They are saying that Bush bungled the war because he was not fearful and resolute enough. Bush's fanatic repetitions and consistency, and the half million Iraqi dead, do not figure in the thinking of these people. David Rose summarized the neo-con attack on Bush in *Vanity Fair* ("Neo culpa"): Bush was "indecisive" (Perle); there was a "failure at the center" (David Frum who had written Bush's "axis of evil" speech); there was "incoherence" (Frank Gaffney); mere "rhetoric," no different then Bush Sr., a waffler who can't lead (Mike Robin); all sell and no performance (Kenneth Adelman author of the "cakewalk" assessment of the war); "a ghastly mess" in which Islamists win (Eliot Cohen). Bush was effeminate, dumb, Texas crony-obsessed, etc., they all cry.

Bush gets this treatment from his very own extremist right. And all this viciousness is for Republican Bush, their main man. Just imagine the sand these strong-worded men will kick in the face of any Democrat.

৩৩

How the Democrats Work It
(Posted 04/03/2007)

The method applies generally (the Iraq War, health care reform, tax reform, ending privatizations, building social services, ending foreign corporate adventures abroad, etc.). The method involves leaning always to the right, cluttering each channel toward action with trash, aborting each ever-reborn progressive hope, tripping up each step toward justice.

The Passage of HR 1591 by 218 to 212 (to continue Iraq war funding) guaranteed that the war remains a bipartisan fiasco. As commonly happens, the bill was advertised for a month as an anti-war bill. House Speaker Nancy Pelosi sold it as "standing up to Bush." The state media—who Robert Fisk calls "the axis of schlock and awe"—followed her struggle for passage breathlessly. Bush played his role to perfection, fulminating against the bill and threatening veto while his war Republicans shouted that such a bill "tied the hands of the commanders on the ground." Quite a show. This show provided Democrats time to deploy their "anti-war" bill deception, a bill that goes "part of the way" (which is a very old, sick, and tired Democratic Party heroic phrase).

What the bill does, as intended, is to weaken opposition to the war and give aid and comfort to whatever war hawk Democrat the DNC nominates for their presidential campaign. The successful campaign for this House bill forced almost every anti-war Democrat to capitulate and vote for funding the war. The "Out of Iraq" caucus fell apart and with it went any chance of building a firm anti-war group in the House. MoveOn lost further creditability as an anti-war group by pushing its members toward support for the House bill, sold as usual on its "tactical merits." Thus, the Iraq War can remain a bipartisan endeavor.

This is what the Democratic Party leadership wanted and what they got. The bill gives Bush all the money he has asked for. It sets a "time-table" that will take the war into late August 2008 (18 months of death and chaos) at least. In addition, most dangerously, the bill as passed stripped out a provision requiring that Bush have congressional approval before attacking Iran. Absorb this, folks. It is how the Democrats work their "anti-war" war-mongering.

There had been significant congressional sentiment against the war (reflecting the 2006 vote and in public opinion). However, Pelosi attached $21 billion in earmark funding beyond Bush's request and scattered rewards around to win over opponents. The *Washington Post* describes Sam Farr of Santa Cruz, CA and Peter DeFazio of Eugene, OR (both previously firmly anti-war with large progressive constituencies) receiving pork. That was for Farr's spinach growers and to DeFazio for funding for schools and libraries. There were words of other "pet project" funding but no details.

There was also the usual rumor of threats. Rewards and threats are the twin children of Congress. The three remaining holdouts in the "Out of Iraq" caucus remained quiet as their group fell apart. This Democratic game is now being played out in the Senate as we speak. Harry Reid has sold Russ Feingold on the

Senate version of this funding bill with a promise to advance Feingold's "Out Now" bill if-and-only-if there is a Bush veto. Senate passage is likely.

On the "left", what do we see? A few in the anti-war movement are in a bit of a snit because the Democrats voted the bill. Their snit is pathetic, even as a tactic. What did they imagine MoveOn was all about? Or Howard Dean? This is the party of the Hillary Clinton candidacy and their snit suggests to me how far we are from building a strong anti-war movement, one whose first step must be repudiating the Democratic Party and demonstrating actual opposition to the wars. It was altogether too kind of Howard Zinn to be "disappointed in MoveOn," He said that "we should not encourage Congress to compromise." Encourage?

The left should not be a wing of the war party, or a party waiting in the wings to endorse the next "lesser evil" or "half-the-way" war hawk. Yet that is what we have. War is a very big deal, much profit, much graft. A left that defines itself by its willingness to compromise in matters of war and peace is no left at all.

Consider, folks, we face the likelihood of an Iran war, a reckless and criminal plan no matter how much the oil corporations, arms merchants, and Zionists may want it. An immense catastrophe in waiting. In the final result, millions of good people will die.

What if the 15 British sailors had been 15 Americans? What if one of the Special Forces groups we have prowling in Iran gets dramatically wiped out? What if the Iranian government should decide that the Security Council resolution in March is the last straw? That resolution, taken against the UN's own Charter, took the side of the biggest aggressor in the region: the United States. We are now conducting two occupations; we are an official "preemptive strike" state (in violation of the UN Charter). We are now filling the Gulf with war ships and loading up our numerous regional bases with armaments and supplies. The enemy is Nonproliferation Treaty member Iran (which treaty we refused to sign), Iran who has invaded no one, being ordered by an avowed enemy that it cannot strengthen it own defensive weapons systems even under direct threat.

A war against Iran already has the leading Democrats foaming at the mouth for war. Hillary has accused Bush of being soft on Tehran; she and Edwards insist Iran is the principle enemy and nuclear bombing is "on the table." Howard Dean (the party's National Chairman and the inspiration behind MoveOn during his brief flurry of anti-war posturing) says that Iraq is diverting attention from the "real threat" which is Iran. Pelosi removes even the provision that Bush must have congressional approval before attacking Iran. Rahm Emanuel promised removal of this provision ("Congressional approval," no less) even before a debate. Obama once suggested "surgical missile strikes" against Iran and says Iran is "a threat to all of us." Even Feingold and others who have consistently opposed the Iraq war sign on to the pledge that we will "not tolerate a nuclear Iran."

How ridiculous to blame all this on the power of lobbying by Zionist extremists. The major supporters of all our wars have not been a few rich, rabid Zionists and their lobbying organizations. To blame it all on them qualifies as a fine Yiddish joke.

We keep hearing cockeyed optimists say such a war, an Iran War, is impossible, insane. We hear that the military are against it, the timing is wrong, and so on. That is the language in which academics face a dire possibility.

Some retired generals have spoken against such a war. But the military does not make policy. Thank heavens for that. A fair number of generals are barely sane. It is not they but the corporations that make policy and the corporations have their criminal, bottom line sanity in place. So why should we trust optimistic reassurances that we will not have an Iran War? These reassurances (from Democratic Party-leaning journalists) are not even reassurances of a forthcoming peace but only reassurances that the next most likely war will not happen.

ᏩᎥ

Hillary Hillary Hillary
(Posted 07/07/2007)

A few days ago my wife and I, along with a lovely friend, stood before the cottage home of William Wordsworth (1770-1850). Profuse roses, wild flowers, the roof being newly thatched under modern construction scaffolding; just ourselves, a handful of English couples, and a small crowd from Japan. It was there at the Wordsworth cottage in the Lake District that Bill Clinton first proposed to Hillary Rodham in 1973. I thought of the Wordsworth line, widely quoted just then about Diana, Princess of Wales, "Then Nature said, 'A lovelier flower on earth was never sown.'" The British press and TV were already anticipating the 10th anniversary of Diana's prosaic death and were quoting that line as we toured England looking at Florence Nightingale sites.

British booksellers say that any book on the former Princess of Wales sells like hot cakes, any book at all. Chain booksellers, ubiquitous in England, display whole sections of them. The British are passionate about their idle interests: that dead Princess, the Queen, gardening, historic preservation, the Manchester Blues, the next PM. Momentous things like that. I believe the death of their empire has been good for them. I found great friendliness, modesty, an awareness of irrelevance, and no more racism and inequality than can be witnessed anywhere in Europe, and less than we witness here. And they seem to read a lot of books.

Nevertheless, I am happy to be home and contemplating Hillary Clinton rather than Princess Diana, taking things seriously as befits a citizen of the world's most powerful country. Hillary may have many empty things to say, but nothing matching the Princess, who said, "The worst illness of our time is that so many people have to suffer from not ever being loved."

At home, I see new Hillary books and wall-to-wall carpet-bombing of Hillary publicity in a month's gathering of magazines. This is just the beginning of a flood. Today's *Times* has her on page one, a "news" article reflecting on how deeply religion matters to her. "Her faith defines her," we learn. *Time, Newsweek*, and others have decided that Hillary sells magazines. *Nation* seems to have assigned each contributing editor an article on Hillary. The Internet testifies to yet more Hillary publicity. She beat opponents to the use of "The Sopranos" finale doing a parody with Bill for *YouTube*; she won the Howard University debate with a variation on "If men got pregnant, abortion would be a sacrament," she appeared with Bill in "Little Bit of Heaven," Davenport, Iowa and won hearts commenting that the Bush Administration requires some cleaning up after. "But I don't mind work, and I don't mind cleaning. Let's get out the buckets and the brooms."

After Hillary wins the Democratic Party nomination and becomes the first woman President of the United States, the books will fly off the shelves like bags of chips.

I cannot possibly support Hillary even as she glows like Diana in the aftermath of George Bush, his war a catastrophe, his government a shambles, his example a deep shame. There is too much evidence that she and Bush serve the same masters, the same oligopoly of great wealth with its all-consuming need for ever-growing profits, for terror abroad, and for fear itself at home.

I want simpler things: universal health care (a moral issue within our grasp and practiced in every other modern nation), taxing the rich at appropriate levels (as was the case prior to Reagan), an end to corporate welfare, all that. I want an end to arms and explosions on the heads of foreign civilians advertised as "security" and "defense." I want a pledge to end the war in Iraq immediately and to rebuild Iraq's infrastructure, destroyed during the Clinton and Bush regimes. I want a pledge not to attack Iran on bogus excuse, not Venezuela, not anywhere else in the Balkans, North Korea, not anywhere in a Latin American because of motion on the left. So, why should I support Hillary? She stands for the opposite of all I hope.

The most recent best book on Hillary—Jeff Gerth and Don Van Natta's *Her Way*—confirms her Republican and right-wing credentials and explains all the support she is winning from the powers that be. Hillary was a Nixon supporter in

1960. That was her High School foray into politics. She next fought for Goldwater in 1964 and entered Wellesley becoming president of the Young Republicans as a freshman. Next, in 1968, came an internship in the House Republican conference with Gerald Ford, and she moved on to support Nelson Rockefeller. Forget any dramatic impact from the assassinations of King and Robert Kennedy, the war in Vietnam, the emergence of the anti-war movement. Hillary next became a "critical" supporter of Gene McCarthy, one of those against the "nonviable" tactics of his large war protestor contingent.

Next, she is a college senior. Gerth and Van Natta acquired a copy of her senior thesis that she based on contacts within Saul Alinsky's community activist organization. Hillary charged Alinsky with excessive radicalism.

At her Wellesley graduation ceremony Hillary gave the first-ever student commencement address (via Dean Acheson's granddaughter) offering criticism of the official commencement address by Senator Edward Brook. Then Hillary went on to Yale. Students were being killed at Kent State and Jackson State by National Guard sent in to quell anti-war demonstrations and elsewhere and my friends and I were hosting veterans of those anti-war demonstrations at our universities and applauding them. Hillary was criticizing the demonstrators for choosing "disruption over engagement."

Then came her romance with Bill Clinton who was following his own ambitious path. He became Attorney General of Arkansas in 1976. Then governor, then president. Along the way Hillary founded the Children's Defense Fund, made sundry compromises, cut her ties with old friends who had introducing her into Democratic Party circles but had then broken with Bill over his shameful Welfare Reform Bill and his other Republican stands on labor and trade. With the Children's Defense Fund in the past, Hillary became a corporate lawyer.

Together, moving quickly on, Bill and Hillary were major participants in the most significant transition of the Democratic Party into effective corporate Republicanism in American history. The unbroken succession reads Reagan/Bush/Clinton/Bush. Now comes Hillary and, to be sure, we will hear again other familiar names: Terry McAuliffe, Madeline Albright, Al Gore, and Iron Bill himself who, like a famous English predecessor, became fifty before discovering that his cock was not in fact a bone.

There is no one in this current election circus more "deserving" than Hillary. There is not a politician in sight who can match her in persistence, self-discipline, staffing, poll appeal, fund-raising, or, in the current electoral dry season, interest making. She has been a national political creature and a significant political player for three decades, tarnished for some, but a famous first lady, a competent Senator, and master at her political craft.

The "A woman can't win" argument is no more than hostile wish-fulfillment, not after Margaret Thatcher, Madeleine Albright, and Condoleezza Rice. Not for the 21st century.

And, just to cut though the commentary, it is already obvious that Hillary will unveil some traditional Democratic Party appeal following her nomination, somewhat shedding her centrist and triangulater skin. A compromise-oriented bandwagon will roll forward, the left will roll over as it did for Kerry (in the current state of our nation any woman seems already a lesser evil) and we will have her for president along with a continuation of her Reaganite politics, the political swamp wherein we are. Bring on the buckets and the mops! Our nation gets Hillary, the leadership with the most money and the correct "line," regardless of any wishes of mine.

∽

Edwards & Two Americas
(Posted 08/13/2007)

John Edwards, among the leading candidates in the Democratic Party horse race, is the only one who speaks repeatedly of inequality and "Two Americas," He is two days into his week of campaigning in Iowa. The major slogan on the bus and banners is "Fighting for One America"—an easy and indistinct slogan— but he is repeating word-by-word his important and pointed rhetoric from 2003. Here is the 2007 version:

> This fundamental unfairness is also at the heart of the Two Americas—one for those on top, the big corporations and a few very fortunate families, and one for everyone else. We have One America that lives by the paycheck calendar; another that never has to look at the calendar before writing a check. One American that's afraid it won't be able to leave its children a better life; another whose children are already set for life. One America— middle-class America—long forgotten by Washington; and another America—narrow-interest America—whose every wish is Washington's command.
>
> If you don't think there are Two Americas, let me share with you three facts. First, the typical CEO makes more by the end of lunch than the average wage workers makes all year—in fact, the

income gap is wider than at any time since before the Depression. Second, the top 300,000 income earners in America now make more than the bottom 150 million combined. And third, in the past 10 years, the number of lobbyists in Washington has tripled to 36,000. That means there are sixty registered lobbyists for each member of Congress. . . .Men in their 30s today earn less in real dollar than their fathers did 30 years ago. For an entire generation, regular workers haven't seen a raise....

The theme comes with no radical, adequate proposals for change. The theme seldom gets even one line in the media coverage of Edwards' campaign; he is referred to as a "populist" as if that word meant "non-serious." No one mentions that Representative Ed Fallon of Des Moines who endorsed him yesterday is a consistent liberal and a 2000 supporter of Ralph Nader. But the message is there and bears repeating. Edwards continues to be the only loud voice against this shocking inequality and Washington's obscene, on its knees servicing of the rich. His is the only voice encouraging people to think along the lines of redistributing America's wealth. He offers an eye-opener for Red State America.

We will see what happens to him. Bobby Kennedy's 1968 campaign—that climaxed in California just before he was assassinated—is said to be Edwards' conscious model. Kennedy's campaign featured opposition to the Vietnam War and lessons from his travels into the impoverished urban ghettos and coal and mill towns, much like the Edwards campaigns. Since the country is a mad house of greed and suffering from that greed, it would be good if Edwards got the next twelve months to draw out this picture of "Two Americas."

৩৩

On Voting Democratic
(Posted 10/03/2007)

If you read my earnest notes reproduced here you are among those who would not be caught dead voting Republican. How could you vote for the Party of the Rich, the party of turn-back-the-clock, of barely pretended pious populism? As a result of your commitment not to support a Party whose every national policy favors well-established "big money" (armament manufacturers, big oil, big pharmaceuticals, polluters, insurance giants, and financial speculators), your only choice is to vote Democratic. Yet, the Democratic Party is the official party of lesser evil, of excuses, and of helplessness. It is *de facto* another form of the Republican Party. Here is a summary of the more recent Democratic Party lack-of-accomplishment. Face the music; listen to the Democratic Party tunes you are stuck humming.

1. Following the 2006 election a year ago, there was widespread expectation that the Democratic Party majority would move vigorously to "bring the troops home" and/or to end or limit Bush's Iraq War. In spite of expectations and words wasted praising Senate Majority Leader Harry Reid and House Speaker Nancy Pelosi, nothing has occurred. In fact there has been continued funding, a troop "surge," yet new funding, and new endorsements for continuing the Iraq occupation to 2013 while plans are put in place for dismembering Iraq and for a ten-year security/occupation agreement (with special attention to the oil fields).

2. Thanks to Democratic Party go-along, the promotion of an attack on Iran has intensified since the 2006 election. That promotion has come not only from Cheney and the Republicans and "Democrats" like Joe Lieberman, but also from leading Democrats including all the Democratic presidential contenders.

3. Following the 2006 Mid Term election, the Democratic Party majority acquired all committee chairs. As a consequence, what? All efforts to bring about corporate accountability (a big issue in the 2006 election run up, excessive CEO salaries, bailouts, corporate irresponsibility, etc. in the aftermath of the Enron and WorldCom scandals) have failed and the talk of accountability has silenced. An obviously pro-corporate Republican Party favors dropping the issue of accountability. There was a widespread (and mistaken) expectation that the Democratic Party would pursue this issue. No. Both parties give mouth breath to "accountability." Neither party has advanced corporate honesty or accountability in practice. Now we have banking and mortgage aggregators in bankruptcy being bailed out while their CEOs continue to collect plus-$150 million/year salaries. The fake congressional outrage has stilled.

4. Legislation and regulatory change since 2006 under Democratic committee chairs have favored the corporations and not the environment. Even since the 2006 Mid Term election Bush has continued his practice of right-wing crony appointments to the agencies and they, in turn, have driven out serious public servants in regulatory and judicial roles, replacing them with incompetent political partisans. The Democrats have looked on, approved, traded earmarks on Bills, and are given a pass on their own misbehavior in exchange for allowing this to happen. Amid confused sentences, the *NY Times* said today, "The Bush administration has an unblemished record of siding with corporations over the rights and safety of American citizens." Had it included "and the Democratic Party majority" we might have had a significant editorial.

5. Foreign policy initiatives and arms sales favoring our repressive and/or terrorist client states (Israel, Saudi Arabia, Pakistan) have increased as have hostile initiatives toward "axis of evil" states (Iran, Korea, Syria, and Lebanon) as well as the not-yet-axis-of-evil states. No one could mistake this for diplomacy, the diplomacy that both parties claim is the preferred approach to foreign policy.

6. Although a number of Democrats survive repeated elections on the strength of their reiteration of old New Deal support for social benefit legislation, the only remnant of the New Deal that actually remains is Social Security and it is under attack. These "traditional" Democrats have delivered nothing in addition over fifty years except Medicare. And it is under attack. They have sat on their seats and grown older while New Deal values were turned back. This has been going on for a generation fueled by cheap local trade-offs, political advantage, and sins overlooked. Their progressivism is, in real terms, a fraud. I think of Ted Kennedy. It is impossible that this man—a Kennedy and a Senator since 1962 and the Party's lead fundraiser—has no evidence against the right, no levers to use against the Bush onslaught, no whistles to blow, no chits to call in. And yet more revelations have come from Seymour Hersh—a mere Jewish journalist—than from Ted Kennedy. Kennedy employs more detectives, researchers, assistants, and secretaries and possesses more friends in Washington than journalist Hersh would dream of having. Yet Ted Kennedy remains close-mouthed. Nothing leaks from his office while Bush flourishes. Big Bill Clinton did exactly the same in behalf of George Herbert Walker Bush (see the book *Secrecy & Privilege* and elsewhere). Bill's wife intends to provide a similar favor for the son, George Walker Bush. Watch and witness it.

7. Each of these notes has the makings of newspaper articles, op-ends, analytical pieces, and talking-head commentary, but mostly you will not see or hear them. The media is neither "left" nor "liberal" in any real sense. Some important media does favor the Democratic Party because to openly support the Party of the Rich would loose its liberal urban audience, especially since the Mid Term election of 2006 when they can represent themselves as expressing the peoples' voice. However, like all highly placed Democrats, the major media, like Ted Kennedy, is willing to let everything go to hell rather than to say what they know about American politics.

Between now and the advent of American Fascism there is only one last major deception that needs to be in place. The next-to-last (already accomplished) is that the Democratic Party is an opposition party. The last will be to sell the Republican Party as "a party of the common people."

OBAMA

Introduction

I would like to have quoted from Barack Obama's books, *Dreams from My Father* (1995) and *The Audacity of Hope* (2006); however, they are right there before you in any bookstore. You would discover in my quotations that Obama has a bit of a lyric bent and some rare honesty. Compare his books to Bill Clinton's *My Life* (2004) or, in nightmare, compare his books to what you might imagine from George Bush.

From Obama you hear a competitors warning against grudges: "Let it go." You hear politicians' savvy: "Put the past behind." These are not simple ideas, certainly not despicable ones. You will learn about his caution and compromise. These are not crimes. Caution and compromise come from people who are unwilling to kill others to stay ahead of the pack, who depend on other ways. We Americans need to heed them. These books are valuable reading, now especially at the beginning of what, if we all have good fortune, may become an eight year presidency.

This current President of the United States is a rare duck, so conventionally political in many way and yet called "an intellectual titan" with some justification, so compromise bent, and yet so patient. Clearly he is willing to give his life to his new job although he does have loves beyond the job (a family, a history, an uncomplicated patriotism). Those loves will take a lot of wear and tear in the next few years.

Obama is a centrist Democrat emerging into a 1976-to-date era totally dominated by extreme right-wing Republicanism, Clinton no exception to that Republicanism. We easily may forget Clinton, but we need to remember that Bush was a reactionary toad in everything that holds a man together (background, experience, and acts). Obama is a truly great change in the character of our presidency.

I believe that what we 310 million people do and say to each other is more important than what Barack Obama says. And Obama has said the same. He has failed to say that what we did not do and did not say in the recent past was more important than George Bush himself. But Obama does not do acqusation much. But now we should do our thing, especially the activists and union organizers among us. The Tea-Party people (with some scattered fascists among them) are doing theirs. The academics are doing theirs (mainly being nice), unorganized labor likewise, the remnant broad left, and so on, right through school teachers, nurses, and soccer moms in their book groups. Meanwhile the young will be making their career choices. I am thinking of every dimension of possible social action. Forget the young who are relationship-occupied and career-occupied.

If the majority of those who vote can elect an African American president, perhaps we are not headed right on down the drain. Yes, there are the compromises. Yes, there are a frightful number who wish him dead. Make no bones about it. He is far more visible then was Martin Luther King. Along with the handful of angry, insane Timothy McVeigh's among us, there are the same right-wing people who winced hearing Martin Luther King so beautifully intone the best values of our entire history and the gospel of Jesus Christ while he took his courageous and important positions on our wars and deprivations. Those who winced at King's major speeches do so at Obama's. They are the ones who, however indirectly, mentored McVeigh's murders and Martin Luther King's assassin. So, there is that.

The United States does deal in death. We are a failed state in profound ways. We do not nurture or educate our children decently, comprehensively, equally. We leave so many so far behind. Yes, Obama is conservative. But I have something of a placid feeling. That is the word I carefully choose. Placid. It comes on like a song. I feel the Obama presidency will release activism, not maim it. To maim activism was Reagan's whole objective: to end "Vietnam Era" activism, labor organizing, and to turn back the clock. That is what his inheritor George Bush and this one party government managed to accomplish. Perhaps we now can get over the Reagan Era terror and begin to move, even the liberal academics.

The progressive parts of our history (the progressive era and socialism, our good unions and socialist organizing, FDR's reforms, persistent progressive voices, even the seemingly lonely voices) form such a powerful image of a good America. It must be taught again. The sense of death-dealing, impoverishment and viciously unequal shares, and a world-wide, militarily-enforced capitalist Emporium must be defeated and untaught.

Here are some of my posts on the 2004 and 2007-8 election runs, on the behavior of the Democratic Party and behavior by the liberals who supported lack-of-effect and irresponsibility, on Bush's toad-life, and on Obama's first year. It ends with our response to the Haiti disaster.

ᖰᖰ

Bad-Ass Democrats
(Posted 02/01/2005)

If you are interested in the Iraqi election, my best wishes. There is disorder on the ground and smooth perfection in the U.S. propaganda airspace, another meaning of "air superiority." Air and land may never meet. The horizon of "withdrawal" is always receding covered by various pseudo-events, alarms, and diversions. This may well go on for years, election after election.

That is because the real issue is our occupation of their strategic, oil-rich country. Our "air superiority" keeps that quiet, keeps it out of the limelight. Meanwhile, back at the congressional ranch where the buffalo roam and seldom is heard an oppositional word, I just noticed that the lead article in the current, left-liberal *Nation* is titled "Bad-Ass Democrats, Durbin and Waxman Show How to Fight Back," all in caps. It is truly outrageous journalism.

I contend that the Democrats are no opposition at all, in fact, part of the problem and no part of the solution. And yet many progressive people maintain their faith and will run back to being disregarded Democratic Party voters at the next opportunity, settling for the "lesser evil" before taking any other action. Pure at heart, I have myself done that.

"Abandon the Democrats," I have said to loyalists, friends, fundraisers and such. They pay no attention. I have explained, "Yes, the Republicans and the Democrats are the main problem. We are a one-party country." And, yes, I have sent 250 word versions of this to *The Nation,* and to all and sundry.

Only an Emily Dickenson could describe the quality of tenuous hope represented in the sort of Democratic Party journalism that *The Nation* uses to sustain support for these folk. They should learn not to cleave to their abuser. Cease being "He Who Gets Slapped."

Anyway, Henry Waxman (65, D. House, LA CA district) and Dick Durbin (60, D. Senate, IL), and young Barack Obama of IL (Durbin's protégé) are the subjects of "Bad-Ass Democrats. The riff is that these Democrats are "filleting" Bush, showing "Congressional Democrats how to be something they have not been since Bush assumed the presidency: an effective opposition." They are "Eliot Ness" going after the administration. They are "marauders" full of "an edgy willingness to battle the powers that be." They know how to "trump the Republicans in the battle of public opinion." They know how to "play to win" in "the nation's most savage political setting." Come on, *Nation*; get an editor who will tone down this flight of fishy fancy.

Mainly, these are only two senior Democratic Party tenured buffalo with substantial staff producing position papers for them, speeches, and proposed legislation, all supportable, on a variety of subjects. Durbin has fought some fights on judicial nominations. There is no more reason to put these guys down than, say, to put Edward Kennedy down, although they are half the men they should be. Would that there were more like them. But there are not even ten. And, in spite of a word or two about young Obama, they do not breed. This is an important point. If there were twenty, and the twenty (make it thirty) did force their party to run like them, they just might pull the party away from the center a smidgen and create some bit of opposition to reactionary Republicanism. Might, I say. In our dreams.

These are the sort of men who made Clinton, who gave us Gore and Kerry walking against Bush's run and hoping to win nonetheless. They only succeeded in making Bush bold.

The *Nation* article makes a point of distinguishing them from Cynthia McKinney, Dennis Kucinich, and Bernie Sander who make "lonely protest votes." Unlike the heroes of *The Nation*! *The Nation's* heroes are wise in "in ways that work." That is to say they are caucus Democrats who have "survival instincts" and are obedient to the DNC. Their strongest actual position is to "lament the lack of congressional oversight." But, unlike Senator Byrd (about to leave congressional octogenarian status in his dust) they do not call that lack "unconstitutional." That would be going too far. That would not "work."

I am not going to look up and rehearse for you the details of their compromises. Presumably, some of that will appear in letters to the editor of *The Nation* in the next issue. Actually, I did not even finish the Waxman piece because its second page has a heavy grey overprint image of a Sherlock Holmes with a signature pipe and magnifying glass peering into the open cap of the Capitol building. Take comfort, *The Nation* says, there is a Sherlock Holmes, whatever it is he is smoking.

Alas, folks, articles like this are not progressive politics, not opposition, not faith in anything, not even a faith in their own left bias. It is nonsense.

❦

Dead Dragon or Crouching Kitten
(Posted 01/09/2005)

Watch out for the concerted efforts to resurrect interest in and support for the Democratic Party following its recent loss. The efforts originate in the party National Committee, the Clintons, the DLC, Democratic incumbents, and the party's professional apparatus and apparatchik wannabees. From there it runs right on through affiliated organizations like Move On, Take Back America, and on to most liberal and left organizations, foundations, and publications.

Here is a small example of how Democratic Party resurrection works from one worthy, progressive organization doing media analysis. Speaking of yesterday's debate on the Ohio voting debacle, the excellent Danny Schecter of *Mediachannel* writes:

> After years of post 911 Democratic deference, patriotic correct-
> ness, pulled punches and namby pambyism, it was heartening
> to see some Democrats rising to the moment, pressured by their
> constituents. Most were very cautious and careful not to suggest
> in any way, oh lord, that the Bushiviks might just be the real
> conspirators stoked with bundles of corporate cash, manipulated
> followers, and a cheerleading media. There was little time for
> an in-depth assessment of what happened but John Conyers and
> his colleagues [Barbara Boxer, Chris Dodd, Harry Reid, Barack
> Obama, Richard Durbin, Debbie Stabenow, Edward Kennedy,
> Ron Wyden, Frank Lautenberg, and Tom Harkin—are all
> named] showed some guts. And the fact they pissed off so many
> Republicans who responded with derision and denial was a sign
> of how rare this kind of stand-up "insurgency" is in the usually
> oh so polite GOP fraternity and sorority that runs the legislative
> branch of this country.

That is how an undeserved resurrection starts to work. Of course it was good to read this site mention John Kerry hiding under the bed, opposing floor debate on electoral abuses, and other acts of avoidance. But, still, here is *Mediachannel* playing *The Nation*, which after every election cycle goes into paroxysms of discovery of gems in the Democratic Party sea bottom. It is not right, this mentioning of "courageous insurgency" by a few Democrats, however equivocal the praise. The real substance of the comment is that when we hear "Please, please, we beg you to give financial support and your feet-on-the-street to the lesser evil, the better evil" you must respond. Why? "Well, because…because…because if you do not there will only be the greater evil." And they call that democracy.

They (echoing Kerry) are saying that realists and all sane folks must realize that America can never ever give rise to a genuine opposition. That would frighten the rich in their mansions. It would bring an end to their financial contributions. Very disaster! To offend the rich? What madness!

Instead of hearing this, we should completely abandon the Democratic Party. I repeat myself. I do not have good answers to every question or the perfect alternative, but I am convinced that without this first step first we will never find answers or see with clear eyes an alternative or help build any organized opposition to what Bush and his vicious, weakest-to-the-wall, rich-loving Republicans are doing to our country.

Praying for another Jesse Jackson will not do. At very least Jackson did work for months and months in unfriendly places and made honest and vigorous statements to the press if asked. But that is not getting far enough away from the fatal, hopeless Democratic Party. The environmentalists (and other single-issue groups) do some fine work but become socially useless when the Democratic Party beckons. Labor has some efforts going (for instance, the democratic opposition within the Teamsters and some SEIU initiatives, maybe something among the dock workers) but they too come when Lesser Evil Democrats call. Organized labor is only 12% of American workers. The university intelligentsia is hopeless. They approve of every lesser evil argument and hop on any Democrat's coach. As liberal, well-educated, and practical men and women they know the Democratic politicians to be their colleagues, friends, and neighbors. And forget organized "left opposition." Only a peek will show you that they also are clipped wings of the Democratic Party.

I have no present answer to future questions. The first step is abandonment of the Democratic Party. Otherwise, watch that Party as it helps bring in Alberto Gonzales at Attorney Genera, funds on-going wars, and blows the chance to reform the broken American electoral process while it agrees-in-advance not to put forward a candidate who will speak honestly to the American people. That is the Democratic Party.

There are some good comedians out there, and some sharp commentators. I enjoy them. However, pissing off Republicans wins no honor. It is just too easy. The Republicans are long schooled in the corporate CEO posture of seeming to be pissed off, always, and always looking ready to blow up, shouting spittle in the face of even the least temerity. That is their style, the corporate CEO style.

Watch out when the drums start beating for the Democratic Party again. Find a different drummer.

∽

Is There Safety in Numbers?
(Posted 04/27/2008)

After the 2000 and the 2004 presidential elections (Gore then Kerry losing to George Bush after a dead heat race), who can sympathize with the anguish of the Democrats worrying about another loss to the Republicans in 2008? They did not run head-on against the Republicans in 2000 or 2004 and appear unwilling to do so this time around. In all likelihood, they will be represented by Senator Clinton of New York running against an elderly Bush surrogate. Ah, the liberal anguish that will follow! Months of appeals for cash and furlongs to the finish line! Only to lose. Here are some relevant numbers. You be the judge if the Democrats deserve any sympathy.

The current president's approval rating is a historic 70-year low of 28%. 72% disapprove of him. Although Bush has been very good to the rich, he has been very bad to the rest of us. We disapprove. Not that it has mattered. His war—unlike his father's war—was based on lies, he accomplished no single mission, his international support now comes from a declining number of old Latin American dictators and a handful of paid clients in the Caribbean and Central Asia. He has accumulated a huge national debt and (exactly like his sainted patron Ronald Reagan) he has grown the size of government, the budget of the military, and hid it all by going bupkis for "Morality in America."

He has contributed only cheap slogans and expensive corporate bailouts while corrupting Justice, the FDA, the FAA, all the regulatory agencies. The whole national economy is in the tank. Not surprising that for the first time in history and for the longest run in history a majority of the U.S. population affirms it "strongly disapproves" of its president.

You would think this means the Democrats have a good chance to come from behind, from out of their generation-long safe trench of Out-of-Power.

And there are other numbers tending the same way. The Democratic Party has a current lead among young voters by 25 points. They now have a minimum 10-point advantage over the Republicans among all voters [Pew Research]. I discounted voters who self-identify as Conservative or Liberal, averaged all the recent Pew poll research categories (sex, age, education, race, region of the country, urban/suburban/rural, evangelical/mainline/Catholic, and all income categories), and found that the Democrats enjoy more than a 17 point advantage over Republican voters.

Yet with all these numbers, seven different polling organizations also give evidence that Barack Obama might win in November 2008 by only a 3.2%. Hillary Clinton, by the same seven polls, will be beaten by Arizona Senator McCain by 2%. Obama runs this assessment as a banner on his web site. But what happened to the 17-point advantage for Democrats? Where is any sign of the 30-percentage point turn against Bush Republicanism?

In a matter of weeks a very substantial Democratic Party advantage has disappeared. The explanation is not solely in the media's commercial need to make every race "neck in neck." It is also in the manner of the Democratic campaign.

Clinton panders and imitates her way toward the forthcoming primaries. Obama seem to fall victim to an onslaught of a mean-spirited media. His own lack of forthrightness plays a role. As expected, he would continue to keep troops in Iraq for years to come, as would Clinton. In addition, although he knows there are Two Americas and that accumulated wealth and annual income separates the two very dramatically, yet he delivers a major speech on race, not on money. I await Clinton's nomination and that of stalwart old Bush/Cheney surrogate McCain. Obama will race Clinton to what is made to seen a dead heat, a photo replay finish. Perhaps you can pick a particular poll or analysis that suggests otherwise. Pick away. I have summarized them all and accurately.

Therefore, 70% of voters disapprove of Bush and roughly 70% of voters were recently inclined toward the Democrats. The Democratic Party will turn that uneven contest into a neck-and-neck race. Then, if past is prologue, we will get to watch them lose in the final breathless yards. Then we will be condemned to hear all sorts of respectful, shallow nonsense about the man McCain simply because he has ascended to the throne as President of our United States.

Four points of analysis of this absurdity:

Point 1: Roughly 50% of eligible Americans will not vote. (2004 produced a 58% turnout and that was the highest since the 1960s). In Congressional elections the percentage falls to 35, in city or county elections to 20. A maximum of 5% of Americans actively participate in political parties or in their campaigns. Something like a maximum of 10% ever makes even a Party financial contribution. That is what one-party democracy brings us.

Point 2: A quite small elite stratum rules our politics and national culture. They are the Republican-inclined elite that have been ascendant since before Ronald Reagan. The interlude of Clinton Democrats was actually republicanism: witness NAFTA, "Free" Trade, Welfare "Reform," no national health program, deregulating telecom and banking, continued de-unionization, lobbyists ascendant, militarization of foreign policy, etc. These elite believe that anything offered to the unworthy poor and middle class is wasted; it will never be returned as a financial benefit to them. They believe that wealth should flow upward, not down the drain. Many below them, but not yet at the bottom, believe that this is God's truth (or else, in place of belief, take some comfort in similar grade school and church lessons).

Point 3: Only a handful of elite make the decisions that shape national policy. We have our elaborate ritual of parties, elections, interest groups, etc. These have little direct or indirect influence. Essentially we are ruled by a class-determined elite closely associated with our major financial institutions and corporations.

They can morph slightly as necessary and they have some slight openness to new members out of their small pool of close associates; however, short of revolution, they persist, replicate, reproduce, and continue to dominate. They are usually the same families, the same vats of money, the same institutions, and more or less the same corporations, decade after decade. They enjoy the benefits of wealth and good education. They have a good grasp of the importance of public policy and are able to argue their own private interests, a rare gift in an America that still believes we are an egalitarian and just society. These few value their unrestrained enjoyment of our money, their media voice, and their public order. They turn it all to their advantage.

Beneath these elite, 90+ percent of Americans bathe in ignorance of the issues, in xenophobia, and in a dumb bias favoring the rich, "their betters." Since they are rich, they must have it right. And, plus, there is always the illusion of the lottery, that newest form of taxation. These folk, the majority, support controls, policing, imprisonment, capital punishment, and general social Darwinism. That is what they were taught in local schools reinforced by local advertising and the local churches. Because this whole picture is so topsy-turvy, so outrageously anti-democratic, they are easily made to feel endangered. As a consequence, they are intolerant yet prideful, apathetic yet confident. They are no longer in any real sense "upwardly mobile." It has been more than a generation since upward mobility was a reality in America. Their work-induced exhaustion, mental vagueness, indiscipline, bad education, and fearfulness can seem boundless. This is the Salt of our Earth, our entire non-professional, non-union, insecure Middle-Earth America. They are much of our voting population.

Therefore, political campaigns—to the small extent that they matter at all—are framed by appeals to the benighted non-elite: does he wear a flag pin, does his minister preach God Bless America, will he or she annihilate Iran and keep the prisons and the borders tightly locked? Does she bowl adequately? Drink beer? Will she save us $30 a year at the gas pumps? Does he engage in happy bluster so beloved by novice journalists? Does he drop the "g" in "-ing" (like slovenly good buddy Bush)? Can she out shoot McCain, having out gunned Obama, before going down in ultimate defeat and back to her Senate seat?

Point 4: The hard-nosed of the elite (and we are coming to know them better) regard a large portion of the American people as without value and dispensable. Their policy toward these "brutes" that serve in the armed forces and occupy the highway-surrounded ghettos and barrios, are the millions of destroyed, underemployed, uneducated "white trash" in small towns throughout America is to offer public hypocrisy and more private exploitation. The elite's judgment of "dispensable" is perfectly reflected in elite-led public policy (public housing should be destroyed; there is no value in universal health care, child-centered public education is a misnomer, as is corporate regulation and social security). They have gone quite far toward destroying all of them. The most brazen and hard-nosed of these elite are simply Nazis.

These tough-minded rich oligarchs have not yet emerged as an actual aristocracy—which, historically, is a necessary condition for social revolution—but they are coming to that. In the event of a massive economic depression, they may again morph toward a seeming, a somewhat greater regard for the public welfare as they did under FDR. However, right now I see no signs of an FDR turn by the American rich. I see signs of emerging aristocracy.

This is history not journalism. None of it should be news to you. The founders of our country were predominantly a Republican elite as well, determined to put in place controls over the masses, prevent direct democracy, insure an opportunity for land speculation (in which they all engaged), and aspire to Empire. The "iron law of oligarchy" is the law that best describes our politics. With the iron law of oligarchy, the elite will defend their sacred property, their sacred capitalism, to your death; a make religion of it.

Consequently, I believe that with or without the proof of numbers we can see how irrelevant and how predictable these elections are. We can note the rise of mass cynicism and the widespread (and damaging) unwillingness to comply with laws. We can note the trumpeting myth of American First ("We are the Best!") while all evidence of that disappears. We can note the widespread intolerance, ignorance, inconsistency, and apathy. Give the dog a name!

The people, the masses, are even unwilling to acknowledge that they have no opinion whatsoever about major public issues. Polling organizations have proven and leaked this revelation. That is why major public issues are not discussed on TV, why impromptu interviews with the public are restricted to three seconds, and why "issue polls" are such mush. Issues are for the elite, the oligarchy. Only they pay careful attention. All this helps explain the demise of Edwards and of Obama, who each has their outside-the-elite uniqueness. It helps explain why all outside contenders and outside discussions are decisively marginalized (Nader, Kucinich, and a handful of other exceptional Senators and Representatives, Governors such as Dean, etc.), and why ultimately our national elections are predictable and meaningless.

This is Political Science 101 available to the elite and elaborated in a number of successful textbooks of American Government, textbooks used year after year in the better colleges and running through multiple editions. The textbooks are sometimes as straightforward about American politics as I have tried to be here. (For example, see the fourteenth edition of The Irony of Democracy by Dye and Zeigler). Others are more scabbed over with respectable excuse-making forcing you to read between the lines. But after High School's abysmal textbooks, good independently published books all tell the same story and are unread by the masses, as are the classics (de Tocqueville, Veblen, the Beards, J.M Keynes, Hofstadter, Burch, Domhoff, Dye, and many others). It is no secret.

∽

The Turn to Obama
(Posted 05/08/2008)

The thoughtlessness of the Clinton campaign this last month surprised me. Her "totally obliterate" Iran remark, her meaningless summer tax holiday at the gas pumps, and her retread of the Rocky slogans ("fighting from behind," "down but not out") were each a follow-on from John McCain campaign themes. McCain already occupied first place among Iran warmongers; he initiated the tax holiday gimmick; he had already worn out the "Come Back Kid" mantle. As the Clinton campaign soldiered on in its centrist outlines, these McCain-derived loser themes were widely reported. What did they think they were doing?

Each ploy set up an easy reply from the Obama campaign. The first allowed Obama to call her "massive retaliation" threat against Iran an "unacceptable act of aggression" in inappropriate "language." Then he immediately named the McCain/ Clinton gas tax holiday an "election-year gimmick" and was able to cite his Illinois experience of the failure of gas-tax holidays to return any real benefit. As for the "Rocky" image, how could this Wellesley-Yale ex-First Lady Party favorite hope to persuade that she was poor-struggling-me up against the son of a Kenyan immigrant who was raised by a single mom, who was educated in struggle at Oxy college in LA and Columbia in NYC, and in south side of Chicago community organizing before well before he ever stood out against the red brick of Harvard Law?

Previously, it looked like the Democratic Party would face us with a 61 year old Washington politician (eight years in the White House, six years in the Senate) going up against a 71 year old Washington politician (twenty-one years in the Senate). She would lose the election. Everything would stay in place. The rich oligarchs who run the country would rejoice.

Personalities aside, I thought, we had two overextended Democratic Party endorsed and funded foreign occupations, a simmering recession brought on by Democratic Party endorsed deregulation and tax breaks for the rich, no progressive legislation since I can't remember when, and, in brief, essentially twenty-eight years of Republicanism. Perhaps then, after another Great Depression and yet another war, an invitation to the new would arrive. After business as usual following on business as usual, perhaps Fire Next Time. And about time. But that picture has changed dramatically.

Many recognized Clinton's bad branding but have not yet absorbed the consequences. As the recent votes demonstrate, all she had secured was the approval of racists and of 65+ uneducated white women, many who had not previously voted and probably will not vote in November. She already had those votes and they did not match the percentage level of voter loyalty by Obama's Black voters. Clinton offered dumb branding in a period of corporate domination when branding is everything and quality is forgotten.

But now we will have Obama as the Democratic Party nominee. I am delighted, on the one hand, and wonder how his corporate-loyal Democratic Party will screw him up, frame him into the usual picture of corporate compliance.

They have a new kid thrust upon them, one with color and a real stake in the world beyond the DC beltway, one who is physically courageous unlike Bush, who is a fine speaker with several cultural styles deployed with natural-seeming ease, a man surrounded with some competent-seeming fresh faces, and someone who has a reputation to build, the major part of a whole career—national and international—to establish. And, finally, here is a candidate funded significantly by small donors.

My theme—Parties are important to the Powerful—asks how the Party of the Rich and its follow along Democratic Party will come down on him, eviscerate his potential, twist their boot on the new plant, make Obama into another example of senatorial business as usual.

Given the Parties in Power, there is little to look forward to domestically and Obama will surely not reconfigure international politics.

Jump to today's news. Putin in Russia has just put on a marvelous display, a Czarist-style coronation of new president Medvedev (Putin's 42 year old, tall, perfect-English, lawyer side-kick) who immediately named Putin the new Prime Minister. Tomorrow this will be followed by a grand Soviet-style military parade complete with tanks and the ICBMs we have not seen since before 1989. A deliberate nationalist two-for-one.

Putin, I believe, is a Russian patriot intent on raising Russia to its rightful position as the most natural ally of the United States sharing domination in a naturally bi-polar—and soon to be tri-polar—world. Over the eight years of Putin's own presidency he took back control of the nation from Russia's mafia billionaires who had nearly destroyed the country in a decade of theft and appropriation. Putin as president grew the middle class from eight to twenty-two million and kicked the major commercial oligarchs off center stage (yes, the same ones who funded his ascendancy). He reintroduced the issue of civil rights, domestic reforms and infrastructure repair, and a living, breathing, quasi-independent judiciary. The oligarchs were rabid thieves with no national loyalty—exactly like their American corporate counterparts—and they had become, until Putin, the face of Russia. That has changed. This week's drama is intended to mark the change.

The uppity moneyed American oligarchs have likewise become too visible, too greedy, destroying our tradition of corporate regulation, defeating every piece of progressive legislation, rewarding themselves at every turn with tax cuts, exemptions, unearned benefits and bail-outs, and picking away at our the remnants of our Constitution and our tattered social-democratic traditions. These oligarchs are easily named (Finance, Oil, Munitions, Chemicals) and Bush has been their absolute flunkey and facilitator. They, in turn, sold him to us like a pair of Nikes, like NASCAR, or a new hair color.

Could Obama, like Putin, emerge as the man to revitalize capitalist America? The man who reconstructs a world order based on competition and multi-polarity, a man who puts the American oligarchs in the shade where they belong and himself takes the celebrity of the entrepreneurial limelight?

In spite of the anti-democratic nature of all branding (which exists to destroy issues, herd us into niches, and reduce everything to idiotic, cheaply conveyed symbols and phrases) we may be in for a revival of traditional politics. How can you not welcome that? It must involve at least some redistribution of the wealth (as with Putin's Russia), some revival of regulatory responsibility, some renewal of the judiciary and the rule of law. Who is more likely to assume that responsibility than a first term Barack Obama?

First, however, the Democratic Party must find it in their Republican heart and Democratic wallets to defeat John McCain, one of their own.

⚭

Obama from England
(Posted 06/19/2008)

Not that it matters, but I cannot see the line of attack the Republican Party will choose against Barack Obama. Could it be simple racism; is there that much racism in America?

We are in England, away from the U.S. media. British media is not as coy as the American press about race. The *Guardian* sent a journalist to the Appalachian states, which Obama lost (some counties as much as 60 points favoring Hillary Clinton). The articles quote local racists in a way that is not done in our press, calm offhand hate speech that is illegal in some U.S. states. Some of the folks quoted say they are "not worried about Obama" because he will be assassinated before he ever becomes president. They encourage that event. How is that for freedom of expression? Complacently, the British journalists quote this stuff without comment. The Great Chain of British Being (Whites on top just below the lower angels) will be restored. They cannot imagine an American that overcomes its racism. "We have never had to."

Others newspapers quote folks that take it for granted that Obama's program, should he win, will be to enslave Whites in retaliation for the 150 years of Black slavery, Jim Crow, and exclusion from the benefits of our sunny national economy. Folks that out of touch. The British press quotes people telling darky jokes (that could only be reproduced here as a satire of extreme ignorance in a little-noticed book) going well beyond your normal street profanity. However—not to mislead you—the usual generous, liberal commentary and speculation also comes in these papers; actually it dominates them. It is England after all, just a bit more free-voiced than we are used to.

At the left end of the British spectrum, their media has voices like John Pilger and Alexander Cockburn. To me, when the do appear here online, they are flutes playing reason rather than the gravel sound of David Brooks, Tom Friedman, William Kristol, and the *New York Times* editorial rhythm section. Pilger and Cockburn—and I would not leave them alone in that—would welcome the collapse of the American empire. They welcome our endless fiddling while Rome burns. They expect nothing of Obama. His domestic program (and they could care less) is at the dull center and his international politics are straight American Empire stuff.

Yet, clearly, all the Brits wonder at Obama's emergence, a Black, and they speculate on the line of attack that to be used in undermining him giving the world the next Reaganite, the next Bush.

The attack used may be similar to that used successfully against John Kerry (bombing his war-hero-become-antiwar-hero image; fixing him as an Eastern Elite Liberal intellectual, out of touch with the millions, labeling "socialist" his Democratic platform). But one British journalist remembered that in 1968 Bobby Kennedy was an Eastern Elite Liberal who also did not speak the so-called "language of the people," running on a social democratic platform well to the left of Kerry's or Obama's. Many believe Bobby Kennedy would have defeated Herbert Humphrey for the nomination and then would have defeated Richard Nixon for the presidency had he not been assassinated. Nixon, after all, was just more routine Republican goods. He spoke haltingly in patriotic generalities in behalf of free trade, empire, and America's world-class inequality ("free enterprise").

The main line of attack, the a few British journalists seem to conclude, will be the simple racist one, continuous reminders that Obama is undeniably a Black man, his wife undeniably an African-American woman, his children Black children. He may—they speculate—run on a Black platform serving the interests of a mere fifteen percent of the population, endangering all other interests. There will be creative insinuations, lies carried, delivered, and aborted at the last minute, all sorts of imaginative media reminders that Obama is "a Black Man"

Yet most British journalists do recognize that Obama, being Black, must run a race-neutral campaign (doubly neutral, in both content and in style). In addition, as with all liberal journalists on both sides of the Atlantic, they carry hints of what most active Black Americans and many who are uninhibitedly progressive assert: Obama will have at his back the powerful spirit of Martin Luther King, the wind of equality and social justice, powerful stuff.

> In King's words (*Where Do We Go From Here*, 1967) Let us remember that there is a creative force in this universe, working to pull down the gigantic mountains of evil, a power that is able to make a way out of no way and transform dark yesterdays into bright tomorrows. Let us realize the arc of the moral universe is long but it bends toward justice.

Frame that as you please, in whatever idiom, it expresses what is hopeful about Barack Obama's campaign for the U.S. presidency and why it is gathering support. There will be "hangover" racism (what I call "a drunk on the subway racism") but most everyone recognizes that it can no longer dictate all our politics as it has for so long. Broad economic justice is the primary issue now, dramatic inequality, pinched and trampled lives—Black and White—robbed and put down so that the rich may indulge themselves freely; and a corporate government that serves and protects only them.

We now watch Obama as a candidate moving closer to Bush positions on all international issues (Iraq, Iran, Israel, Venezuela, Cuba, and Sudan). We realize that his somewhat pale improvements on the national policies of Reagan-Bush Era (in health, environment, regulation, fair taxation) are not going to count for as much as we might have hoped. But at least one significant step will have been taken. We will have shown that our long history of racial injustice is not our nation's major issue even thought it may be made into our nation's current major diversion.

The emerging issue is social injustice, the horrid crimes of the rich against the poor. I believe we would have been a step ahead with John Edwards as the presidential candidate. Even without Obama, the struggle for racial justice was making headway. But never mind that. Social justice must come. Injustice shows clearly in the numbers measuring American public health. No one can erase them. So, let us turn the page. Any breathless anticipation of a grand turn against American Empire, as one progressive British journalist anticipates, is not yet on the horizon.

ᕲᕯ

Obama Back at Home
(Posted 08/17/2008)

All Americans of any liberal inclination, all American minorities, and all of the world's people felt a warming, like a first blush, at the possibility of Barack Obama as President of the United States. That had something to do with renouncing our racist heritage. It had a bit to do with reluctance about more of the Clinton duo. It had something to do with the quality of Obama's presentations after eight years of George Bush. However, it had most to do with Obama's early opposition to the Iraq War and our perception that he, as an African-American, would provide some populist focus on America's problems.

The blush is fading.

Now I hear "politician" and disappointment. From his supporters I hear "Why can't we all just get behind Barack and make Bush III impossible?" To others Barack Obama is sounding more and more like someone who thinks he can ride to victory on the magic carpet of celebrity.

Everyone has now heard from Barack that "the choices we make in November will shape the next decade, if not the century," heard from him of "the free market" and "America's competitiveness in the 21st century," heard Barack about Middle Eastern-bred terror, terror, terror. From Barack we have heard about the "American dream" reflected in his personal "improbable story." We have heard from him about "this defining moment" and American self-reliance and independence.

All this was repeated in speeches this month and last month. It is typical running-in-place campaign language. The Obama proposals and programs are not all that exciting in a country that, after all, does have great reform and progressive traditions.

A great many ordinary Americans already know that they are forced into self-reliance by slavishness while the rich enjoy all the benefits of a guardian government and are not required to pay their fair share. They know Washington D.C. is running the global marketplace in behalf of the corporations. Meanwhile Barack Obama is running on class harmony and the fumes of "change you can believe in." He is not an opposition; he is an advertisement.

His opponent, John Sidney McCain III, is remaking himself into a candidate named "War Hero." He is zeroed in on winning in November. Hillary Clinton, if we are to believe Maureen Dowd, has not given up and is planning a *coup d'etat* at the Democratic Party national convention in order then to lose to Senator War Hero. Perhaps that was a joke; I sometimes cannot tell.

Ralph Nader—relegated to the blogs maintained by newspapers in a kind of Internet-only, late pages opinion section—is organizing demonstrations, continuing to get his independent and progressive candidacy for president on state ballots, and trying to push his way into the forthcoming debates in order to fill abandoned space for a progressive agenda.

I say to my friends—those of "Why can't we all just get behind Barack?"— that they should get in touch with their inner Karl Rove. They should vote Nader while making it possible for Obama to win big.

1. On every possible occasion repeat your opponent's full name: John Sidney McCain III
2. Ask Obama to give a major stirring speech on *Women in America* comparable to his speech in March on *Race in America*.
3. Give up on the white male vote. Neither Carter nor Clinton won the majority of that vote when they were elected and Obama will not.
4. Ignore the Republican Party platform. It is corporate America speaking.
5. Ask Obama to quit mentioning his points of agreement with McCain; quit saying things like "the most interesting [thing] that's going on these days is the debate between John McCain and John McCain." Ask Obama not to nitpick at McCain but to oppose him, oppose the whole right wing, pro-corporate, war-mongering, closet-racist, dishonest essence of the man. McCain is Bush III. Make a point of it. This is especially important when everyone already knows both candidates are for solar and wind power (both run ads using the same stock photos), for Israel (unique but similar photos), children (ditto), health care (ditto), helping home owners (ditto), and both are for keeping campaign spending and special interest in line, next time or someday.
6. Suggest to Obama that on all matters of foreign policy he repeatedly use the words "strong" and "strength," but skip all his repetitions of "terror, terror," and "terror" (which shows weakness and worry). Show knowledge

of where/what/who and ask McCain questions he cannot answer. That should be easy. And supporters should explain to Obama that he is running against an elderly War Hero, a hawk right-winger with vast, not-to-be-matched experience in sucking up to white male know-nothing racist American voters. Give up on those votes. And, in utmost seriousness, they should urge that Obama:

7. Talk about inequality. Talk about forcing the rich to carry their share. Talk about the federal government's responsibility for infrastructure, health care, and education. Talk about strengthening the regulatory agencies (FDA, FTC, FAA, SEC, EPA, etc.) and building a real government, one that serves the people against the corporations instead of the opposite. I say this without much hope.

Really, I did not expect Obama to run such a pale campaign. Sunday's *NY Times* did a page one titled "Seeing Tougher Race, Allies Ask Obama to Make 'Hope' Specific." In their vague way local party leaders are asking Obama to address Issue 7 above. They are saying that mouth-breath on "hope" and "change" is not enough.

He must know that some of Edwards' populism is golden in spite of Edwards' personal implosion? He must know that routine speeches, written pretty much as McCain's speeches are written, will soon be distinguishable only in delivery? Delivery is not all. Or—my actual fear—Obama is simply a machine politician, authorized by the DNC and DLC trailing their string of failures, willing to squeak by as long as nothing excites, upsets, or advances the commonwealth.

I am always saying "We live in interesting times." Sometimes that seems way overblown. Now there seems nothing to do but give copies of Nader's DVD "An Unreasonable Man" to all my relatives this Christmas. In the coming months and into 2009 I plan to continue—in spite of my weak qualifications—looking into and writing about issues of social medicine. Next year I plan to travel to interesting places (like Canada, Ireland, and Scotland).

That's for places. As for times, I cannot even imagine rereading Michael Moore's *Mike's Election Guide*, Garrison Kellor's *Homegrown Democrat* or the many similar election-cycle Democratic Party books, I find myself rereading pre-1976 books for the immediate vitality of them. 1976 is about the year John McCain entered Washington politics and Barack Obama was shooting hoops in a Honolulu prep school gym. It is the past. The Obama campaign is making the past look exciting.

❧

Obama from Mile High Stadium
(Posted August 29, 2008)

Listening to the season's news commentary you also may have had enough of secondary issues: abortion, guns, gay marriage, stem cells, and race. You may also join me in having had enough of demands that Barack Obama go on the attack, or at least "paint a more specific picture of his presidency." The media operates like a sports bar. Drinks are forced on you when you dare to say you have had enough. "What do you mean, 'enough'? Are you too good to drink with us?"

Obama's contribution last night at Mile High Stadium was an attempt to put the secondary issues behind. The Democratic Party primary campaign is over. Here I am, he said, the candidate, just as you see me. He was trying to raise the political discussion to a level above Limbo. He spoke of "the hope that we confess," a resonate phrase from Martin Luther King. A bold riff on the four-letter word he has overused.

Before several tens of millions, he very nearly shouted out "Enough!" Yes, enough. There has been no major domestic political change since Ronald Reagan came to dominate our national politics making his first run at national prominence in 1976, then forcing Gerald Ford and Jimmy Carter into one- term presidencies. What Reagan initiated back then, George Bush has taken to the extreme. Now we pray—or confess the hope–for a turning point. Now is the time for putting some flesh on the dry bones of our desire for change.

Assume that Obama wins in November and assess the accomplishment of his first 100 days. Throughout his career Barack Obama has been a cautious and moderate liberal, not far from the Democratic Party center, not much out of line although to the left of the Clintons with the Party leadership (Nancy Pelosi, Rahm Emanuel, *et al*) or with major media such as the *New York Times* that so obviously inclines toward moderate Democrats and moderate Republicans. So Obama comes to us out of a weak center.

No one from this center could manage to support the populist, "Two Americas" candidacy of John Edwards. None could support an avid reformer like Ralph Nader. They cannot even thank Nader for his lifetime of advocacy for consumers and against corporations. This center could not support impeachment of Dick Cheney or George Bush, bring an end their lie-based war in Iraq, or make even a small beginning toward taxing the ultra rich. They could not call our far-flung soldiers back home from throughout the world. They could not rebuild our National Guard (you would think that was a no-brainer) against the hurricanes, floods, collapsing bridges, and miscellaneous, random attacks on America. They could not restrain the short-term greed of a few dozen finance moguls. That would be going too far, too far from Reagan whose politics own this era.

They are chained to posts, guarded by dragon corporations who occasionally throw them scraps. Their Republican colleagues, the Grand Old Party of the Rich, require no chains or guards. And all the weak centrist moderates support Barack Obama. One wonders if the leading men and women of the Democratic Party center—as well as many native Oligarchs and some in the corporations—are thinking of Barack Obama as a temporary man, a flash in the pan, an electrifying centrist Black candidate who must inevitably fail in his first term. All understand that, after all, he is facing all the problems created by thirty years of Reaganite politics and made sharper, uglier and extreme by the eight years of George Bush: economic crisis, record inequality, failures abroad, deteriorating health care, deteriorated public education, services, infrastructure, and environment. "A one term president," they are thinking. No major changes; and a man with no coattails to ride.

Yes, I will bet you this is the thought of many who are the source of Obama's funds. Naturally they contemplate McCain without much enthusiasm. And, they know better than anyone how obstruction has been build into our sick system of national government where a tight, revolving circle of political appointees, lobbyists, corporate hires, and professional advocates (numbering is the low hundred thousands) run the government in behalf of the corporations while elected officials (numbering 500 or so) put on their show of opinion and misspent votes.

Yet Obama does inspire some hope for change. All it will take is his first 100 days as President to determine if that hope has substance. Here are four issues we can use to measure Obama's first 100 days. His entire presidency hangs on its beginning. These are the problems that must be addressed very early in his new presidency.

1. **Regulation.** In behalf of the corporations, Bush has destroyed the American regulatory environment and it must be rebuilt. The destruction began with Reagan, but Bush has brought it to nearly complete collapse. The agencies do not regulate. They are deliberately crowded with incompetents who will be very hard to remove. The agencies do the will of the corporations they are supposed to monitor, corporations whose tendency to an excess of the short-term profit seeking the agencies were created to restrain. Bush has set up tiers of bureaucracy at the top (Office of Regulatory Affairs, OMB "Reviews," the Council on Competitiveness, etc.) all designed to slow down and interfere with regulation. His political appointees have the primary function to inhibit regulation and to gut their agencies with review processes. His political appointees are now all scrambling to have their jobs

reclassified from "appointment" to "career" (i.e., into Civil Service career positions) from which they will be impossible to dislodge. Obama must find mechanisms to disrupt these reclassifications. Then he must appoint agency leaders willing to fire incompetents and restructure their agencies in line with the law. If he cannot alter the tier upon tier of Bush functionaries—whose whole expertise is preventing or disrupting change—nothing in the regulatory environment will change. His presidency will fail.

2. **The Rule of Law.** The Democratic majority in Congress is already conducting numbers of popular hearings and investigations. Will there ever be prosecutions? Will a President Obama sit through the early months and months and months of already underway investigations and do nothing? These investigations are revelations of corporate-induced public harm, of deliberate failures of oversight, scandals of stealing, scandals of lies, illegal secrecy, and misrepresentation. To sit through investigations while not putting in place prosecutions will complete the circle of meaninglessness as many—perhaps as most—expect. Will he forgive and forget? Or will he use the process to teach America what must be restrained, where the public interest actually lies, who the public enemies actually are? If he simply disowns the past then in two years most of the country will believe everything is his fault. They will not reelect him.

3. **Inequality** Poverty and inequality in American is a story only beginning to be told. Obama may not thank Edwards for this but inequality—along with population growth—is the driver of social change. A succession of presidents, Republican and Democrat, has tamped down the record levels of poverty in the U.S. by tinkering with and misrepresenting national statistics. Only the shocking health statistics survive their tampering. None wanted to be a poster child for unequal America. Now the continuing regressive tax policy, the layoffs and outsourcing, the rising cost of necessities (especially housing and transportation), and the record corporate profits, along with the transparent crimes of the finance giants are all combining to make the cost of inequality real. No one presidential office is to blame and Obama's will not be to blame. But the American people did blame Jimmy Carter for the oil crisis and stagflation. We now blame Bush (or at least Reagan's man Greenspan) for the housing bubble. The next president will be held accountable for the collapses yet to come. Obama must immediately make it known that he is attacking inequality, not continuing it. He cannot do that without immediately making known the extent of inequality. Change will require a tax policy way to the redistributionist left, of anything he has yet hinted at.

4. **Health Care.** Then there is Health Care. Listen to the speeches at the Democratic Party convention. Health Care was central in Kennedy's speech, in Hillary Clinton's, and in others. The leading Democrats use the word "universal," they invoke comparisons with a fully socialized, single payer health care (such as Medicare, Medicaid, such as the VA, and such as every developed country has had and tested for many years). People are going to get it. They are going to expect, in the first 100 days, something beyond Obama's current weak words about making health insurance "available" to all Americans. Everyone else is talking about Health Care as "a right of all Americans" not as something to be made "available" by hugely profitable insurance corporations. Health Care is a particular weakness of the Obama program. Even Hillary's compromised plan was always better. It is entirely possible the McCain campaign could decide to trump Obama on the issue of national health care. It would not take much.

After Bush—a slow, shameful, and unrepresentative man—I am electrified by Barack Obama. The potential of his candidacy is enormous. At the same time, the evidence accumulates that he is just another centrist Democrat, a moderate, one who parades with the slogans of "Change" and "Hope" as do they all.

President Obama will need to hit the ground running, a man of a first 100 days (matching LBJ's first 100 days, exceeding JFK's). If not he will sink under the weight of these major, seemingly intractable and unaddressed issues outlined above. There has to be some redistribution of our national wealth. One instance only: Obama has promised 4 million "green" jobs. That is not nearly enough. FDR created 6 million jobs back when the population was one third of what it is now.

Obama will inherit a damaged economy, powerful economic rivals, an entrench bureaucracy put in place by right-wing Republicans and never altered by Bill Clinton, an incapacitated Congress long in the pockets of corporate interests, and a diversion and slogan-addled public too busy with work and media to pay much attention.

Obama seem to me to have brilliance and a calmness that places him above anything the Democrats have offered in a long time. Biden seems a good companion. Yes, there is a world of people out there who are more radical and possess who knows what unseen skills. But for now, we have Barack Obama, a step up from anything I expected the Democratic Party to be able to offer. Our first African-American president, a brilliant speaker, appealing humanity, a dignified liberal presence, and believably the very opposite of Bush and McCain. That fills many Americans with an undeniable hope. The collapse of the American empire can wait—because clearly Obama will not change our corporate foreign policy, in any event—while I look forward to enjoying some Obama success over eight years, eight years that will surprise a number of his current nasty supporters, supporters who have, for the time being, ordered "Hands off Obama."

༄

Anyone for Tennis?
(Posted October 16, 2008)

Driven to extremes by his declining poll numbers, John McCain finally stepped on the line in last night's final debate of the 2008 presidential campaign. He uttered the words "class warfare," and "spread the wealth." No credit for this most important piece of public honesty goes to Barrack Obama.

Obama has always tamped down the reality, avoided the phrase "two Americas," carefully referred only to "corporations" having their taxes raised and "corporations" do not actually hold the wealth at issue. He has never uttered the word "redistribution." Obama is guilty of obscuring and softening the reality of class war. Last night before millions McCain let that cat out of the bag:

> The whole premise behind Senator Obama's plans are class war-
> fare, let's spread the wealth around.

True enough, unless Obama is only feinting to the left. If not, welcome premise. And Obama found himself forced to somewhat greater clarity about who he will tax and who he will not tax, in whose behalf he will make new public expenditures, whose side—at least apparently—he is on. Here is his reply:

> Now, Senator McCain, the centerpiece of his economic proposal
> is to provide $200 billion in additional tax breaks to some of the
> wealthiest corporations in America.

> What I've said is I want to provide a tax cut for 95 percent of
> working Americans, 95 percent. If you make more [oops, Barack,
> don't go there]– if you make less than a quarter million dollars
> a year, then you will not see your income tax go up, your capital
> gains tax go up, your payroll tax. Not one dime. And 95 percent
> of working families, 95 percent of you out there, will get a tax cut.

We're going to have to invest in the American people again, in tax cuts for the middle class, in health care for all Americans, and college for every young person who wants to go. In businesses that can create the new energy economy of the future. In policies that will lift wages and will grow our middle class.

This FDR stuff from Obama is welcome, as is Senator McCain's brief plunge into partial truth with his one-liner about class warfare. Most people readily excuse Obama's moderation. If you want to win an election in Reagan's American—after more than 30 years of dominant Republican propaganda-making, deregulation, taxation for the poor, government as the "enemy" nonsense, incentives for the rich, excuses such as "stimulating business," "growing jobs," "trickle down,", etc.— you must be completely vague, especially now with the added shove by a major economic crisis.

There are two more weeks of this to come: From McCain about Obama: "He will raise taxes," "Joe the Plumber," "an explosion of spending," on and on. Obama will have to reply and repeat his now famous numbers—a quarter of a million dollars in annual income—.the 95% of Americans with below $250,000 annual income who will see no tax increase. He will have to specify his spending and frame spending not in JFK's terms (a visit to the moon and Peace Corps), not Reagan's terms (star wars, national security, a bigger fleet of aircraft carriers), but in FDR's and today's Main Street terms (jobs, higher wages, rebuilt schools, local infrastructure projects). This kind of rhetoric has become the language of Obama's candidacy since he—so unlike Kerry in 2004—was allowed by his failing Party to actually win the primary. This rhetoric, and not merely the language of "hope" and "change," is moving Obama's campaign forward.

Other Democrats like Bernie Sanders, Dennis Kucinich, and a handful are somewhat more explicit and educational about the class war reality than is Obama. But Sanders and Kucinich are not running for anything (they have secure seats in Congress) while Obama, also a moderate Democrat, but also a man educated as a leftist, is seriously running for President of the United States in what still may be a close race.

The long-running silent and one-sided war over shifting wealth from the poor to the rich is about to receive a little publicity. That is my hope. The corrupt and corporate broadcast media have not contributed to this exposure; it came from McCain and Obama themselves and was forced on them by current economic circumstances. All of us for whom wages, jobs, mortgage and retirement savings matter greatly and capital gains, interest income, dividends, depletion allowances, investment insurance, estate and even income tax matter little or nothing have ignored the war being fought against us.

Blame that on habit, training, lack of education, systematic propaganda in all media, apathy, happy trust in things unseen, whatever. It does not matter. The very rich—for whom capital gains tax, income tax, estate tax, deregulation, speculation, and asset accumulation are the very breath of life—may be about to come in for a bit of exposure.

The class war—admittedly wearing today's media-designed sheep's clothing—is on. Some of my friends say that it feels more like the match that followed when Humphrey Bogart, in an early role as a stage actor, rushed onto stage set of a garden party in whites and waving racket to cheerily call out "Tennis anyone!" I think they are wrong.

Note that the two names Obama gave in replying to McCain about who he actually pals around with on economic issues were Warren Buffett and Paul Volcker. You have to believe Obama's names were quite deliberate. It was Buffet who said recently "There's class warfare, all right, but it's my class, the rich class, that's making war, and we're winning."

This was in a *NY Times* (Nov. 26, 2006) report by Buffett on those who work in his office in Omaha. He revealed that he himself (with CEO salary and immense income from dividends and capital gains) paid a smaller fraction of his income in income taxes than the secretaries, clerks, and executives in his office.

The outspoken former Fed Chairman Paul Volcker also belongs to the class that is winning. He is the one who raised Fed interest rates to 22% (now it stands at one and a half percent) ending any chance for a second term for Jimmy Carter. Volker is the man who knows more than anyone about Iraqi and Saudi oil money. He is the one who saw the current crisis coming as early as 2005 and pointed out that overall wage revenue will definitely fall (that is, because of the growing unemployment) and that there is a 75% chance of a currency crisis (a collapsed dollar) within five years.

This will be no tennis match. These guys know class war. Of course, they do not share with us their full thoughts. Neither does Obama. Hardly anyone does. Nevertheless, it seems time to abandon my quibbles with Obama's campaign. I think we should all vote for him. The purpose is not to "save capitalism." The alarm over the financial system's "very survival" is being exaggerated out of the immediate financial self-interest of the very rich. The real tragedy is inequality, job loss, foreclosure, debt, and lost retirement savings. This real tragedy will remain with us for years to come, Obama aside. The Reagan Era years were obviously not a time of any flourishing radical social movements. My hope is that

Obama's eight years, if he can diminish Reagan's sway over hearts and minds, will open up the opportunity for a younger generation to move toward socialism through new radical social movements. Such movements will be their accomplishment, not any president's.

❦

He Is No Lesser Evil
(Posted 11/03/2008)

The media has given this election its usual simplification: a race between two animal emblems with cheers and speeches. Tomorrow it goes down to the wire leaving us with less to look forward to than the cheering warrants, but more than the last several elections. True, both candidates supported the $700 billion Wall Street bail-out initiated by Bush's Treasury Secretary, both are belligerent toward Iran and Russia, both are ready to surge in Afghanistan, both are pledged to rally round Israel's racist and reactionary state menorah, both endorse "free trade," neither endorse universal health care free of the insurance industry's bite, both go to the wire without a promise of electoral reform, bankruptcy reform, or any immediate employment stimulus. Yet this election could not be more different from 2000 or 2004.

An old slogan, "Don't Vote; they're All the Same," no longer applies. Obama is not a lesser evil with all the usual nasty implication of that phrase.

Many will genuinely celebrate this outcome with good reason. I have been glued to this media event like no other in my lifetime, as well as holding signs, talking to neighbors, all that good stuff.

This election has had the usual measure of fraud and chauvinism, but also a measure of promise. Barack Obama is coming to dinner! When I compare him to recent potential guests (Al Gore, John Kerry, Hillary Clinton, or a George Bush surrogate), I am delighted. Not dishes as at the socialist feast I look forward to sometime in your future, but better than gnawing on "Lesser Evil."

Mainly, for me all this is because an Obama's victory will give us a new look at our divided American. The meaningless Red and Blue state distinction is breaking down. Obama has promised a posture of bipartisanship, and in some ways that may help break down of the meaningless Republican and Democratic distinction. This has to happened before the actually significant rich vs. the rest of us distinction comes into focus.

The Republicans will rub Obama's nose in their intense partisanship, no matter his mild talk. He will follow FDR in leading some kind of capitalist economic "recovery" while ignoring the very poor (as did FDR) and set a "bipartisan" legislative agenda which will fail. However, the effort will help highlight the real divide in American.

Also, some traditional political clichés about the south and west are breaking down in this election cycle. Unless Obama completely abandons his own organization (among his young supporters, Hispanics, other minorities, and in the south) that break down will continue. Unless the media works overtime to suppress the truth, their usual story book demographic tales will not be swallowed so readily. We will immediately be a nation with a Black president, and soon to be a nation of the children of immigrants in which "minorities" is the majority.

The valuable question "Who benefits?" will be a bit harder to suppress after this election. When, since the sixties, has the word "socialist" been bandied about so widely? The talk of socialism will continue. The "socialist" issue is about simple fairness, the rich should pay their fair share. The question "Who benefits?" can move beyond the irrelevant kibble of plaintive intellectuals. I believe the issue of classes and of rich vs. poor will sink in a bit deeper because of Obama's victory. More if we talk it up. More if it is encouraged by some presidential speeches. But I will not hold my breath until that happy day.

The true Janus face of America should become more visible following this election: America comic and tragic, earnest and hypocritical, generous and reactionary, rich and poor. I am not just waxing lyric over Obama's victory. Some of my friends on the left are altogether too anxious to get back to their own business-as-usual. They should do that, of course, keeping up the good fight. But that does not require their repeated predictions that Obama's accomplishments will be even less impressive than were Bill Clinton's which were nearly nonexistent. Clinton appeared briefly as a populist (up to about the summer of 1993. It was as shallow as a well-reserved Southern accent and the speaker then faded to the center right. The difference? Clinton lacked the quality of the popular support Obama is about to receive.

In any event, and if Obama fades to the center, I will come to understand the Rev. Jeremiah Wright's acute frustration with the contradictory face of America. Out of that frustration and anguish, he cried "God damn America!" If I were given to passionate outbursts, I would cry the same; but I remind Rev. Wright that, surely, God is no Biblical literalist. He has "lifted up" and "cast down" nations only in the imagination of mortal chroniclers. As usual, we are on our own as God intended, or so I was taught by my Quaker grandmother.

We are our own tragedians and comedians; God's fools, if you like that metaphor, Reverend. Americans are the thieves as well as the victims, the sow's ear as well as the silk purse, sharpie and his mark, pimp and john, rich and poor. We are a Janus thing, a class society divided against itself, laughing and crying, most people not knowing which way to turn or who to turn against. White working class men glare hatred at Black professionals, imagining that they have it better. All the numbers, race to race, prove that they have it much worse, but that is confusion for you.

Anyway, tomorrow we vote (or have already). There is the failing rival, a man of years, exhausted, giggling and now relaxed (Have you noticed?) in his last days. McCain is finally at ease with his old self, making repartee, affecting intimacy with thousands, using smiles, eyebrows, and jerky gestures. He was not much of a man of words.

Against him is the new child, the man of promise, shy even of 50, perfectly at ease, toning down the multitudes ("There, there!" he says, "We don't need that. Just vote.") Thus, he inspires. He is already the victor.

The Republican machine—a leaking balloon of imagined vast self-importance—with a candidate who is no slouch even unsupported (McCain has eight major political campaigns, two for president, under his belt) running against a populist sleeper awakened by the clamor of the masses (like some charmed character out of a Washington Irving story). That is Obama, who calmly pulls along the remains of his Party to a stunning victory. That is something!

Is it a fraud of true democracy? Yes it is. But make your marks on the ballot and go on from there. We will see what can come from talking a bit more widely about fairness, about robbery by the very rich, about socialism.

༄

Heroic Pictures, Desperate Times
(Posted 11/24/2008)

The heroic pictures are appearing (Obama and his hawkish Secretary of State against a broad blue horizon with clouds above, his Vice President standing in the distance). You see the pictures everywhere. Our new president-to-be, skating on the "fluid poetry" of his winning presidential campaign, is being given his visual space, his introductory media adulation, his hundred days of grace in advance of nay-saying, racism, budget-cutting, defense-spending, and backlash.

However, witness the Obama appointments. We seem to be looking at yet another Clinton Administration.

There is nothing wrong with another Clinton Administration for saving Wall Street from the consequences of its excess speculation and profit-taking. Obama is assembling such a group, all possessing talent for organization. They will avoid an economic catastrophe while not imposing any onerous hardship on future economic speculation or profit-taking.

Ten years ago Obama's new Secretary of the Treasury, the NY Federal Reserve Bank's Timothy Geithner, was there saving the world when the Asian Banks threatened to bring down the international financial system. He served under Bill Clinton's Treasury stars Robert Rubin (since of Citigroup and now heading the Council on Foreign Relations) and Larry Summers (since of Harvard and now into hedge fund management) who remain as Obama advisors.

The Asian crisis was caused by Kabuki excesses of speculation, a plot no one could follow but similar to the recent speculative U.S. excesses in derivatives and structured whatevers. Geithner, the Fed, and the IMF brought that international economy back from the precipice. Too bad so many fell off the edges of the carriage in the process. But that is only if you are looking backward. Obama, of course, is not looking in that direction.

The Clintonians put trade, the deficit, and the budget—as Obama says—"back on track." Wall Street continued to enjoy the low-wage nineties and a good part of the benefit-cutting and shipping jobs abroad of the Bush years. Now, in this bigger crisis, the really big capitalists seem willing to impose a necessary hit on the smaller capitalists and on us all. Their only requirement is that their pain be widely distributed, extending to massive unemployment, the destruction of retirement savings and of suburban home equity. They are pleased especially since Geithner sees no reason for an excessive swing back to regulation.

Adapting the California cliché to the circumstances, Wall Street moguls can say "I feel my pain." Narcissism alone does not make the rich into bad people. That is only the way they think about the world. Poverty has always been an anomaly to rich people. They find it difficult to make out why people who want dinner do not just ring the bell. (That is Walter Basehor's remark that I rediscovered in Lewis Lap ham's little 1998 book *The Agony of Mammon*).

I have not yet read Niall Ferguson's new *The Ascent of Money; a Financial History of the World* but I heard him promoting it on NPR the other day. The extreme human and moral distinction between those whose surplus accumulated wealth goes up and down a bit and those who have no surplus wealth escapes him. One is the subject of "financial history;" the others are just the poor who are always

with us, undeserving of thought, much less of 800 pages of exquisite consideration. The rich are so habituated to shifting wealth from the great majority of us to
their own very cozy minority that they don't notice that this shifting has human
and moral consequences. "Hang the Rich!" was never a bad slogan.

Anyway, on the issue of economic recovery work is underway and in good
hands. "Back on track," "putting America back to work" (an enlarged armed
forces, building windmills, $15/hour road work, yet more service jobs, is prob-
ably what we are looking at), "we will hit the ground running," "not a moment to
loose." All are Obama phrases in what appears to be his version of an established
Bill and George presidential idiom.

On the issue of foreign affairs things do not look so rosy. That Secretary of
State at his side wants her own war.

Aggressive imperialism has not been taken off the agenda. Obama puts
national security first, per the Constitution (although the framers were thinking of
security against British colonialism). National security is reflected in the appointments of Clinton, Bill Richardson, and a set of Hummers about to be named to
national security posts. Obama's ploy is to open his new administration with a
double win for the powers-that-be: economic recovery and reinvigorated national
defense. A two-fer.

Hillary has always been a Hawk. She applauded bombing the Balkans, held
firm for "the nuclear option," sometimes more gently phrased, and would "obliterate Iran," Her significant campaign impact (forget any populism, feminism, or
health and children words) was to condemn Obama as "naïve and irresponsible" on
the national security front. He was "weak," she had implied, with all the hawk's
irrational implicit "Prove me wrong; I double dare you." Her campaign—quite a
long one, you will recall—did indeed take the anti-war option off America's social
table. What is left of an anti-war "left" once its troops run to Clinton and Obama?

When Hillary saw her presumption-of-nomination evaporate she turned up
the Masters of War demands. Her opponent is "soft" on terror, a mere "diplo-
mat," loading the word with scorn. He is not a true defender of Israel "by any
means necessary"; he is naïve in "talking to tyrants without pre-conditions," too
respectful of the UN, hesitant at the 3:00 AM phone call. Would that he were.
In response Obama slipped away from her bad by mouthing all the clichés of
Imperial America to the extent that the anti-war aspect of his campaign simply
vanished in a puff of words. Then he appointed her Secretary of State!

Now that she is Obama's Secretary of State, will she follows the flight of her
fellow hawk, Madeline Albright who was her husband's Secretary of State and
would have been her own had she been nominated? That is Madeline Albright,
firm for a Cold War NATO of bombardiers, firm on the Bill Clinton sanctions

against Iraq. Albright assessed the consequent deaths of hundreds of thousands of Iraqi children as "worth it" and apologized only for the way she framed her answer. That Albright, a Reaganite Cold Warrior who led in the UN against condemning Rwandan "genocide," who fought repeatedly with Secretary-General Boutros-Ghali—the last Secretary-General of any independence—until his replacement was secured. And so, too, we will have Hillary, not for a moment the kinder, gentler Madeline Albright.

Then there is Bill Richardson, temporarily with the Commerce appointment. We must wait to see where this loyal back-up man is used next. Richardson had been Clinton's Energy Secretary and then his UN Ambassador. Many folks seem to like him; the media assess him as "tireless and warm." But please remember the Richardson pumping for an Iraq war at Davos in 1998. That is in 1998!

Lewis Lapham attended that Davos summit and recorded the following quotes. Richardson did the rounds seconding Albright. "Saddam Hussein is Hitler, God damn it," he said. "The man wants to be bombed." "We're preserving America's credibility, not allowing the UN to be so contemptuously insulted." War on Iraq at that time, he admitted was "not an easy sell." "How do you sell it, Bill," he was asked:

> First I take our best diplomatic shot. I say that Hussein is Hitler, that the diplomatic options have been exhausted, that we don't mean to obliterate Iraq but merely to bring it into full compliance. Then I move in with the killer argument—look, I say, if you don't support us, get out of the way because we will send the bombers no matter what you decide to do.

He said he was sick of hearing about "serious consequences." He wanted war. "How much bombing?" he was asked:

> We have three kinds of bombing—pinprick, substantial, and massive. Pinprick won't do. We would want the bombing to be substantial.

Asked if this shock and awe might not produce a negative Arab reaction, he answered, "We'll take a big hit in the Arab world. But we can live with that. . . . There may be some spillage."

"But what if China vetoes the bombing in the Security Council?" Richardson answered "We'll go ahead and bomb anyway," claiming we had "wonderful information" from sources inside Iraq, substantial damage showing up on satellite photographs and perhaps some sort of popular uprising. "Who knows?"

On and on he went, fierce and determined, an off-the-cuff spokesman for war doing his part in 1998 while Newt Gingrich talked up new economic bubbles in other rooms at the Davos summit.

Today the media is more controlled than in 1998. The old new national leaders are more careful in how they phrase things. All the Democratic Party's "anti-war" liberals are on board for this ride along the precipice. And we now have Barrack Obama to put a human face on Empire.

In spite of the heroic pictures, in spite of my cheerful pessimism/optimism, the same state capitalism is at hand with much the same managerial personnel. State capitalism—as much as it wants to skirt the catastrophe created by its own greed, as much as its moguls are willing to take their hit if they must—state capitalism is incapable of good will, compassion, or even much of a human mask. Do not forget that a President's stand on war gives it bloody color to his entire program.

War still holds the key to the heart of those who rule us. They are hired as defenders of corporate America. We missed the chance Ben Franklin hoped for (to "crush in its birth the aristocracy of our moneyed corporations") and now fewer stand against them. That is, in part, owing to Obama's charm and his domestic promises.

త

Can You Say 'Obama to the Rescue'?
(Posted 03/23/2009)

A hero's arrival is an episodic thing at best and, like Shane (Alan Ladd in the movie), a hero does not even turn and wave as he rides off into the sunset. Best case, the hero might leave behind some good advice. Shane told young Joey (played by Brandon DeWilde) to "grow up strong." The implication was: be like your father, a man of integrity, one who fights steadily for the rights of homesteaders against the cattle barons.

We, too, should grow up strong. Watching President Obama with a child's hope in your eyes is indeed childish. The only thing Obama is giving us is a bit of opening to be ourselves. We need to remember that our imagined heroes often turn their back on "the little people," that they do not even look back and wave. They are an episode. We are the full story.

Most good leftists voted for Obama because of his story and what we might guess were his private inclinations. They gave encouragement to our efforts toward social justice. Certainly he will be a much better president than Bush, but more than that there was his social justice inclination expressed alongside his ambition. Now he is giving us the opportunity to make our own movements in the direction of that inclination. He himself will ride away. Heroes are men of exotic personal skills and great personal ambition. They use their ease and their determination, even studied flairs of anger, but usually maintain themselves with compromise and a vast indifference.

At least that is my take on Shane and all the cowboy heroes.

Here are Paul Street's reflections on Obama thus far. You might well have skipped Street's new book *Barack Obama and the Future of American Politics* and can hardly be faulted for that. "Obama" is like the word "Cooking"' in book title land these days. Street is also the author of *Empire and Equality* (2004). He is not cocky and leaves a trail of good names, his reading, behind him. He is a habitual teacher. I clip here from his website where Street describes the Obama violin model of politics, "you hold power with the left hand and you play the music with the right." "You campaign and gain office with populace-pleasing progressive-sounding rhetoric but you make policy in standard service to existing dominant corporate and military institutions."

> Obama's violin performance is being expertly marketed by dominant media. We are told by the *Times* that Obama is making "a radical departure from the past" even as he proposes to increase the so-called defense budget, even as he makes it clear that he will be leaving 50,000 so-called "residual" troops in Iraq well past August of 2010, even as he increases the level of violence in Afghanistan and Pakistan, and even as he cannot pay elementary honest attention to the legitimate grievances and claims of the Palestinian people.

> Obama is a "radically progressive departure from the past," we are told from on high even as he says he will cut the federal deficit in half but cannot bring himself to embrace the elementary bank nationalizations that are obviously required in the current economic crisis. Even as he refuses to advance the obvious cost-cutting social democratic health care solution: single payer national health insurance. Even he can only set up a middle class task force but not a poverty and inequality task force. Even as he

promises to spend untold billions and trillions on further bankers' bailouts executed with zero citizen oversight and direction.

Obama is a radical progressive break, we are told, even as he does not utter one word about the overdue labor law reform he campaigned on, the Employee Free Choice Act. Even as he fails to advance such basic elementarily progressive measures as a moratorium on foreclosures, a capping of credit card interest rates and finance charges, and the rollback of capital income tax rates to 1981 levels, Even as his tepid and inadequate stimulus plan is over-loaded with business-friendly tax cuts and woefully short on labor-intensive projects that will put people to work right away. And even as he asks for twice the amount of money to sustain the criminal invasions of Iraq and Afghanistan as he proposes to set aside per year as part of a reserve fund that might pay for just more than half the amount required to give us uninsured health coverage... in 10 years. [Even as he pays a presidential visit to Caterpillar, the company that sells occupation and apartheid bulldozers to Israel and the first major U.S. manufacturer in decades to break a major strike with scabs.]

Looking back, Street sees Obama as the ideal establishment candidate for a ruling class at peril: he is Black, from African parentage, with a Muslim name, a "community organizing" resume, a solid family, and a degree from Harvard Law. These are hardly the normal establishment credentials but enormously useful for a corporate/military spokesman at the present moment. Thus Obama passed the corporate vetting. It gained him $37.5 million in campaign funds. In the final tally 75% of it from donations over $200, with $900,000 from Goldman Sachs whose gold watches adorn so many wrists in the Obama Administration. It gains him an outstanding corporate media approval that was probably even more costly (from the same sources). Street misses the one-term president issue, but never mind.

Also Obama does not lack the familiar Clintonian corporate-friendly moderation. Today Larry Summers is fronting for another give-away (hedge fund moguls will buy toxic assets, he suggests). Timothy Geithner, a deregulator, announces a vast new program of regulation that he will administer. And the hundreds in DC, who specialize in promising bogus "defense" against bogus "threats" for their armament manufacturing and oil interests, go to work each day with enthusiasm and smiles. Nobody is actually worried. Flexible capitalism (which by essence and definition cares nothing for equality or justice) is at stake. Now it has a leader, Obama, thought by many to be a hero. All the essential ruling class interests are intact. A few cripples may fall beneath the wheels of the American carriage but the basic mode of transportation with the masses pulling rolls on. Well more than 80% of Congresspersons are stake-holders in the corporate cause. They are still riding in comfort.

We "little people" would not have given Hillary Clinton or Joe Bidden an inch but will give Obama a mile. And when he delivers only reassurance, smiles, and that fleeting sense of pride we will have lost a great opportunity if we have not used this Obama Moment for social action. That action in no way depends on him; nor should. Clearly, he is another centrist. If we do not use the opportunity, then in 2012 everything goes back to the fascists and their backers. Who can we blame for the missed opportunity? Not Shane.

I think, reading these times, all of you should join some cause, take the risk, spend a few dollars, put your back to the wheel of change. Why not? This is the time. There will be no "Great Depression." That much is clear. Going forward the main interest of the powers-that-be will be harvesting the government's new money, our money. In their last throes, if it gets to that, they will turn the fire hose of inflation on us; but that is not yet. Presently it is just harvesting the giveaways.

As Shane advised, "grow up strong."

ॐ

The Ship of State Today
(Posted 11/03/2009)

Some see our ship of state floundering, water logged by right-wing bluster, attacked by deficit terrorists, sinking in leftover oil and gas wars, its crew untested, a ship weak in captaincy. Our captain, they say, lacks resolve, tenacity, perseverance, and so on and on.

I do not see it this way.

If the ship were floundering one indicator would be the corporate elite running in panic about the deck tying down their properties? No. There are the usual bulls and bears doing business as usual. Do they step out bravely to die in the name of "free enterprise"? No. They are falling into line for President Obama's bale-outs, nodding sagely over his Wall Street appointments, skinny-dipping in the calm water for his stimulus money, lining up investments for his Green enterprise, that "vast ecosystem of entrepreneurial business" that electric cars will require or some other environmental fancy. Could it be that these corporate elite looked into the terrifying eye of the potential economic storm, contemplated the failure of all their greedy aspirations, and concluded, "He's our man"? Something like FDR for our time.

Have the nay-saying Republican politicians seized the helm in these troubled waters? Hardly. They work for the failure of this first Black president. They play deficit terrorists and war hawks. For those who can believe anything, they promise "getting government off our backs" and the return of "values." They train their audience in disruption and overuse of the word "betrayal." Their audience, who can believe anything, had their minds blown out by eight years of Bush-Cheney lying triumphalism. These are mainly conservatives from under populated states and counties who may furnish some worrisome proto-fascist candidates down the line. However, we should not imagine those candidate's qualifications will exceed those of Sarah Palin.

If the state were floundering, another indication would be progressive folks mobilizing in the face of the dire emergency. I do not see that at all. A healthy segment of them, far from crying alarm, are quietly running for local offices, building their modest reform organizations, attempting their own version of bipartisanship, limited aspirations, and compromise. The Obama model. Tonight they will watch the HBO special "By the People" with pleasure or perhaps go to the new show "Obama Mia!" with some self-satisfaction; they played a good role in helping Barack Obama win this first year as captain of the ship.

As for the grander progressive objectives—Medicare for all, out of Afghanistan now, full gay rights, punishment for the wicked—those will have to wait on post-election mobilizations, if any. Progressives may become discouraged a bit by the midterm elections. They are a hesitant lot, reflecting the Democratic Party, part of whose base they form. In any event, the captain now has two additional years to deliver on his promises, a change of course, not sharp but one you can believe in.

Third quarter GDP growth is significantly up. The Dow has been generally up since Valentine's Day. The President and all the wise men did say that employment rebound would take a minimum of two years. Today is the cusp of the second year and already some job recovery is beginning. An orchestrated announcement, no doubt, but most of the numbers seemed real. Yesterday's *Times* reported this significant stimulus-money job growth and the Republicans denounced the million-job gain as a fraud. The House Majority Leader said, "The trillion-dollar 'stimulus' isn't working, and no amount of phony statistics can change that." John Brehner must pray on bended knee for more layoffs. His charge is to give his defeated Party some chance in 2012. His financial support, you may have noticed, comes from corporate and Wall Street segments who do not believe in the future, only in past contracts.

The Minority Leader and Republicans of his ilk hate the progress toward even an inadequate health care reform. They decry deficits (against their history of giving votes for any military expenditure). They deplore a deliberate foreign policy (calling it "cowardice" and "flip-flopping"); they breathe hatred toward Hillary Clinton as our first competent and consistent Secretary of State selling rapprochement in every direction. They are outraged at Obama's indifference to neighbor-against-neighbor cultural issues (his "lax" attitude toward homosexuals, HIV-positive travelers, those bankrupt because of loan sharks or medical catastrophes, and even his forgiving attitude toward those doing routine, minor rip-offs on the federal treasury with ear-marks for which Republicans themselves are famous).

I cannot give a run-down the Obama's administration appointments, but there are interesting power-figures who will appear in forthcoming dramas. Arne Duncan in Education may be one. He brings ten years of success with the Chicago Public Schools. His evidence-based program will unfold shortly; and I like his insistence that teachers, principals, and superintendents be held accountable to some significant extent (and not only "parents & poverty") when students fail to learn.

Another is Eric Holder (the nation's chief law-enforcement officer). Holder has vast experience and a consistent stand against large-scale commercial gun and drug trafficking, for closing Guantánamo, on developing clean (rather than politically tainted) prosecutions of congressional crime, and also he defends keeping state secrets. The Right portrays all these as government intrusions. Best of all, Holder has stepped directly on the Right's attempts to bring fundamentalist Christian intolerance into American public life by making a vigorous defense of Obama's new federal "hate crimes" law.

Another might be chief of staff Rahm Emanuel. His sketch history suggests that Emanuel would have secured (as price of his acceptance of the job) the promise that he holds the individual careers of this vast modern administration in the palm of his hand; and, probably, as well, that his views would carry weight concerning improper, anti-Obama congressional and military behavior. Thus far, thanks to him, it has been a year not marred by the typical new-administration leaks and sniping. Achieving this was his charge and he accomplished it.

The one major first year leak—when General Stanley McChrystal's secret recommendation to Obama for a troop "surge" in Afghanistan appeared in the *Washington Post*—seems to have resulted in a quiet but quite effective put down for McChrystal. Nothing direct was reported but I suspect McChrystal's ambition to replay General Petraeus and his Iraq "surge" in Afghanistan—and then go on to be mentioned as a Republican presidential contender for 2012—will not meet with success. Obama's aim is to wind down both Bush wars, not to provoke another with Iran, and to "peace process" rather than saber-rattle here and there. Clearly, his Secretary of State is on-board for all of this.

Bad as are the very rich in their routine self-interest and their rejection of "doing good," most of them are not locked into the ugly Bush past. However, unlike these private oligarchs, the Republicans, the fringe right, and some of the stone progressives cannot get over all those Clinton/Bush years. Their political imaginations are lock-jawed onto corruption and the technically illegal, onto 9/11, and onto scaring folks with a scattered international hate crime cartel named "Al Qaeda." They are either charmed or far too repelled by Cheney's bluster (the predictable hack bluster and negativity of a corporate mogul, once our Vice President) and by the swarming lobbyists fingering their pockets full of petty cash. Such things flourish under the politics of fear, crusade, Mission Accomplished lies, and Us-vs.-Them ideology that were the Bush-Cheney hallmarks. But those things are in the past, while the present real danger still comes from the military-industrial complex and the very, very rich who are invested in it.

The above is my snapshot moment in the course of empire. It is a network of for-profit private corporations and their government that has done much harm to American labor and to the world. Obama, as a reformer, will not transform this empire, but already he has changed some things. Of course, "some change" does not make a political slogan.

Let me mention that in his first weeks, nearly a year ago, Obama signed Executive Orders to close Guantánamo, to ensure compliance with our treaty obligations including the Geneva Conventions, and to give all detainees access to the International Committee of the Red Cross, as well as ordering the CIA to close all existing detention facilities. He has also taken steps to put us back into the United Nations where we have been effectively absent or in conflict for nearly 20 years. Examples are: we have been without membership and withholding funding from UNESCO from 1984 to 2003; rejecting the International Court of Justice through the 1980s and "deactivated" and not participating in the World Court 2002 to date; allowing the Gates Foundation to thumb its moneyed nose at the World Health Organization.

What has been the progressive contribution recently? Yes, what has it been? Many did get behind Obama's election slogan of "Change you can believe in" a year and more ago; but it was mainly Obama himself who brought in the young, new voters and the Black and other minority population. I find it dramatic, but not surprising, that he has now taught some lessons in neutralizing one's enemies, making concessions as required, and proceeding with the speed of a patient man toward his campaign promises.

I suggest that we let the existing members of Congress wallow and let the fringe Right go to their paranoia hell alone. Obama is not a revolutionary but he is beginning to be stable and consistent.

My hope is that progressives, for their part, begin to talk openly of the alternative to Obama's centrism and to capitalist empire. That would be an American socialism. In the wide world outside our borders there are many models from which we can learn something. And, in honesty, please note that Obama's voice is the most prominent one encouraging all of us to make international comparisons (as in his health care and education speeches).

Presently we do not stack up well against the rest of the developed world in health, education, or, in many cases, in humanity.

I would like to see serious progressives build a popular front directly for socialism, elect some additional socialists and build new reform and pro-socialist NGO's and community initiatives. They might also do popular union organizing and take up the thousand ways in which feet-on-the-street can make a difference.

At the center will be Obama's administration, perhaps eight years of it. That will not create a hostile environment for admired social change. In our historic rope pull contest between the classes the left must have feet planted in the ground of socialism and arms outstretched. All the evidence is that Obama has decided to appear as a firm and conscious centrist, patient and slow-moving toward his better ambitions. I am sure that trying to push him "to the left" is a lazy and ineffective progressivism and a waste of all our time. Progressives or anarchists without an explicit socialist orientation are wasting the people's time.

༄

The Haiti Disaster
(Posted 01/14/2010)

I want make a secular contribution to go along with all the prayers for Haiti and for Haitians as they survive through their recent disaster. We do posses secular, mortal instruments:

> **Partners in Health**, Dr. Paul Farmer's organization, has its origin, center, and much of Farmer's life focused in Haiti. Their health teams in Haiti were involved from the first moments, effectively and without aid bureaucracy pass-through. They are fully invested and are a worthy place for your contributions.

Doctors without Borders whose Haiti medical teams were involved from the first moments of the earthquake disaster, with additional medical activists streaming in with supplies and expertise. Their administrative and fund-raising overhead is remarkably low.

Disasters such as their hurricanes and this earthquake are "natural" only if you ignore where the world slums are built. But no one imagines that U.S. invasions and governmental policy are "natural catastrophes." U.S. policy has long been primarily responsible for creating Haiti's *Hideous Dream* (as Stan Goff called it in his book by that title, quoting Shakespeare).

Now begins our vast and wealthy country's aid response to the earthquake. I hope U.S. government aid will come close to matching, in dollars, the outpouring of aid and philanthropy from Haitian-Americans and all of us together with our small individual contributions. I hope it will match, in dollars, the United Nations contribution. But, if not, that is no reason for reducing our individual aid.

Perhaps we should hang out heads in shame for passively accepting our corporate-ruled nation's Haiti policies over all these years. Perhaps the thing is to make our small contributions now as Haiti faces its latest disaster. And perhaps now is a time to make a beginning to dealing with those whose racist hatred and corporate idolatry have inspired and supported every cruel thing our government has done to Haiti. They are the likes of Pat Robertson, TV evangelist, who has long preached against the very being of Haiti (on Wednesday repeating that Haiti has been cursed by a "pact to the devil"), Rush Limbaugh, talk radio leader, who yesterday once again denounced aid to Haiti ("We've already donated to Haiti, it's called U.S. income tax"), and those already beginning to decry "Haitian refugees" and the use of even a single Florida hospital bed.

We should do everything good we can for Haiti because, in truth, Haiti is a real threat to everything that is bad in America.

Haiti (1701-1804) accomplished the first successful armed slave rebellion and achieved independence shortly after the American Revolution, this while surrounded by slave nations created and policed by Europe and the United States. Throughout America, Haitians immigrants furnish models of the social gospel in action (those Sermon on the Mount values) while not collapsing their Christianity into exclusivity, eliminationist hatred—that is David Neiwert's accurate term—and the shameful fundamentalism that is so common in America.

Haitians have survived the health effects of extreme and unjust inequality. They have survived our racism and the years of major media distortion of their culture (said to be" exotic" and "perverse"). They survived at least two CIA and U.S.

military overthrows of their democratically elected governments, kept faith with their unique inland state "monopolies" that originated in their early independence history, and, to this day, they believe in genuine democracy. Yes—although the phrase is not usually used in this way–Haiti represents "the threat of a good example."

We now have a man at the bully pulpit with a background that should enable him to speak to the nation about Haiti, saying all the above things and more. This would be a teaching moment, a great anti-racism, pro-immigrant, anti-poverty, Social Gospel moment. The moment will pass; I know that. President Obama will direct giving to the American Red Cross, with its long history of using Haiti's disasters to help overcome its habitual deficit spending and with no history of opposing U.S. government crimes in Haiti.

The moment will pass. Nevertheless, we should do whatever we can as individuals and take pride in whatever acquaintance we have with Haiti and Haitians.

www.ingramcontent.com/pod-product-compliance
Lightning Source LLC
Chambersburg PA
CBHW062136280526
45788CB00001B/188

* 9 7 8 1 4 5 0 5 8 5 2 8 6 *